SPEAKING OUT

No AR

Students at the Children's Theatre Company performing the peace play *Tinarina the Runt Who Refused to Grow.*

SPEAKING OUT

Storytelling and Creative Drama for Children

Jack Zipes

Routledge

New York • London

Published in 2004 by
Routledge
270 Madison Avenue
New York, NY 10016
www.routledge-ny.com

Published in Great Britain by
Routledge
2 Park Square
Milton Park, Abingdon
Oxon OX14 4RN
www.routledge.co.uk

Routledge is an imprint of the Taylor & Francis Group.
Printed in the United States of America on acid-free paper.

ISBN 0-415-96660-4 (hard cover : alk. paper)
ISBN 0-415-96661-2 (paperback : alk. paper)

10   9   8   7   6   5   4   3   2   1

Library of Congress Cataloging-in-Publication Data
Catalog record is available from the Library of Congress

To
Maria Asp and Wendy Knox,
two wise friends,
who have inspired me
and taught me more than they realize

Contents

THE IMPORTANCE OF CHILDREN'S THEATER

Prologue

Building Bridges

Have you ever thought about how the Twin Cities got their names? Minneapolis and St. Paul are strange names, and they certainly don't seem to be twinlike. But there's a story to all this, and what I'm about to tell you is the unvarnished truth.

Years ago, years before the Mississippi River cut the cities in two, years before there were thousands of lakes, years before the cities even had names, there were two farmers who lived on some land with beautiful green meadows and rolling hills. One of them, old Minnie, well, she was a crusty widow who had outlasted her husband and five sons. Tall and willowy, she was a survivor and managed a large farm with forty cows that she milked every day by herself. The other farmer whose land was right next to Minnie's property was called Paul. Not Saint Paul. No, he was a rascal, that one. He was always playing tricks and causing fun in the neighborhood. But he was also a hard worker, and over the years, he and Minnie had always been friends, though she frowned on his chasing after young women.

"Why don't you get married and settle down?" she asked him one day.

"No fun in that," he responded. "Besides you're the only woman I want."

"Well then," Minnie joked. "Let's get hitched, even though I'm thirty years older than you. I'll settle you down."

"Let me think a couple of years on it," Paul replied. "Don't want to rush into things."

The truth is Paul was a bachelor and always wanted to remain a bachelor. So he kept avoiding the subject and having a good time with Minnie, helping her out, and swapping stories until one day Minnie came to him and told him she had lost a cow and asked him whether he had seen it.

"Nope," he replied. "Not seen a thing."

"Well, if you do, you'll tell me, won't you?"

"Sure," he said.

Well, for the next week Minnie kept losing cows until she had only twenty left from her herd. Finally, she went to Paul and asked him again whether he had seen any of her cows.

"Are you playing one of your mean tricks again?"

"Well," he said, "there are a few stray cows that I've picked up on my fields this past week." And he took her into his barn and showed them to her.

"They're mine!" she said.

"Afraid not," he replied. "They were on my land, and what's on my land belongs to me."

"You're joking," Minnie laughed.

"Not joking this time," Paul said. "Times are tough, and I need more cows to keep the farm going."

"What about me?"

"What about you?"

"I thought we were neighbors."

"Sure we are, but you'd better start looking after your cows much better."

Well, Minnie had no choice but to leave without her cows. There were no police in those days. No judges or courts of law because everything was open territory. That is, until Minnie went to a small lake on her land and opened it up so it began to flow like a stream between her land and Paul's. Then she went to some other small lakes that fed into hers and opened them up, and before you knew it, there was a gigantic river that split off her land from Paul's.

"The woman's crazy," Paul complained. "Hey, it was only a joke," he yelled to her from across the river. "I'll return your cows to you."

But Minnie wouldn't listen to him anymore. She was blinded by rage at his stupid joke.

Well, now Paul got angry, and he was especially angry because the river was making marshland out of his meadows, and he couldn't send his cows out to pasture. So, one day he asked around to see if there was a master carpenter who might help him build a fence to protect his property from the river. Soon, a strange man appeared. His name was Sam. Some people called him Simple Sam, because he dressed in overalls and a T-shirt and carried his carpenter's kit wherever he went. Sam never said more than "yes, sir" or "no, sir," and he never took money for payment, just food and lodging. Of course, I forgot to tell you, he was a huge man, Sam was, and it took a barrel of food to keep him going all day.

Paul told him to make the fence as strong and tall as he could. He didn't want to see Minnie's face anymore, and he wanted to protect his land.

"Yes, sir," Sam said.

"How long will it take you? A week?"

"Yes, sir," Sam said.

So, off Sam went, and Paul could turn to some other things on his farm.

Finally, after a week had passed, Sam was finished, and Paul and Sam celebrated with a gigantic breakfast. Paul said, "Now show me what my fence looks like."

The two of them strolled down to the river, and Paul could not believe his eyes.

"What? What?" he cried. "That's not what I asked for!"

Right before him stood a bridge, a large wooden bridge that spanned the river from his land to Minnie's land. On the other side was Minnie, who was just as astonished to see the bridge as Paul was.

"You're a saint," Minnie cried out to him and approached. "It's a lovely bridge, and thanks for sending back my cows."

"But, but," Paul stammered. However, he didn't finish because he melted when he saw Minnie's smile and realized what a fool he had been. He had missed Minnie's friendship more than he realized.

"Hey, Sam," he shouted, "look who's here." But when he turned around, Sam was gone.

"Who's Sam?" Minnie asked.

"Just a friend," Paul remarked. "I guess he's gone off to build some more bridges."

Well, now you know the truth about how the Twin Cities got their names. Paul went on to help people build a large city on his side of the river, and Minnie helped people on her side. People came from other countries and other parts of the United States. Many people came, and they built homes all over and used the bridge to visit one another just like neighbors. And Minnie and Paul made sure to build other bridges that crossed the river so they wouldn't miss each other anymore. They were friends for the rest of their lives, and some say Minnie and Paul kept building bridges even after they died.

Preface

Professional storytellers and their disciples have come to believe they are one big loving family. Storytelling is more than a profession, it is their religion. They are convinced that if everyone learned how to tell stories to communicate their genuine feelings, the world would be a better place. At least this is the impression that I formed after attending the National Storytelling Network Conference, held at a vapid Sheraton Hotel in Arlington Heights, Illinois, from July 8 to 14, 2003. It was a strangely unfamily-like place to hold such an intimate conference—twelve miles from O'Hare airport in a dismally synthetic, generic hotel surrounded by an austere industrial complex, about forty minutes from bustling downtown Chicago. Yet seven hundred or more gifted storytellers, who use their art in various fields as therapists, teachers, librarians, community organizers, park administrators, actors, and even professors, flocked from all over Canada and the United States (and a few from Europe) to participate in a lovefest and to celebrate the sacred nature of storytelling.

Now, before I continue with my very personal comments on this familial gathering of storytellers, I must be honest and confess that I come from an eminently dysfunctional family and am prone to believe that family life in the United States can be nothing but dysfunctional. I become suspicious when I see love and care all around me. I was the smallest in my family and was called "the dwarf." Unlike the famous youngest sons in fairy tales, I rarely saved the day but often ended the day hung on a clothesline by my toes. My younger sister, who weighed four hundred pounds and stood six feet tall, won a sports scholarship to Ohio State to play right guard on one of their championship football teams and later went on to run a construction company. My older sister had the nastiest tongue in the Bronx, which is saying something. She was six feet one, lean and mean, and threw the javelin for Texas A&M until she spiked a spectator. She gave up the sport to take up fund-raising for the Republican Party in Texas. Nobody ever dared refuse her requests, and now she runs a cattle ranch. My older brother was a giant. At six feet ten and 280 pounds he won a basketball and wrestling scholarship to Arizona, but he managed to flunk a special course called Science for Jocks as well as some other similar classes and had to leave school. So he enrolled in the merchant marines to avoid the military draft, but he never boarded a ship because the merchant marines recruited him to play on their basketball and football teams during the Vietnam War. Later he attended NYU business school and learned to bribe the instructors to pass his exams. Eventually he joined my father's real estate firm and seemed to find tons of money on the streets, especially in front of gambling parlors. As for my father, he is too difficult to describe. Let me just say that he barked when he spoke and walked around his office with a bottle of whiskey in one hand and a cigar in the other. His favorite suits were bright plaid, and he always wore blue suede shoes. My mother did not particularly admire my father and didn't see much of him. After she overcame the trauma of raising three giants and a dwarf, she spent most of her time in the Lower East Side of New York City organizing tenant strikes, some of which were aimed at my father's properties. Eventually she divorced him and moved to Florida to lead the gray panther chapter on Collins Avenue in Miami Beach. By the time I graduated from college I was disowned by my father because I had decided to study English literature, and I was discarded by my mother because I was not radical enough. My sisters and brother were happy that I got what I deserved.

This brief account of my family background should help explain why I was taken aback by the waves of family love that swamped me when I arrived at the National Storytelling Network Conference. Mind you, this was a conference with workshops on "Creating 'A Land Twice Promised': Performance Process of an Israeli-Palestinian Dialogue," "All Together Now: Communities Meeting Challenges and Creating

Healthier Futures," "Business Storytelling: Adding Meaning to Meetings," "Stories Inside and Out: Incarcerated Mothers and Family Literacy," "The House between the Earth and Sky: Storytelling and Folklore with High School ESL Classes," "Story Partners, A Way of Life for Teenage Parents," "Grab the Space, Kids! Teaching Children to Communicate Effectively," "From Experience to Story: Evoking, Structuring and Telling the Personal Story," and "Bad Boys of the Bible: From Fortune to Misfortune to Forgiveness." The keynote speakers were Studs Terkel, famous raconteur and philosopher of the people, who interviewed the dynamic political activist, Tim Black, who spoke about his struggles against racism; Susan O'Halloran and David Hernandez, notable storytellers, who gave a presentation titled "The Illusion of Diversity: Re-Imagining Our Community's Commitment to Change"; Syd Lieberman, writer of many children's books, who lectured on "Lions and Tigers and Bears, Oh My: The Storytelling Adventure"; and Naomi Shihab Nye, the remarkable poet and singer, who recounted "The Stories of Our Lives."

This was not a dull, ordinary academic conference or business convention. People embraced each other incessantly in the hallways. They sang before and after dinner. They told stories late into the night. They danced with uninhibited gaiety to the rhythmic sounds of an Afro-Cuban band. They gave standing ovations to all the keynote speakers and constantly applauded. The storyteller, who introduced Naomi Shihab Nye, exploded with fervent emotion, and Naomi responded by hugging her and greeting the audience with "I love you! I knew as soon as I arrived that I would love you! You are all doing such wonderful and important work." The audience responded by telling Naomi how much they loved her. In fact, the audiences were always enthusiastic, eager to learn, eager to compliment. I did not hear one argument or disagreement during the five days I spent at the Sheraton. Not even the staff argued. It was as if I were living in never-never land.

But I would be unfair if I were to say the family of storytellers was living in an unreal space. What was difficult for me to grasp—as well as for my European friends who were stunned by the tidal waves of love—was that the unreal atmosphere of love and harmony concealed the real and material contributions that the individuals, probably many from dysfunctional families like mine, were making to various groups and associations. Clearly, most of them were upset and disturbed by the growing poverty in the United States, the collapse of caring communities, the destruction of public education, and the brutal indifference of state and federal governments whose policies are making the majority of people more desperate. Without being explicitly political, most of the storytellers regarded themselves as healers and educators. They insisted that a "good" story had a moral or social purpose and could enable listeners to gain greater self-awareness and a deeper social consciousness. To tell a story, any story, was first and foremost a mode of sharing problems and troubles and of community building to offset the alienation we all feel. Stories, they tried to demonstrate, could be used for empowerment, consciousness raising, self-discovery, therapy, education, and, of course, for the very sensual pleasure one feels in articulating a dilemma or conflict and in presenting a potential solution. The slightest story was to be revered and was meant to touch other souls.

The irony of the entire conference was that the public displays of sincere storytelling that sought to strike a family chord often came across as insincere and self-serving. Although the storytellers idealized their art in their workshops or tried to transform storytelling into a sanctimonious art the way priests, ministers, rabbis, and politicians do, they were more realistic and concrete when they talked to each other on a one-to-one basis. At breakfast, lunch, and dinner, I met extraordinary individuals who were down-to-earth and were using innovative forms of storytelling in hospitals, schools, nursing homes, libraries, parks, museums, youth centers, and businesses to bring people together so they might better communicate with one another. Not all their work was meaningful, and many of the "professional" storytellers, sporting their wares, liked to think of themselves as stars and behaved like celebrities. Yet the majority of the people were humble and modest. They had come eager to improve their craft and to make contacts so they might feel part of a movement. And perhaps the effusiveness of their emotions reflected their deeply felt need for family and support at a time when the idyllic family and community appear to be disappearing.

Perhaps this is why Studs Terkel received such a warm reception. There he was, all ninety-one years of him, gravel voiced, hard of hearing, swapping tales with Tim Black, who had worked closely with Martin Luther King Jr. in the 1960s and had participated in many political movements in Chicago. Sitting down in front of hundreds of storytellers as though they were in someone's home, they joked and told anecdotes about how they had endeavored to make the United States a better place. Even when Studs talked about how he had recently been robbed and then pleaded with his naive robber to give him enough money to buy a cup of coffee in the morning, and even when Tim recalled how he had fought in World War II and had been compelled to put up with racists in the army, their words radiated with optimism, and the audience could sense how cunning and defiant these old rascals were. Their tales were not fairy tales with happy endings. Their open-ended stories were about struggles to overcome oppression and injustice.

The audience was glued to their every word. After an hour, Studs, who was obviously getting tired, stood up and said in a gruff voice, "We'd better quit while we're ahead." And they did, but the storytellers, who listened, haven't quit. They are back out in the world, spreading words of hope. No matter how they gush, I reflect that I would rather belong to their dream-borne and idealized family than those real families and governments who spread lies and pretend to believe earnestly in the lies they spread.

I am dedicating this book to those professional storytellers, those educators and healers seeking to restore a sense of community in the United States and Canada. It is also clearly dedicated to the nonprofessional storytellers, especially the young, who are seeking narrative forms as a way to speak out about themselves. Like my first book, *Creative Storytelling: Building Community/Changing Lives,* this one is not a self-help book but a self-reflective and critical one, intended to complement *Creative Storytelling*. It is based on my experiences in Minneapolis and St. Paul, where I have been involved in various storytelling projects, especially Neighborhood Bridges, during the past fourteen years. It is also based on workshops and talks that I have given in the United States, the United Kingdom, and Italy that have brought me new insights into the manifold uses of storytelling.

I have divided this work into four parts to share what I have learned about storytelling, basically as it has manifested itself in the United States. The first part, "The Necessity of Storytelling in Education," deals with theoretical reflections about the art and purpose of storytelling. It includes the essay "The Wisdom and the Folly of Storytelling," which I previously published in my book *Sticks and Stones,* and I have revised and included it here because it is so pertinent for understanding the present state of storytelling in North America and Europe. The second part, "Neighborhood Bridges," is a descriptive history of the Neighborhood Bridges storytelling program, which I direct in collaboration with the Children's Theatre Company of Minneapolis. This program, oriented to the needs of children and schools, is one of the more unique storytelling programs in the United States. In the third part, "Spreading Tales, Opening Minds—Sample Sessions," I present a detailed analysis of several of the sessions in the program, including exercises and tales, in the hope that storytellers, theaters, schools, and other institutions might appropriate some aspects of our work and use them. The final section, "The Importance of Children's Theater," is a critical discussion of contemporary children's theater and creative drama in the United States. Because the Neighborhood Bridges program combines creative drama and storytelling in innovative ways, it is thus important to distinguish the type of nonspectacular theater we are trying to develop with young people from the spectacles that, I believe, blind audiences. The sense of storytelling that we try to instill in children cannot be accomplished if we do not explore and use all the arts, especially creative drama, which involves all the skills and talents of the children and opens their eyes to their potential.

At various times I make a distinction between professional platform storytellers and educational storytellers that may be somewhat unfair to platform storytellers, who often work in schools, community centers, and libraries in innovative ways and perform on stage or at festivals to entertain. In fact, many gifted platform storytellers are dedicated to using storytellers in schools to enable children to develop a critical and creative consciousness, and I want to apologize in advance if I, at times, seem unjust in my criticism of platform storytellers. But it is also important to make a distinction between storytellers who focus their energies on spectacular performance and those storytellers who use story in unspectacular ways to interrogate social tendencies and to animate children to become creative and critical thinking individuals.

This book is the result of long and intense collaboration with the children, teachers, teaching artists, and the staff of the Children's Theatre Company of Minneapolis. Unless otherwise noted, all the tales, legends, and stories in the book are my own or my own translations and adaptations. In the Neighborhood Bridges program, we use them in a consistent manner to explore genres and modes of narrative, and the teaching artists and teachers who use them are free to adapt them according to their talents and needs. In this regard the texts offered in the book are models for experimental storytelling. Through experiments we learn about ourselves, and through speaking out we learn to communicate and form communities.

The proceeds of this book will be donated to the Neighborhood Bridges program to further the work of the children. I encourage storytellers and anyone who reads this book to use our methods and stories freely and to experiment with all features of our program. It is through such a process of sharing that we can foster the folly and wisdom of storytelling.

Acknowledgments

It is impossible to thank all the wonderful people who assisted me in one way or the other in the writing of this book, and I hope that I do not omit anyone. If I do, I want to begin by offering my apology.

Maria Asp, Sharon De Mark, Carol Dines, Rhonda Geyette, and Gregory Smith read a first draft of the manuscript and made numerous useful suggestions for changes and corrections. All of them have been dedicated to Neighborhood Bridges and have contributed to its development in Minneapolis and St. Paul. I have benefitted greatly from their familiarity with the program, their experiences, and their critical acumen. Peter Brosius opened the door of the Children's Theatre Company to the Neighborhood Bridges program in 1997, and it would not be what it is today without his support and also without the valuable guidance of Teresa Erying and the entire staff at CTC.

Among the teaching artists who have worked with Children's Theatre Company (CTC) and Neighborhood Bridges whom I have enjoyed collaborating with are Aimee Bryant, John Bueche, Paul DeCordova, Signe Harriday, Jennifer Holt, Leif Jurgensen, Ann Kim, Wendy Knox, Michael Lee, Katy McEwen, Isabell Monk, Casandra Scott, Matthew Vaky, Carla Vogel, Kate Weinrieb, David Wiley, Joe Wilson, and Emily Zimmer. They have brought tremendous energy and remarkable skills to the program, and I have learned a great deal from their inventive experiments.

My heroes in the public schools are the teachers who have been committed to the Neighborhood Bridges program and have gone out of their way to support it: Meg Axe, Becca Barniskis, Mary Bussman,

Brigid Butler, Jessica Carr, Jean Carson, Roberta Carvahlo-Puzon, John Cearnal, Ruth Craft, Sara Dotty, Melanie Figg, Sonya Fish, Rhonda Geyette, Janet Glocker, Julie Gray, Jane Greene, Lisa Haines, Uve Hamilton, Jessica Hansen, Jan Hyman, Larry Johnson, Nancy Johnston, Mary Jones, Jennifer Knutson, Jenny Kraft, Jason Mann, Carrie McDaniel, Rochelle McTier, Leah Pagel, Lisa Robb, Cathie Schreifels, Joanne Toft, Dammian Tucker, Crissha Walton, Kate Weidenbach, Jeff Wendelberger, Kia Yang, and Michelle Zimmerman. Their work in the Neighborhood Bridges program has been greatly supported by the principals of their schools: Louis Boone, Armando Comancho, Jane Ellis, Jim Lemmer, Kris Peterson, Sue Poston, and Sandra Wood. Special thanks to Rhonda Geyette and Julie Gray for providing material that they have used in their classrooms.

Without the backing of the former Minneapolis superintendent of schools, Carol Johnson, and the arts education director, Judy Hornbacher, we would not have been able to make contact with various schools and integrate our program into their curriculum.

My colleagues at the University of Minnesota—Rick Beach, Sonja Kuftinec, Eva Nderu, and Kyla Wahlstrom—have participated in Neighborhood Bridges and made connections that have been very important for the program. Throughout the years, CTC has provided superb education directors of Neighborhood Bridges, such as Kati Koener and Tamara Goldbogen. It is now in the more than capable hands of Sharon De Mark, education director, and Gregory Smith, assistant director. Without their work and the entire staff at CTC, Neighborhood Bridges would not be able to flourish as it has. In particular I want to thank Linda Jacobs, Deb Pearson, and Yvonne Carranza, who have gone out of their way to make the program more effective.

Many friends and educators throughout the United States and Europe have made important contributions to this book and my work, and I want to express my deep gratitude to Michael Apple, Roberta Asieri, Audrey Favorito-Robinson, Lella Gandini, Herb Kohl, Michael LaFlamme, Salvina Rago, Baji Rankin, Pat Ryan, Joseph Sobol, and Mike Wilson. Finally, I should like to thank Prudy Taylor Board of CRC Press for her careful work as project editor and overseeing the book in its final stages.

Throughout the years I have shared my storytelling and writing with my wife, Carol Dines, and my daughter, Hanna Zipes. Without their encouragement and understanding, I would not be able to commit myself to Neighborhood Bridges as intensely as I do, and I feel that my commitment is their commitment as well.

The Necessity of Storytelling in Education

Fig. 1.1 Students at Powderhorn School with teacher Jeff Wendelberger at the conclusion of their festival play about a new society.

1

THE UTOPIAN TENDENCY OF STORYTELLING: TURNING THE WORLD UPSIDE DOWN

Narrative fiction creates possible worlds—but they are worlds extrapolated from the world we know, however much they may soar beyond it. The art of the possible is a perilous art. It must take heed of life as we know it, yet alienate us from it sufficiently to tempt us into thinking of alternatives beyond it. It challenges as it comforts. In the end, it has the power to change our habits of conceiving what is real, what is canonical. It can even undermine the law's dictates about what constitutes a canonical reality.

—Jerome Bruner, *Making Stories*

It would be misleading to argue that every story told is utopian or to assert that there is an "essential" utopian nature to storytelling. There is, however, a utopian tendency of telling that helps explain why it is we feel so compelled to create and disseminate tales and why we are enthralled by particular stories. In his monumental three-volume work *The Principle of Hope,* the philosopher Ernst Bloch argued that real-life experiences are at the basis of our utopian longings and notions. Because our daily lives are not exactly what we want them to be, we daydream with a certain intentionality and glimpse another world that urges us on and stimulates our creative drives to reach a more ideal state of being. It is our realization of what is missing in our lives that impels us to create works of art that not only reveal insights into our struggles but also shed light on alternatives and possibilities to restructure our mode of living and social relations. It is through art that utopia, designated as no place that we have ever seen or truly experienced, is to be realized as a place truly inhabitable for humans, a real humane place different from the brutal artificial places we inhabit and the earth that we are in the process of destroying with dubious notions of progress.

All art, according to Bloch, contains images of hope illuminating ways to create a utopian society that offset our destructive drives. Obviously, not every work that presumes to be art is artful. Nor do all works of art necessarily contain a utopian tendency. But inspiring and illuminating images of hope can be detected in low and high art, in a Beethoven symphony or in a rock-and-roll song, in a grand Shakespeare production or a Broadway musical. The utopian tendency of art is what propels us to reshape and reform our personal and social lives. In fact, Bloch pointed out that there are concrete utopias, short-lived experiments, that have given real expression to new social and political relations that are more just and pleasurable than our present ones. These concrete utopias set the building blocks for the future, for once hopes are tested and realized, we cannot betray them for long. We can never fully deny what has been concretized. Among his examples are such major events in the world as the American Revolution of 1776, the French Revolution of 1789, and the Russian Revolution of 1917, as well as the Fourier experiments in France and the Brook Farm "commune" in the United States, all which have left traces of how we might shape the future. These revolutions and experiments—and there are many more that can be cited, such as the experiments and projects that sprung from the student movements of 1968—did not entirely succeed because the proper socioeconomic conditions to maintain them did not exist. Yet the very fact that they came into being for a short time reveals a great deal about the validity of our utopian longings that we continue to concretize in different ways.

These longings are recorded in the spoken and written word. These longings are the source of ancient religions and rituals as well as new cults. The belief in a better and just world has always been with us, and this utopian belief assumes myriad forms. For instance, the belief in miracles and life after death articulated in religious legends and myths stems from utopian longings. Salvation is predicated on the notion of a just world in which the oppressed will be protected and guided by a powerful and compassionate divinity. Hundreds of thousands of tales in all religions have been spread with hope that we shall be redeemed after this life. But the more interesting utopian tales, in my opinion, focus on the present world. The utopian tendency of sacred stories is clear from the beginning. What is not so evident is how our profane and secular stories have a utopian bent to them and are perhaps more appealing and significant because they restore miraculous power to human beings. In other words, they suggest that ordinary people can take power into their own hands and create better worlds for themselves, if they know how to use their gifts. There is no need to wait for the promised land.

Stories help us navigate ourselves and locate ourselves as we interact with others in our endeavor to create ideal living conditions. They help map out the terrain of utopia. They reiterate messages that we sometimes forget. In our most common stories, the utopian tendency is constituted by the actions of an ordinary, quite often naive character who manages to overcome obstacles or an adversary to achieve some kind of success. We know these characters as Hans and Gretel or Joe and Mary or Peter and Molly; ordinary people with ordinary names. A good example is the cycle of Jack tales that has been spread in the oral and written tradition in England, North America, and elsewhere. In his wonderful collection *The Jack Tales,* Richard Chase remarked, "It is always through the 'little feller' Jack that we participate in the dreams, desires, ambitions, and experiences of a whole people. His fantastic adventures arise often enough among the commonplaces of existence, and he always returns to the everyday life of these farm people of whom he is one."[1] The most famous of the Jack tales is, of course, "Jack and the Bean Stalk," which depicts a resourceful Jack, who literally grows and grows up through his encounter with the giant and manages to gain a treasure in the course of action. There is another tale, "Hardy Hardhead," which is perhaps more interesting because it has many different variants in Europe and contains utopian implications. Here Jack asks his mother to take leave so that he can free a king's daughter who has been bewitched. If he is successful—many men have died trying to free her—he can marry the princess. When Jack enters the forest, he meets a "weezedly" old man, who gives him money and a ship that can sail on ground. On his way to meet the ship, he takes on board five men: Hardy Hardhead, Eatwell, Runwell, Harkwell, and Shootwell. These men have talents that will help Jack defeat the witch. He returns home and gives back the money to the old man. The narrator informs us that he does not know whether Jack married the girl, but at least she was no longer bewitched. As for the ship, the narrator confides in us that he knows for a fact that Jack kept it because he has taken it sailing several times.

This is a delightful tall tale with many utopian motifs such as the collective action of the six men whose talents are used to liberate an oppressed girl. In the Grimms' version, "How Six Made Their Way through the World," the hero is an ex-soldier, mistreated by a king. He and his five friends defeat the king's daughter in a race and make off with the king's treasures that they share together. In an Italian version, "A Boat for Land and Water," retold by Italo Calvino, the hero is a youngest son. Here, too, he is helped by an old man in the forest, and after the young man completes his task, thanks also to five gifted friends, he builds a palace that houses his father, brothers, and companions, not to mention his bride. In a Sicilian tale, "How St. Joseph Helped a Young Man Win the Daughter of a King," collected by Laura Gonzenbach,[2] it is the gracious saint who enables a humble man to bring together talented men. In turn they help the young man overcome an unjust king and win his daughter. The theme of all four tales is the transformation of a young man and the realization of a just cause through collective action. The implication is that miserable conditions can be changed and evil can be overcome. There is hope for the oppressed, and this hope is carried by ordinary people like Jack, the soldier, and the youngest son. Naturally, they have some extraordinary help, but aren't the miracles in these tales symbolic of the powers that reside in us, hidden potential that we have not learned how to mine and use? The magic help from the outside is actually an energy or potential within us that we need to recognize in order to transform ourselves and to pull ourselves up by the bootstraps. The hero receives a call from the outside in the form of an announcement. This call is actually from the future and sends the ordinary protagonist on a mission that will change his life forever, turn his world upside down, and bring more justice to the world around him. The miraculous transformation is a fairy-tale motif that can be found in all types of stories from antiquity to the present. Not only are ordinary men made extraordinary, but also female protagonists are transformed into talented and beautiful individuals. This motif is pervasive in our mass-mediated commercials, where quick, slick stories are told on TV and movie screens about beastly men turned into princes by the proper use of the right shampoo or the scraggly woman who looks like a queen after she uses the right lotion. Drinks, running shoes, beverages, and cars are all magic gifts that can allegedly change our lives. Here, of course, we see the perversion of the utopian quality of storytelling. Utopia cannot be attained simply on the basis of individual transformation and enrichment by commodity consumption. What is needed, as Thomas More long ago pointed out, is social and political change, and there are unusual cycles of tales that address the radical transformation of society and the conception of a paradise on earth such as Atlantis, the Golden Age, Shangri-La, and Cuccagna (also known in different languages as Cockaigne, Lubberland, Luilekkerland Cocagne, and Schlaraffenland—all connoting the land of milk and honey).

Schlaraffenland or Cockaigne as a utopia means nowhere. It is not a real place but rather a fictional and moral land. As Herman Pleij pointed out in his brilliant study *Dreaming of Cockaigne*, "The Land of Cockaigne here on earth: nearly every aspect of this dreamland which no one actually believed in, appears to have had a concrete counterpart in everyday life. Or, to put it differently, it looks as though Cockaigne was experimentally tested and put into practice in all milieus throughout the Middle Ages and early-modern period. ... The escape to paradise—a golden age, Cockaigne, or El Dorado—belongs to all times and all cultures, and those dreamlands always reflect the private yearnings and ideals of their creators."[3]

Indeed, Schlaraffenland or Cockaigne was created out of all sorts of intentions. In the Middle Ages, there seems to have been a real demand for a paradise in the here and now. Some tales envision a perfect community or government that does not exist because of the corrupt nature of people in the world. The storytellers' intention in portraying such a society is to show more clearly and more freely the incomplete nature of humankind and the foibles of monarchies, aristocracies, and democracies. Others seek to represent the misery and struggles of human life. Such poverty generates wishes for a more plentiful existence. This is perhaps why storytellers and writers created and continue to create such countries or islands where one can have everything without work. For instance, in Schlaraffenland tales, there are images of seas full of wine, streams of beer, forests with fried chicken, and fish hanging from the branches. One need only picture Pieter Breugel's famous painting of *The World Turned Upside Down* (1559), also known as *Netherlandish Proverbs,* to imagine what is meant by the Schlaraffenland or Cuccagna as the land of milk and honey. Indeed, Breugel was so intrigued by the stories of "Luilekkerland" that he painted the *Land of Cockaigne* in 1567.

The excess behavior of the characters in the Cockaigne stories is somewhat disturbing. People eat, sleep, drink, carouse, exchange roles, and turn the world upside down. Chaos seems to be the ruling principle of Schlaraffenland. Yet there are some historical factors that must be considered if we are to understand why the characters in these tales seem so voracious, boisterous, crude, and lustful. Most of the familiar tales in the Cuccagna, Cocaigne, and Schlaraffenland cycles arose during the sixteenth, seventeenth, and eighteenth centuries, and they are connected to the Carnival, Mardi Gras, and folk traditions when the common people were permitted on the day before Lent to become "kings for a day." That is, all the people were allowed to let their hair down and assume the roles of their rulers and oppressors, to dress up and do as they pleased without fear of being punished. In addition, given the great famines during this period, feasting became a major part of the celebration, and to eat to one's content became part of the celebrations. To break all the rules of decorum and to live for pleasure was also a political act, for it was during this time that the daily life and work were becoming more regulated and rationalized. Leisure time was becoming more and more a luxury, and peasants were compelled to treat time more like money. With the rise of the middle classes and mercantilism, the socioeconomic system demanded more work and accountability and less time for pleasure.

Perhaps one of the more interesting documents about the milk and honey tales is actually a sixteenth-century Italian folk song titled "A Chapter That Tells about the Existence of a New World Found in the Sea Oceano," which was based on different folktales. In the song that was probably sung and told by sailors, the narrator begins by reciting how seafarers found a beautiful land in the sea Oceano where nobody ever dies. There is one mountain made out of cheese, and on the top is a kettle a mile wide. In this kettle macaroni is cooked. When the macaroni is ready, it spurts out of the kettle and rolls down the cheese mountain to a house with forks where people can eat as much as they like and drink wine out of the springs. All the trees are filled with cake and cookies, and a river of milk flows through the land. Everything grows there without difficulty: grapes and figs, melons and other fruit. The woods are filled with fried chicken and other game. The weather is so wonderful that clothes are not needed, and all the boys and girls run around naked. For them, decorum is foolish and crazy. Everyone is young and lives for a thousand years. Then they die in their sleep. There are no sicknesses, pain, and suffering. Each person lives cheerfully and enjoys each second of the day. Everyone has what he or she wants, and if someone were to think about working, the others would hang the person and heaven would not save him or her. Everything grows by itself, and the donkeys are tied with sausages. Nobody has anything on his or her mind other than dancing, singing, and making music. The king's name is Bugalosso because he is the fattest, laziest person there. In fact, he is so fat that he never moves or exerts himself. Money streams from his rear, and when he spits, he spits out marzipan. Instead of lice, he has fish in his hair. There are no peasants there because everyone is rich. When one wants to sleep, one only has to find a bush equipped with sheets and pillows made out of down. It is not necessary to worry about having too many children to feed, because when it rains, it rains ravioli. The houses are made out of the finest gold, and all the fields are shared and free. What a wonderful land, sings the teller. The sun and moon never set. The people never quarrel or fight. The song ends with the singer commenting something like, "Oh what a beautiful place, Oh what a glorious land! How stupid it is to stay here any longer. I would like to head for this island and live near the beautiful mountain. Whoever wants to go there, I'll tell them the way. He only has to take a ship in Mameluke Harbor and then sail over the sea of lies. And whoever arrives there will be king of those fools."

Despite the wonderful irony of the song, it has a powerful appeal because it articulates the real needs of the common people and illustrates their wishes and desires. Typically, the contours of this utopia are depicted in the extreme so that there is a burlesque and grotesque quality to the narrative. This radical manner of introducing the motif of utopia, also to be found in tall tales and trickster tales, is intended to burst the seams of the status quo and provoke listeners to move ahead in their lives with laughter and optimism. The utopian tendency in storytelling does not accept things as they are and seeks to expose human foibles, hypocrisy, and injustices.

There are many types of utopian tales, and the utopian tendency of ancient tales about paradise has led to the science fiction and fantasy tales of the present, including many dystopian narratives. But the tendency, as the tales reveal, is not simply in the narratives themselves. The tales are articulations of the utopian tendencies within us that we cultivate from childhood to death in our endeavor to seek immortality. One need only watch children at a playground to see how early the utopian tendency in storytelling develops. Left alone to play, children will begin talking to themselves and will invent magic kingdoms and narratives to express their wishes and desires. Or they will join with other children to act out a story or play a game that has a story line to it. A playground filled with laughing and somewhat "wild" children is not unlike Breugel's *The World Turned Upside Down* or a land of milk and honey. As they talk and run about, the children seek to grab hold of their lives and map out their destinies, not knowing where they are going but knowing that there is a land or home out there that will suit them. As Oscar Wilde once said, "A map of the world that does not include Utopia is not worth even looking at, for it leaves out the one country at which Humanity is always landing. And when humanity lands there, it looks out, and seeing a better country, sets sail. Progress is the realisation of Utopia."[4] And one might add, the tendency toward utopia is kept alive through storytelling.

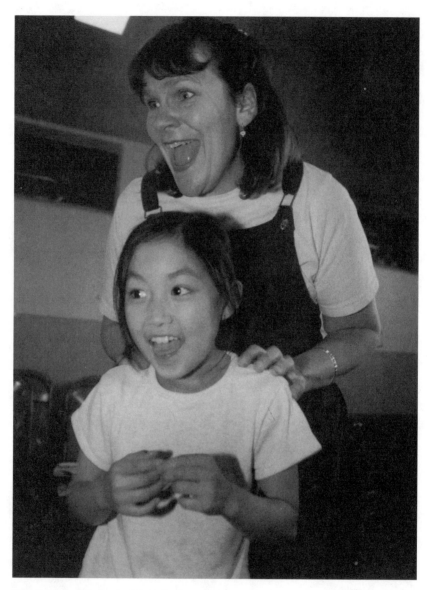

Fig. 2.1 Teaching artist Maria Asp coaching a student at Lucy Laney School.

2

THE WISDOM AND THE FOLLY OF
STORYTELLING

In his 1987 novel *The Storyteller,* the Peruvian writer Mario Vargas Llosa explored one of the vexing contradictions of contemporary life, namely, that the more we advance to civilize the world, the more it seems we breed intolerance and barbarism. In particular he raised the question of whether genuine storytelling and *communitas* are possible in advanced civilized societies. Vargas Llosa sent his narrator, who has a writing block and is suffering from ennui, on a trip to Florence where he visits an exhibit of photographs of the Machiguenga Indians in the Amazon jungle. As the narrator gazes at a photo of an *hablador,* or spiritual teacher, telling a story to a group of Indians, he realizes that the man looks a lot like Saul Zuratas, a friend from college, who had disappeared from his life some twenty years earlier. An outcast because of a blemish on his face and because of his mixed Jewish and Indian ancestry, Saul had developed a close relationship with the Machiguengas while doing anthropological work in the Amazon. Impressed by their spiritual dignity, he had decided to live with them and help them resist colonization.

What Vargas Llosa's narrator finds baffling is how someone raised in contemporary Western culture could become an *hablador*—a task that would involve, among other things, mastering the Machiguengas' demanding art of storytelling:

"Talking the way a storyteller talks," the narrator says, "means being able to feel and live in the very heart of that culture, means having penetrated its essence, reached the marrow of its history and mythology, given body to its taboos, images, ancestral desires, and terrors. It means being, in the most profound way possible, a rooted Machiguenga, one of that ancient lineage who … roamed the forests of my country, bringing and bearing away those tales, lies, fictions, gossip, and jokes that make a community of that people of scattered beings, keeping alive among them the feeling of oneness, of constituting something fraternal and solid."[1]

In contemporary Western society, we are not exactly suffering from a shortage of storytellers and stories. Every day we are inundated by one tale after another on TV and radio, in newspapers and magazines, at work and at the family dinner table, over phones of all sorts, and over the Internet. But despite this deluge, something important is missing. As Vargas Llosa revealed, we have lost the gift of genuine storytelling, which every Machiguenga understands implicitly and which was an integral part of Western culture until the early part of the twentieth century. It's the gift of using the power of story to share wisdom and build a meaningful sense of community.

For us, stories have become commodities, and they are used to market the interests of big corporations and politicians or to promote ourselves. It is somewhat of a pathetic, if not deplorable, situation. On June 25, 1999, the following headline caught my attention: "Biotech Industry Bets Its Future on Storytelling." I read that Jeremy Rifkin, the ecology activist, had unexpectedly been invited to attend an industry meeting at the headquarters of Monsanto Company. It was not Monsanto's idea to seek his input, as the company was quick to tell anyone who asked. The fifty-four-year-old Rifkin was called in by Ulrich Goluke, a consultant hired by Monsanto, and thirteen members of the World Business Council for Sustainable Development to help them paint a portrait of the biotechnology landscape of the year 2030 and how it evolved. The exercise, known as story building or more formally as scenario creation, is a specialized form of crystal-ball gazing that big corporations in the United States and abroad are increasingly turning to as an early warning system for how their strategies could go astray.

" 'Every child knows you get the really big issues across with stories,' Mr. Goluke said."[2]

Ad agencies use cleverly written stories to "move product." News commentators discuss the creative aspect of advertising. Newspapers and magazines print sensational stories to titillate their readers. TV talk show hosts coax people into divulging their most intimate stories on the air and to do preposterous things, all to score big ratings. People who commit atrocious crimes sell their stories to book publishers for unspeakable amounts of money. Politicians are trained to tell stories in the fashion of comedians to entertain audiences. Even worse, they train themselves to lie and to believe in their own lies. Comedians imitate politicians trying to act like comedians. Even the new breed of professional or platform storytellers in North America and Europe are caught up in the game. They charge high fees for their services in schools, libraries, and community centers and perform in a manner that has more in common with Hollywood, Las Vegas, and Broadway than with the talking circles of the Amazon rainforest. Though many of them are gifted, their primary mission is not to share wisdom but to amuse, distract, and entertain and to celebrate their art.

Without idealizing the past, let's recognize the significant qualitative difference in the manner in which tales were told and used up to the twentieth century. The work and customs of small tribes, villages, towns, reading circles, court societies, and small communities shaped storytelling, but today market forces, mass media conglomerates, governments, and the Internet determine how stories will be spread. There is an intricate "web of dictation," an arbitrary set of rules based on profit and power, that limits how far and how deep storytellers can go. In his 1936 essay "The Storyteller," written when fascism was enveloping Europe, the renowned German literary critic Walter Benjamin outlined how the capitalist market system had created enormous barriers to the free exchange of experience. Therefore, one of the key roles of storytellers, according to Benjamin, is to be subversive, to pierce through the myths of the ruling elite in order to free people to recognize who they really are. At other times in history, the myths that came to be challenged were those of Greco-Roman religion, feudalism, Christianity, and communism. But now a new—and more insidious, some would argue—myth looms: the myth of freedom and democracy. This myth is at the core of what I call the Pinocchio syndrome, best exemplified by our current president of the United States, but he is not the only one who knows how to twist and distort words to form calculated lies.

We think we speak freely in free societies. We think there's a free exchange of ideas in model democracies. Yet our ideas are often prescripted, our words often petrified before we speak them. Roland Barthes demonstrated how words are frozen in myths that endorse the ruling ideologies of a given society. He argued,

> Myth is constituted by the loss of the historical quality of things: in it, things lose the memory that they once were made. The world enters language as a dialectical relation between activities, between human actions; it comes out of myth as a harmonious display of essences. A conjuring trick has taken place; it has turned reality inside out, it has emptied it of history and filled it with nature, it has removed from things their human meaning so as to make them signify a human insignificance. The function of myth is to empty reality: it is, literally, a ceaseless flowing out, a haemorrhage, or perhaps an evaporation, in short a perceptible absence.[3]

Linguistic standards, word choices, expressions, and gestures are molded into a semiotic system manipulated by politicians, religious leaders, and corporate heads to create myths that serve to consolidate the power structure. This system fosters the thoughtless consumption of products, faiths, and laws that inhibit the free expression of ideas. But, as Benjamin pointed out, the web of dictation is not seamless. By challenging and exploding the putative truths of the myth of freedom and democracy, we can make room for truthful and imaginative expression. Here is where genuine storytelling comes in.

Benjamin maintained that the ability to exchange experience, what he called *Erfahrung*, which means the moment in which one learns something about oneself and the world, is at the heart of genuine storytelling—and that ability, which at one time seemed inalienable, has all but disappeared because shared experiences are not the basis of story anymore. According to Benjamin, traditional forms of storytelling have been eclipsed, and shared experiences mediated by a wise storyteller have given way to individualized experiences that reflect the growing alienation in society. In this respect, Benjamin and Vargas Llosa are very close in describing the predicament of storytelling and the genuine storyteller in contemporary Western society, and this deep concern in the fate of storytelling has been echoed even more strongly in Karl Kroeber's thoughtful study *Retelling/Rereading:*

> The world is becoming with accelerating swiftness a single culture, and narrative has always been rooted in localisms—the personal, the family, the tribe, even the nation. In a unitary worldwide civilization perhaps narrative discourse has little or no significant function. Walter Benjamin thought that story was obsolete in societies in which mechanical reproduction is popular as well as feasible. But even he did not foresee the extent and rapidity with which reproductive technologies would spread. In a world capable of instant electronic transmissions and rapid and inexpensive reproduction of images, for example, the patience required of a narrative audience, its willingness to let a story unfold at its own pace, may not be a valuable attribute.[4]

The threats to genuine storytelling are many—homogenization, depersonalization, fragmentization, and obsoleteness—but it is perhaps misleading to exaggerate them, and I would like to step back a moment from the critiques of the transformation of storytelling by Benjamin, Vargas Llosa, and Kroeber to reexamine their premises and to discuss the potential impact of storytelling on children. There tends to be nostalgia in their works for a type of storytelling that is practically impossible in today's advanced technological society that fosters globalized networks. Storytelling has transformed itself in accordance with socioeconomic changes, perhaps not for the better, but there is still the possibility for "genuine" storytelling, despite the general tendency to make every story the same; that is, devoid of its subversive and antiauthoritarian qualities, which, for Kroeber, is the essence of storytelling. My focus is on the situation of storytelling largely in the United States, but I also discuss some of my own experiences in Europe to question the notion of genuine storytelling and what it means for children more broadly.

There is no doubt that the art of storytelling and the types of story-telling that have existed in Western societies—and in the East as well—have undergone immense changes since the 1930s. Yet I believe it was a gross exaggeration on Benjamin's and Vargas Llosa's part (whereas Kroeber is much more perceptive)[5] to suggest that genuine storytelling has declined with the decline of integral communities, what the Germans call *Gemeinschaft*, which suggests commonality within a community. As I have argued, there is a nostalgic tinge to their writing that leads them to espouse a myth about past storytelling or storytelling in small communities. I am reminded here of a poignant tale by Her-mann Hesse, a storyteller who venerated the past and Asia, in which he portrayed the suffocating conditions and the darkness experienced by people living in a tribe deep in a forest at the dawn of civilization. "Der Waldmensch" ("The Forest Dweller") depicts the degrading conditions under which the people of the forest tribe live because their priest, Mata Dalam, hated the sun and spread lies about light so that they all feared him and the sun. In particular, they are scared to leave the dark-ness of the forest and are held under the spell of the stories of Mata Dalam, who becomes more and more tyrannical in establishing ritual and law. When Kubu, an intelligent and curious youngster who repre-sents the dissatisfied young people, tries to expose the lies of the swin-dling Mata Dalam, he finds himself expelled. Hesse then described Kubu's situation the following way:

> So he [Kubu] walked around the forest and pondered his situa-tion. He reflected about everything that had ever aroused his doubts and seemed questionable, especially the priest's drum and his rituals. And the more he thought and the longer he was alone, the clearer he could see. Yes, it was all deceit. And since he had already come so far in his thinking, he began drawing conclusions. Quick to distrust, he examined everything that was considered true and holy. For instance, he questioned whether there was a divine spirit in the forest or a holy forest song. Oh, all that too was nothing. It too was a swindle. And as he man-aged to overcome his awful horror, he sang the forest song in a scornful voice and distorted all the words. And he called out the name of the divine spirit of the forest, whom nobody had been allowed to name on the pain of death—and everything remained quiet. No storm exploded. No lightning struck him down![6]

In fact, as Hesse went on to narrate, Kubu leaves the forest and discovers the truth and beauty of the sun. He becomes enlightened because he breaks the spell of the alleged wise priest/storyteller and tears through his web of fabrications.

I mention this tale because much of what we call traditional storytelling was (and continues to be) swindles, lies, and untruths. Many of the traditional tales were told as religious and political propaganda to uphold and correspond to rituals that either celebrated a particular kind of totemic worship or reinforced the power relations of the dominant families or groups in a tribe or community. And many tales were also told in reaction to the status quo. In my own research on the interaction of the oral storytelling tradition and the rise of literary genres such as the fairy tale, fable, and legend, I have found that we know very little about the lives of "genuine" storytellers or genuine stories and how they functioned in the oral tradition. Most of the research on storytellers in the oral tradition is speculative because so little was written about them until the nineteenth century. Moreover, few scholars have dared to question the dangerous tyrannical aspect of priests, priestesses, shamans, holy men, administrators, court officials, scribes, and so on. We know next to nothing about the common people who spread and listened to stories. If we just examine storytelling since the rise of Christianity in Europe, we know that all types of tales were told from the medieval period to the present, and there were many different kinds of storytellers, some paid by aristocratic patrons whereas others were members of a family or community who freely told their tales. The tellers came from all sectors of society—slaves, priests and priestesses, peasants, fishermen, sailors, soldiers, spinners, herb gatherers, troubadours, wandering scholars, housewives, merchants, innkeepers, hunters, actors, heretics, criminals, bandits, administrators, and scribes. People told stories in all walks of life, and they fit their stories to the situation. Oral storytelling was always functional and purposeful and remains so today. There were no doubt genuine storytellers who grasped the essence of their cultures, and there were probably many among them who used the power of story to fabricate and to maintain power.

If we turn our glance to this history, we can see that there were all types of settings in which tales were told in spontaneous and organized moments. Marriage, birth, and death ceremonies called for different kinds of tales. Numerous religions and ethnic groups developed particular creation stories to explain how the earth was formed and how the gods came into being. Festivals and holidays were all associated with particular stories. Soldiers recounted great heroic feats that became legends. Farming and the conditions of life in the country formed the backdrop of tales told at harvest time or around the hearth. Merchants and travelers spread rumors and stories about bandits, duplicitous priests, and miraculous events. Each craft or trade, such as blacksmith, tailor, spinner, and so on, and profession, such as priest, peddler, sailor, merchant, midwife, and doctor, had stories associated with it. Aristocrats organized court spectacles and pageants that included storytelling. Rulers sought entertainment through storytellers, and aristocrats and bourgeois women formed salons where artful conversation and storytelling played important roles. Factories, churches, synagogues, temples, bathhouses, brothels, shops, prisons, schools, hospitals, saloons, and many other settings were the places that generated generic kinds of tales linked to the experiences that people had in these places. Hundreds, thousands, and millions of tales were told there and continue to be told in similar settings today. They were disseminated to instruct, warn, satirize, amuse, parody, preach, question, illustrate, explain, and enjoy. The meaning depended on the teller and auditors in a given social situation.

So what is genuine storytelling? Kroeber argued, "Genuine storytelling is inherently antiauthoritarian. Even a true believer in an official dogma cannot help articulating a received truth in his own fashion—for stories are told by individuals, not groups. Inherent to all such individuation is the potentiality for subversion, especially because a story is 'received' by individuals, no matter how large and homogeneous the audience of a telling, each of whom simply by interpreting for himself or herself may introduce 'unauthorized' understanding—all the more dangerous if unintended."[7] But are we to believe, then, that we are all potentially subversive? How do our claims about truth test the ethical standards of a society through our narratives? Is there an ideal social context in which tales are to be told that is much more preferable to others? Can the quality or value of a tale be separated from its function?

These questions demand sincere and frank answers, and I want to try to briefly answer these questions before I turn my focus to the changing function of storytelling and the storyteller in the past thirty years, and how these changes may have an impact on children.

The notion that there is such a thing as genuine storytelling has always been appealing to me, and in previous essays on storytelling I tried to define the possibilities for genuine storytelling. But on further reflection I now fear that I, too, fell under the sway of Benjamin's "storytelling," and perhaps that of Vargas Llosa, for it is difficult to distinguish between genuine and artificial storytelling, except in the most obvious cases. In fact, a tale that resonates as genuine may often depend on the artifice or art of a storyteller to engender an aura of genuineness. A sincere and honest story can be boring and does not necessarily reveal the essence of a culture or the essential purpose of the narrator.

But the impossibility of defining the genuine storytellers or genuine stories does not mean that they do not exist or that we should abandon the project of seeking to know what distinguishes genuine from artificial. We could begin with a simple definition: the frank presentation and articulation of experience and knowledge through different narrative modalities in order to provide a listener with strategies for survival and pleasure and to heighten one's awareness of the sensual pleasures and dangers of life constitute genuine storytelling. Kroeber insisted on the importance of retelling and the ethical nature of genuine storytelling: "All significant narratives are retold and are meant to be retold—even though every retelling is a making anew. Story can thus preserve ideas, beliefs, and convictions without permitting them to harden into abstract dogma. Narrative allows us to test our ethical principles in our imaginations where we can engage them in the uncertainties and confusion of contingent circumstance."[8] But then such genuine storytelling has probably always taken place and is still all around us. Again, this is not to say that there is no such thing as genuine storytelling, but the definition will most often depend on the critic's ideological perspective.

For me, genuine storytelling is not only subversive but also magical in that it transforms the ordinary into the extraordinary and makes us appreciate and take notice of the little things in life that we would normally overlook. Genuine storytelling is more often spontaneous and unrehearsed than it is planned and studied. This is not to say that it is unnecessary to remember and recall tales we have told in the past or that we should not create a repertoire of tales that we like to repeat in an artful manner. Rather, I mean that a tale or genuine storytelling arises out of a particular occasion and suits that occasion for both teller and listener. It is the coming together of the teller and audience that creates a genuine aspect to a moment that, unless recorded or taped, remains fleeting. Even then the living moment cannot be re-created. This is why one cannot categorically define the genuine tale or genuine storyteller, for it is the sociohistorical context that gives rise to the event. And this is also why one cannot determine what wisdom or ethical principles the teller will pass on to the listener and what the teller will learn from his or her audience. Surely, *all* tales teach. Even in the most banal joke or anecdote there is something to be learned. But the wisdom of a tale depends on the teller's clear realization that what he or she is telling may be folly. To speak, to take center stage, to appropriate the role of storyteller, to be the focus of attention is to assume power and command the minds and imaginations of listeners, however briefly. The storyteller persuades listeners by any means possible (incantation, music, rhythm, gesture, tone, instruments, costumes, and so on) to enter a realm for a moment and to abandon themselves to the conceptual power (or lack of power) of the teller. In any event, the teller seeks to convince listeners that there is some iota of truth, something that the listeners can carry away with them that might make them more insightful. Paradoxically, the storyteller—and here I am trying to define the genuine storyteller—must be convinced that the tale may be folly, that he or she may be creating a hoax. The genuine storyteller is a skeptic, a doubter, whose wisdom is conveyed by the realization that there may be no wisdom or ethics to be passed on. It is by challenging the truth value of the very words that the storyteller speaks that he or she becomes genuine and that wisdom may be conveyed.

There is obviously no ideal social context in which a tale can be or should be told. The telling can occur across a kitchen table or on a bed as a good-night story. It can occur on television or on a stage; it can be a confession or a declaration. With children it can be in a classroom, on a school playground, in the halls of a school, in a car, at home, on the streets, at a ball game—there are all kinds of occasions that may call for a story, and no occasion is preferable over another, although I would argue that some social contexts are intrusive and manipulative and are purposely intended to prevent critical and imaginative thinking of the listeners. In such instances, the quality or value of the tale is diminished. If the storyteller wants to be absolutely convincing and to gain power over the minds of the people in the audience, the tale itself will suffer, no matter how artful the teller is. It is in the absolutism—the absolute art of the teller—that deceit enters. The same tale can be told over and over again by different tellers and it will never be the same. Its value will depend on the occasion and how the teller responds to the occasion, and it will also depend on whether the teller seriously questions the efficacy and message of the narrative and the occasion. Obviously, if a tale is told spontaneously to suit an occasion, there is no time for immediate self-reflection on the part of the storyteller, but there is time for reflection, and it is in the critical reflection after a tale is told once or twice that value is revealed.

The value of telling tales to children has been a subject of debate for centuries. There is a well-known expression in English that seems to serve as a marker to determine whether a tale should or should not be told to children. We generally say that something is not fit for children's ears when we hear foul language or when the story contains a disturbing and horrid event. Ever since the twentieth century—and this has not always been the case—we have sought to protect our children from hearing and seeing what we deem to be inappropriate and harmful. Exactly what is appropriate and harmful has always been a matter of taste and a matter of social class, just as the mastery of language, spoken and written, has been subjected to taste and class. Storytelling for children in the United States became the domain of librarians, schoolteachers, church educators, and recreation workers, mainly women, up through the middle of the twentieth century.[9] It was also regarded as the mother's duty to tell good-night stories to soothe the souls of children before they went to sleep, although fathers also participated in the good-night ritual. In some cases, gifted regional storytellers practiced their craft outside institutional settings, but there was no deep-rooted tradition of folktale telling in the United States with two exceptions: the great storytelling tradition of Native American tribes (largely eradicated or silenced in the U.S. public sphere) and African American storytelling customs (also torn apart and confined in the United States). These traditions were not destroyed, but they underwent transformations and became important means (often subversive) to maintain community connections. The Europeans who settled the United States told stories, of course, but the notion of creating a special status for the storyteller or conventionalizing storytelling customs never took deep root except perhaps in the church, which explains why so many different religions in the United States speak with such power. Local secular storytelling was maintained in the United States as an underground tradition. This may have something to do with the lack of fixed rituals, changing communities, and socioeconomic mobility in the United States. In many countries throughout the world, the vocation or profession of storyteller has been and still is highly regarded. In the case of the United States, there have always been storytellers but no such thing really as a professional storyteller, and more often than not, in the early part of the twentieth century, the storytellers read aloud from books in libraries and schools at appointed story hours or they more or less memorized literary fairy tales and stories written for children.

All this changed somewhat radically in the 1970s. In his important book on the revival of storytelling in the United States, Joseph Daniel Sobol focused on the period from 1970 until approximately 1995 and pointed out,

> The resurgent mythological imagining of the storyteller as artist and cultural healer provided the impetus for storytellers to move out of those institutional settings and out of their family and community backgrounds to form a network of free-lance professional performers. These new professionals are supported largely by those earlier institutions—libraries, schools, and recreation centers—but also by a national network of storytelling festivals, modeled on the National Storytelling Festival in Jonesborough [Tennessee]. In the process they have developed a web of connections among support personnel in established "art worlds"—publishers, media producers, arts councils, arts journalists, and public sector folklorists. All of these interlocking networks of storytellers and support people have come to constitute an "art world" of its own.[10]

Ironically, for the first time in U.S. history, professional storytellers began trying to establish ritual and myth in a "demythologizing time."[11] As Sobol incisively remarked, the storytelling movement emanated from the civil rights and antiwar movement of the late 1960s and the diverse cultural radicalism of the 1970s when many different ethnic groups in the United States began seeking their roots and when the disenchantment with U.S. politics and the inability to change the society led many people to seek spiritual and ecological solutions to social problems. By the beginning of the 1980s, the fracturing of the myth of the American Dream and the questioning of the moral values of U.S. society caused by the strife of the 1960s and 1970s also led to what Christopher Lasch called the age of narcissism and produced massive cult movements, a strong conservative religious revival based on traditional family values, and the rise of right-wing militia groups, identity politics, and New Age cults. Many people were willing to try anything to bring about inner and outer peace or to stake their claims as to what it meant to be American. In addition, many ethnic groups sought to recuperate anything they could from their past to discover what it meant to be Native American or African American.

One of the "things" people began to explore was storytelling; to be more precise, storytelling as a mode of bringing about a new sense of community and new sense of self. Therefore, the organization of the storytelling, its professionalization and institutionalization, which owed a great debt to the foundation in the early 1970s of the National Association for the Preservation and Perpetuation of Storytelling in Jonesborough, Tennessee—now called the National Story Network—was most instrumental in creating formal and informal networks of storytellers and a new myth about storytelling in the United States. Of course, as Kay Stone, in her fine study *Burning Brightly: New Light on Old Tales Told Today* (1998), pointed out, "The dramatic rise of organized storytelling is not only a North American phenomenon. ... Organized storytelling, both as a child-centered activity and as a performance art for adults, has continued to flourish in countries of continental Europe and the British Isles, and in other parts of the world, most notably in Asia (especially Japan) and Australia. ... The folk revival on this continent is yet another expression of the hunger for an imagined era of the lost simplicity."[12]

Sobol and Stone agreed that many amateur storytellers who turned professional, that is, began to use their storytelling as a means to earn their living, had been drawn to storytelling because they had experienced intense personal and spiritual insights—almost epiphanies—that had ignited their desire to tell tales: they longed to bring about harmony and community against the growing technologization of society, and they yearned to heal wounded souls. Call the period from 1980 to the present postmodern, postindustrialist, or globalist; there has been a growing sense throughout the world that the imagination has taken a backseat to rationalization, that alienation and fragmentation are determining factors in the psychic and social behavior of most people, and that most public talk is shallow, hypocritical, and deceitful.

Therefore, an underlying motif of the new professional storytellers in the United States (and probably elsewhere in the world) was to recapture talk, to purify talk, and to make talk serve the people and spiritual ends rather than to induce people to buy products or buy and sell other human beings. In the eyes of many of the revivalist storytellers, the purpose of the storyteller became something mystical. Even divine. Sobol claimed that the revival of storytelling was "an idealistic movement and remains so at its deepest wellsprings. It consistently invokes a revival dialectic—basing itself on artistic and communal ideals located in an imagined past to heal a present brokenness and awaken an ideal future. The storyteller is the mediating image of restored wholeness, a prism of heightened presence through which these idylls of past and future can shine, clarifying the social matrix for at least the duration of the performance event."[13] This is undoubtedly the positive side of the professionalization of storytelling in the United States, and storytellers began entering hospitals, old-age homes, prisons, businesses, asylums, parks, reservations, churches, synagogues, and even shopping malls to demonstrate how stories could transform people's lives and engender a new sense of communal spirit. They performed for large and small crowds and organized their own festivals, shared stories and experiences, and expanded their outreach to work in some instances with Jungian therapists and in other instances with teachers, clergy, and social workers, often offering workshops to train new "disciples" of the revivalist movement.

In every movement, however, there is a period when cliques and ruling groups form and when the movement grows beyond the expectations of its founders. For clearly understandable reasons, the leaders, who invested much time and energy into developing a movement, have sought to keep their position and maintain control of their organizations. Unfortunately, many storytellers who have become well-known or even famous have developed a distorted sense of their power and have sought to become cultural icons or gurus. Moreover, the necessity to accommodate the needs of the institutions that the storytellers were serving because they were receiving payment led many storytellers to become commercial and to neglect the original spiritual impulse of the revival. More and more storytellers have tried to transform themselves into star commodities and advertise their wares as though they were indeed magical. The competition among storytellers has contaminated the sense of artistic community. The commodification that afflicts so many storytellers has led to a situation where there are two large camps: those commercial storytellers who perform largely for the sake of performance and who have forgone any sense of cultural mission, and those professional storytellers who continue to reflect both on their role as storyteller within the situation into which they insert themselves and on their stories and who question the value of storytelling that they urgently want to pass on to their auditors. Of course, generalizations about storytellers in a country as large as the United States—or in any country for that matter—are bound to have numerous exceptions. But the major point that I am trying to make—one that gets blurred at times—is that as soon as the storytellers in North America began a vital movement, organized themselves, and became professional, they also began threatening to undermine their very own movement because they had to subject themselves to market conditions that transformed them into entertainers and performers, compelled to please audiences and their customers, certainly not to provoke, challenge, or confront them.

Given this situation, storytellers are faced with a nonchoice: complying with the market system and seeking popular success, or complying with it and resisting it at the same time. For instance, there are those who regard children and schools as clients, and for the right price they will come to a school, do a performance or two before large audiences, answer some questions, talk about multiculturalism or some distinct ethnic culture, and then leave the youngsters (and teachers) in awe. The learning experience for the youngsters and teachers is minimal. They remain passive. And why not? What has happened in their presence? The storyteller could be any kind of good performer. The children could get the same thing sitting in front of a movie screen or before a stage. This is not to demean all performance or platform storytellers. Many platform storytellers are dedicated to work in schools and are advocates of progressive education. They also take great pleasure in performing. There is always a place for artful performances and amusement in our lives and the lives of children. But I think that it is crucial for storytellers working with the young to question both themselves and their stories and to use their skills and repertoire to enable the young to become their own storytellers.

There are many superb storytellers who are doing exactly this kind of critical reflection in the United States and throughout the world. For instance, Lynn Rubright, a professor and storyteller in St. Louis, reported on a three-year federal grant she received in 1971 for her Project TELL (Teaching English through Living Language) in her invaluable book *Beyond the Beanstalk: Interdisciplinary Learning through Storytelling*. The purpose of the project was to demonstrate how storytelling and other arts can serve as pivotal approaches to teach reading and writing, and it resulted in training and transforming students and teachers. She listed some of the basic agreements among teachers who have used storytelling in their classes. Here are just a few:

- The more teachers and their students open themselves to playful experimentation with stories, the more possibilities there are for varieties of renderings to unfold.
- Through storytelling workshops, teachers recognize and experience their own potential as skilled storytellers, and by modeling storytelling in their classrooms, they enable their students to become more effective storytellers, too.
- Storytelling, combined with dramatic play, allows children to try on many roles, helping them develop their ability to empathize, increasing understanding of those different from them.
- Teachers are often surprised at the insights children reveal as they ponder the complex meanings of fables, folktales, and other literature they have heard or read.
- When children tell stories they often reveal gifts and talents that have gone undiscovered with traditional approaches to learning.

- Storytelling offers many children an opportunity to develop skills and excel in oral expression, gaining respect that they had not experienced before from peers.[14]

What is crucial in Rubright's ongoing work as a storyteller is her awareness that storytelling is a means to bring students and teachers together and to develop their skills and talents. It is not to highlight the prowess of the storyteller as priest, shaman, guru, or healer. The storyteller's role is more that of an animator who uses story to empower his or her auditors and to establish a realm in which the students can explore themselves and the world in imaginative and critical ways. There are indeed numerous methods and approaches to storytelling and helpful guides to becoming a storyteller such as Margaret Read MacDonald's *The Storyteller's Start-Up Book,* Doug Lipman's *The Storytelling Coach: How to Listen, Praise, and Bring Out People's Best,* Rives Collins and Pamela Cooper's *The Power of Story: Teaching through Storytelling,* and Judy Sima and Kevin Cordi's *Raising Voices: Creating Youth Storytelling Groups and Troupes.* But the point in working with students is not to train them to become future storytellers but to provide them with skills and confidence. Through storytelling they can learn not only that what they have to say is significant but also that they will have to struggle to have their viewpoints represented or interwoven into the stories fabricated around them.

There is a plethora of ways to empower young people through story, especially in schools. In England and Ireland, Michael Wilson, professor and storyteller, Patrick Ryan, Liz Weir, and many others have sought to animate adolescents to form their own storytelling clubs and circles and to guide them so that they would acquire the skills to collect and tell their own stories. The cooperative work with adults, especially with teachers, is crucial, especially when the children are between the ages of five and twelve. Throughout her work in Chicago, the gifted writer and teacher Vivian Paley demonstrated how she has managed to draw children to stories, to draw out stories from children, and to be inspired by them to reflect on their interactions, problems, and needs. One of her books, *The Girl with the Brown Crayon,* is a fascinating account of how Reeny, a five-year-old girl, is attracted to the books of the illustrator and writer Leo Lionni, and because of her great interest, the entire class begins listening to and reading all of Lionni's books. In addition, discussions of the stories lead to discussions of race, gender, and identity. The classroom is transformed into a laboratory of life through the conversations and stories that the children and teachers tell.

Transforming the classroom into a laboratory, theater, or playroom is important because it breaks down borders and boundaries. Children can trespass, and in doing so they can become acquainted with unknown dimensions of their personalities and the material conditions surrounding them. In Pistoia, Italy, a municipal laboratory called "Di Bocca in Bocca" ("From Mouth to Mouth") explores the local Italian oral tradition in six-week programs. Because Italian schools often end at 1:00 in the afternoon, children are often left to themselves or are looked after by parents in the afternoons. Several years ago, the city of Pistoia organized free municipal programs that focused on storytelling, mask making, designing, and other activities to enable children to learn more about the oral tradition in their region and to bring about a stronger sense of community. During 1998 to 1999 I made several trips to Pistoia to witness a fairy-tale project in which the storyteller Marisa Schiano used her story to animate the children to form their own characters by using masks and outfits. Then the students created their own stories using what they had made. The long-term work with the students involved writing and acting out of stories that were collected in little pamphlets or hung on the walls. Sometimes schools visited the laboratory space in the mornings, but most of the activities took place in the afternoon.

In my opinion, however, it is preferable to transform classrooms and schools during the time that the children are at school. But the choice of a venue for storytelling with children depends on the customs and regulations of a particular country or community. In the United States, storytelling for children now takes place in bookstores, recreation centers, churches, synagogues, parks, and other domains outside the school. Yet I think the school is the best venue of all because it enables the storyteller to establish a relationship with the teacher, students, school community, and parents. The storyteller, who returns again and again to a particular class, goes through a learning process. That storyteller can then help train teachers to use the techniques and methods of storytelling to develop the critical and creative talents of the students.

In the twin cities of Minneapolis and St. Paul I am involved in a project called Neighborhood Bridges in collaboration with the Children's Theatre Company of Minneapolis and eight to ten urban schools. Each year for five years I have worked with more than fifteen actors—whom I coached as storytellers in a special program to introduce children to different genres of storytelling, acting, and writing—several teachers, and two classes of fifth graders. The overall goal of the program is to transform their classrooms for two hours each week so they can try out and test their skills in storytelling, improvisational skits, writing, and drawing. In the process they have produced some printed stories and created their own plays, which they have performed for their schoolmates, parents, and teachers, and they have traveled to the other school at the end of the year to build community bridges. The effects, as Lynn Rubright already noticed in her work, were multiple and probably not always recognizable with regard to the future development of these students. By this I mean it is difficult to measure quantitatively the improvement in the lives of the students and teachers, but anyone involved in a storytelling program or experiment of this kind will see immediately that in the long run this kind of storytelling will be a significant impetus for individual growth. Through storytelling programs centered on critical literacy, young people acquire the confidence to stand before others and articulate their views, to invent stories, to write and illustrate their own narratives, to appreciate and question the tales they hear from others, to move and use gestures that dramatically aid their articulated views, and to think for themselves.

Yet the focus of school authorities and politicians tends to be on testing, more testing, and rote learning. Storytelling as a means to strengthen learning and cultivation of skills in all disciplines has generally been neglected by schools and teachers, who generally are receptive to innovative storytelling when exposed to it. For most school officials, parents, and politicians, storytelling is performance or platform storytelling; good and healthy amusement for the children but not related to the learning processes that they hope will make the children successful—successful in their careers, successful and responsible citizens, and successful consumers. But performance or platform storytelling has very little to do with genuine pedagogical storytelling, or, if I might add, with genuine storytelling as I have defined it.

It is not my intention to examine the manifold ways in which market conditions and relations of work have penetrated families and schools except to say that the corporate model of doing business generates models in the public and private spheres that influence our behavior. We tend to treat other people as objects and are treated as objects ourselves. We learn very early in our lives that the primary goal in life is to win at all costs, to make our bodies into perfect machines as sports stars or sex objects, and to use language to our advantage. Existence has become almost monadic; that is, we tend to lead encapsulated lives and develop little trust in our communities—if we have communities. In my estimation, the effect has led to growing violence among all age groups and in all social strata in the United States and to an intensification of the reification and alienation in all walks of life. At the same time, the discontent that many people feel—as Freud might say, *das Unbehagen,* in his great book *Civilization and Its Discontents*—has produced a deep longing for tranquility, harmony, spirituality, and community. As various critics have noted, this longing that is connected to a lack or gap in our lives has been part of the driving force behind the revival of storytelling in North America and in the world. In reaction to the work and living conditions that undermine the possibilities for creating communities and fixed traditions, storytellers have tried to foster a mythical and mystical sense of community in and through their stories. This intention is certainly understandable, even laudable. But to my mind, genuine storytelling today cannot pretend that ideal communities and cults are within our reach. If it is to capture the essence of our contemporary societies, then genuine storytelling must reflect conditions that produce alienation and invent plots and strategies to combat the conditions. It need do this not with pessimism but with the hope that suffering can lead to joy and that candor can lead to wisdom. Mythological storytelling in unmythological times only masks the dilemma in which we find ourselves today.

A few years ago, while visiting Germany, I saw a disturbing TV documentary on storytelling and sects. Part of the show focused on a group in Hamburg that gathers to tell stories about their actual experiences watching and listening to fairies. Another segment featured a group of men who congregate regularly in a forest to run around naked, commune with nature, and tell stories to strengthen their bonds of brotherhood. In the final segment, male and female witches gathered in the woods to celebrate medieval rituals that endow them with spiritual powers as storytellers. In all the interviews with the storytellers and their followers, the people appeared to be sincere. They believed devoutly in the stories they concocted. Their folly in my eyes was wisdom in theirs. And the truth of the matter is, both their folly that I perceive and the wisdom that they feel result from the same widespread malaise. The folly and wisdom are of our own making, and we often confuse the two.

When people form secret societies, they are striving to fill gaps in their lives left by a technological society that discounts human feelings. The problem is that they are often unaware of the extent to which their behavior conforms to market expectations and unknowingly helps sustain a myth of freedom because, on the surface, they appear to be acting freely. However, in my opinion, most of these groups' rituals are little more than conditioned responses to intolerable circumstances —responses that are tolerated by society because they do not endanger the status quo. On the contrary, these groups reinforce it by serving as so many zany sideshows for the rest of us—just another form of entertainment—while confirming that our norms are normal and good.

In a world in which entertainment has also been largely commodified by large corporations, genuine storytelling, and especially storytelling with and for children, has a special mission: to expose the wisdom and folly of all storytelling and to reveal to children how storytelling can empower them to grasp the forces acting upon them. If our young are to have a chance to ground their lives in any kind of tradition, they must learn hopeful skepticism, how to play creatively with the forces dictating their lives, and how to use storytelling to reshape those conditions that foster sham and hypocrisy.

Fig. 3.1 Students at Tuttle School preparing for a play.

3

How Storytellers Can Change Education in Changing Times: Stealing from the Rich to Build Community Bridges

The best storytellers are thieves and forgers. They steal their tales from everywhere—books, television, films, radio, the Internet, and even other living human beings. Sometimes they steal tales from their own experience that they revise, adorn, and dress in such a way that those who might have witnessed the real incidents would never be able to recognize them. Storytellers appropriate their stolen goods, make them their property, and re-present them as if the goods were their own material, which, in many ways, they are because storytellers always forge the tales they steal anew. They conceal their thefts by pretending their stories are their very own or by claiming they have borrowed them from some source and added their own original touches to make them their own. Some storytellers maintain their stories are absolutely true and original, whatever these words mean. But the truth of their stories depends on artifice. Put more positively, truth depends on art—the ability of storytellers to transform their material and make stories relevant for themselves and the people to whom they are giving their stolen goods. Theft and forgery are crucial ingredients for the making of a good storyteller, and storytellers are indeed morally good if they steal and forge to repay society for their crimes, that is, with the intention of changing their community and enriching it with their stolen tales. A good storyteller is an incorrigible thief and at the same time is the social conscience of society because he or she is critically aware of how theft and exploitation determine our traditions and govern our lives.

I, too, like to consider myself a rogue storyteller, a cunning thief, capable of being charged with grand larceny, and this is why I want to begin this chapter with a tale that I am stealing from Carl Ewald, a much neglected Danish writer of the late nineteenth and early twentieth centuries. Disturbed by the many wars that erupted in Europe during his lifetime, he wrote the following tale to provoke readers to think about the causes of violent conflicts. It is a tale worth telling and retelling.

> There was once a time when wars spread throughout the world causing havoc and great destruction. Hundreds of thousands of people were killed. Hundreds of thousands starved to death and lived in poverty. The land, the forests, and seas were devastated. The animals and plant life all but disappeared. At one time the people had placed their faith in their leaders, who had insisted that war was the only way to defend their communities, customs, and religious values. They had God's blessing, their leaders insisted, and the people had soon come to believe in the righteousness of war more than they believed in the words of God. Yet, gradually they realized that the wars had torn apart their communities and did not hold them together. They did not know how to get their presidents, ministers, and generals to stop using barbaric weapons to settle disputes that brought death to their families and friends, for their leaders did not listen to their cries for peace. They ignored their pleas and arrested anyone who protested against their wars of liberation. Finally, the people from different countries came together secretly, for they feared the wrath of their leaders, and decided to send some deputies to God to ask for his help.
>
> When the deputies arrived in heaven, they were upset and asked God why he was allowing their leaders to continue their wars and create such misery and suffering on earth. Why had he

allowed the earth to be ruled by presidents, ministers, and generals?

God looked sternly at the deputies and said in a booming voice, "I don't know a thing about this. I created you all equal. Good bye!"

When the deputies heard his answer, they sat down in front of the gates of heaven and began to cry and plead for his help. When God saw this, he took pity on them and let them enter heaven again. Then he summoned an archangel and said, "Get the book in which I listed all of the plagues that were to fall upon human beings. Check to see whether there is anything in all my writings or spoken words that condones the behavior of presidents, ministers, or generals."

Then God ordered the deputies to wait outside the gates of heaven, and they sat there the entire day because the book was very thick. Finally, the angel returned to God and told him that there was nothing in all his words and writings about presidents, ministers, or generals.

"I'm sorry," God said as he turned to the deputies. "I cannot help you."

"Please, please!" they cried. "Please have your angel search some more."

So God spoke to the archangel and said, "Get the books in which I've recorded everything human beings must suffer for their foolish acts and prayers so that they might learn the wisdom of my words. Check to see whether I wrote anything about whether presidents, ministers, or generals should rule the earth."

The angel spent two weeks carefully searching God's words and writings. Then he returned to God and gave him the same answer, whereupon God turned to the deputies who were desperately expecting his help.

"There is nothing in my words or writings," God declared, "to justify the wars or actions of your leaders. Presidents, ministers, and generals. They are your own invention. If you're sick and tired of them, it is up to you to get rid of them. I cannot help you."

Upon saying these words, he dismissed the deputies and sent them back to their war-torn earth.[1]

Now one might ask what all my talk about storytellers as thieves and my theft of Ewald's tale about peace has to do with storytelling, higher education, and building bridges in the community. There are connections to be made, and I shall try to make them next.

When I talk about a storyteller as a good thief, similar to our image of Robin Hood, who allegedly stole from the rich to give to the poor, I am introducing a moral category that can be applied in more general terms to make social distinctions to clarify how occupations function to determine a person's professional behavior in capitalist society. Opposed to the good thief is the crook. He or she assumes a role similar to that of the captains of industry and our political leaders, who pretend to act on behalf of the people but who are more interested in power and self-aggrandizement. These distinguished men and women do not give back anything to society; they take, hoard, and protect their treasures. They will kill or hire people to kill for them to maintain their privileges and power. Their actions are not abnormal or strange, for they behave in accordance with the basic principle of capitalism that depends on the exploitation of human labor for profit. The difference between the good thief and the bad crook is that the good thief admits that we are all obliged to rob in some way and somehow wants to offset injustices and repay his or her crime by helping the disadvantaged and maintaining a subversive tradition of human compassion and responsibility, whereas the bad crook refuses to admit his or her involvement and culpability and continually seeks ways to deceive the majority of people with slogans like "compassionate government." Because it is difficult to rationalize the bad crook's actions, he or she uses the forces of the mass media, government, and courts to gain more of a stranglehold over the minds and lives of common people.

It may seem that I am being too simplistic or too contentious in drawing these political parallels, and certainly, any critic of U.S. society must be more prudent and more sophisticated in analyzing the complex nature of how governments and corporations function. But even though I am generalizing about the socioeconomic conditions in the United States, I believe there is great relevance in grasping the moral difference between thieves and crooks and how that difference is played out or can be played out when storytellers consider teaching, working, and learning within the different institutions of education. Without a critical analysis and understanding of what is happening in our schools and universities, and without critical self-reflection about the social roles they occupy, storytellers will essentially contribute to the goals of the crooks, which are to make consumers out of children and to take their own profits from regulated human labor and manipulated mass consumption. Let me say it up front: there is nothing wrong in storytellers earning a living and making some profit from their storytelling, but there is something wrong if the art of the storyteller does not help in some way to combat cultural and political conditions of homogenization, conformity, and planned "cretinzation" of our young.

Before I elaborate about the possibilities of storytellers to insert themselves as good thieves, whether they be academics or creative artists, into the university and to provide bridges to contribute to communities, I want to try to present a succinct critique of the conditions of education in k-12 schools and higher education. I also want to insist that it is important not to make a great distinction between k-12 schools and colleges and universities because whatever is happening in our elementary, middle, and high schools has a direct effect on higher education, and vice versa. Indeed, the same students trained in the k-12 schools are then prepared at universities to take over those schools, and in turn they have a profound influence on k-12 education, which had already predisposed them to specific attitudes and created specific expectations. There is a dialectic at work here that unfortunately does not tend toward fostering enlightenment and a more humane civilization. Consumer capitalism, which forms and informs the basic tenets of the institutions of U.S. education, is incapable of articulating and realizing conditions for human compassion and autonomous communities. This is why storytellers must be subversive good thieves, talking against the grain. Any moral storyteller worth his or her salt recognizes this important role as soon as he or she enters a school or a university and must deal with vast problems. These obstacles to teaching and storytelling range from the heavy-handed bureaucratic administration and inane rules and regulations to the rationalized production of students who are being trained for a market that actually offers relatively few chances for self-development, unless one learns how to assume the habitus of elite groups that manage our social, political, cultural, and economic institutions.

So what is happening at our schools and universities?

In *Educating the "Right" Way: Markets, Standards, God, and Inequality,* perhaps one of the most important recent critiques of the changing conditions in public education in the United States, and not only in the United States, Michael Apple discussed how the powerful forces of neoliberalism, neoconservatism, and authoritarian populism have brought about gradual restructuring of education by demanding a return to traditional forms of teaching, reintroduction of Christian values and prayer, responsible teaching controlled by testing and set curriculums, vouchers to allow for greater choice among customers of schools, and privatization of education. Overseeing these policies is a new managerial and professional class that has altered the role of the state. Apple commented,

> We can think of this as involving three strategic transformations. First, many public assets have been privatized. Public utilities are sold off to the highest bidder; schools are given to corporations to run. Second, rigorous competition between institutions is sponsored so that public institutions are constantly compared with supposedly more efficient private ones. Hence, even if schools and other institutions are still state funded, their internal procedures increasingly mirror those of the corporate sector. Third, public responsibilities have been shifted onto the informal sector, under the argument that the government can no longer afford the expense of such services. In practice this has meant that a good deal of child care, caring for the elderly and infirm, and so much more has been "dumped" onto the local community and the family. This is one of the reasons that it is crucial to realize that behind a good deal of the new managerialism and the importation of business models into the state is a specifically patriarchal set of assumptions and effects, since it is largely the unpaid labor of women in the family and in local communities that will be exploited to deal with the state's shedding of its previous responsibilities. At the same

time, while some aspects of the state are indeed dumped onto local communities, other aspects of state control are enhanced and made even stronger, especially its control over knowledge and values in the schools and over the mechanisms of evaluating institutional success or failure in such cultural production.[2]

Apple is well aware that these negative tendencies have not taken root throughout the United States, and that as a cultural force field of conflict, in which educators on the left, right, and middle have staked out their positions, education is in a constant process of change. But his fear about the commercialization and privatization of schools is not unreasonable, for the recent developments in public education may bring about a limitation of critical discourse, prevent project-oriented learning, preclude innovative programs in the arts such as storytelling, and transform children into nothing but discriminate consumers and gear them for participation in a workforce bound by the interests of corporate conglomerates. For instance, more than 40 percent of the schools in the United States have signed contracts with Channel One, which offers televisions and other technological apparatuses to schools, providing that the schools contractually oblige their students to watch only the news programs and advertisements of Channel One. In other words, the "stories" disseminated by Channel One condition and influence the modes of seeing and grasping the world, limiting the perspective of students. Besides the introduction of commercial television, many schools offer programs that teach for jobs and the market. Functional education is at the heart of the new "reforms." State and national testing, which have become excessive in the past twenty years, dictate what and how children are to know so that rote learning of facts of history, literature, math, and science is favored. The boards of education determine what textbooks will be used in each state according to ideological preferences, often producing censorship and elimination of viewpoints that may run counter to religious and political interests that dominate in a particular region or state. In her important book *The Language Police: How Pressure Groups Restrict What Students Learn,* which reads like an urgent appeal to stop and prevent a growing disease, Diane Ravitch commented, "The censorship that has spread throughout American education has pernicious and pervasive effects. It lowers the literacy level of tests because test makers must take care to avoid language as well as works of literature and historical selections that might give offense. It restricts the language and ideas that may be reproduced in textbooks. It surely reduces children's interest in their schoolwork by making their studies so deadly dull. It undermines our common culture by imposing irrelevant political criteria on the literature and history that are taught."[3] All kinds of censorship have an impact on the publishing industry that derives millions of dollars from sales in schools so that publishers will self-censor the textbooks before marketing them in the public domain. More and more parents, especially of the white middle class, have come to view themselves as customers of schools and have demanded that teachers be held more responsible for the learning progress or defaults of their children because they believe the teachers are failing their failing children and should be held accountable. Tests and private and state control are, they believe, effective ways to guarantee children will have success in college and then in the work world. Yet they do not examine their own responsibilities, nor do they become involved enough in guaranteeing that public education will be duly supported.

The constraints placed on school administrators and teachers along with the reduction in available funds due to state and national budget crises and the present recession are enormous. In particular, teachers are under great pressure to perform according to standards determined by the state and by the exams the children will have to undergo, and they are so burdened by paperwork and other responsibilities that they have very little time if any to experiment in the classroom or to develop arts programs, especially storytelling and creative drama. Even the residency programs that bring artists from different fields into schools have been curtailed in most states. It is generally well-known that when there is a budgetary crisis and schools must cut positions, and programs, the first teachers to be dismissed will be the art and music teachers or the media specialists. Rarely is a second thought given to how the arts might be incorporated in daily teaching to improve the learning skills and respond to the interests of the children. In fact, much of the storytelling that is done within schools is separate from the curriculum, or it is done in the library by the media specialist who simply reads a story from a book. What often passes for storytelling is passive listening by the children who are encouraged to read by a teacher reading a book with the intention of setting a good example. This is a form of entertainment and rote teaching if it is not coupled with an interactive component. Even the storytelling programs at high schools and the contests that are held within states bear the marks of rote learning. I remember visiting Mankato (Minnesota) a few years ago, and two girls about sixteen years of age approached me and asked whether I would listen to the tales they were going to present in a state contest held by a group of high schools. I agreed and was aghast when I heard them tell two Grimm fairy tales word for word from memory. They also had pat gestures and predictable intonation. When I asked them why they had memorized the tales and acted them out in such a prescribed way, they told me that they were expected to tell tales according to certain standards; otherwise, the judges would take points off from their performance. They could not freely play with the tales and tell them in innovative ways. They could not use their own voices. There was a *correct* way to tell tales just as there are always *correct* answers on tests, and the tests themselves are never to be questioned or challenged.

Fortunately, what I call a "locked" approach to learning and education is unlocked to a certain extent in higher education. Depending on where a student will attend college—if he or she does—the emphasis on positivism, testing, and rote learning will be questioned. Unfortunately, the testing continues, and grades mean more than the acquisition of knowledge and learning how to think for oneself. Sometimes freshmen students are indeed confused when given the freedom to think, for U.S. colleges and universities do encourage students to think for themselves and determine what they would like to make out of their lives. It is difficult to make generalizations about the educational opportunities that students receive, for they will often attend colleges and universities that reinforce their own religious persuasion or philosophical beliefs. However, in my experience of teaching at four major state universities, one private university, and several universities in Europe, I have seen how students are presented with diverse possibilities for learning how to think critically and imaginatively if they take advantage of the courses offered to them. The U.S. higher education system is exceptional in the world because it is so diverse, provides all kinds of possibilities for students of different backgrounds, and has a wealth of resources. Nevertheless, as in the k-12 schools, there have been clear signs that our colleges and universities are already turning themselves into vast corporations that serve the business world and are limiting the opportunities for students to explore the different fields of knowledge in depth and to understand the connection between learning and concrete existential concerns. There have been a series of excellent books that have studied how universities are gradually abandoning their role as learning institutions: Bill Readings, *The University in Ruins;* Sheila Slaughter and Larry Leslie, *Academic Capitalism: Politics, Policies and the Entrepreneurial University;* Wesley Shumar, *College for Sale: A Critique of the Commodification of Higher Education;* and Stanley Aronowitz, *The Knowledge Factory: Dismantling the Corporate University and Creating True Higher Learning.* Just this past year, Derek Bok, a former president of Harvard, published a devastating critique of the negative transformation of U.S. universities and colleges in *Universities in the Marketplace: The Commercialization of Higher Education.* However, in a review of this book, the new president of Amherst College, Anthony Marx, was even more radical than Bok:

> As chilling as Bok's warnings are, they could go even further. For instance, the competing for admission selectivity and higher rankings has produced too much anxiety among applicants and too little socioeconomic diversity in the student body. Institutions also increasingly compete with one another for star faculty, paying large salaries to attract celebrity professors who demand lighter teaching loads, setting the stage for all faculty to make similar demands and undermining the focus on teaching. Bok does not address an even more important problem, how market competition has encouraged elite institutions at the top of the educational pyramid to ignore their social responsibilities and interest in helping to improve the primary and secondary educational systems below them. But such efforts would not bring in funds: They may require time and resources. And the country at large suffers from the way that education, like society as a whole, is divided into rich and poor.[4]

The keyword used by most administrators today is *cost efficient.* Higher education is expected to model itself on the corporate world, and departments in all fields are ordered to cut costs and make profits by drawing as many students/customers as possible to their classes.

Programs and departments are downsized or eliminated if they do not produce according to market needs. Many students who work and need five to seven years to complete their bachelor's degree are being obliged to complete everything within four years as if they were on a conveyor belt and had to function according to the needs of the university and not their own interests. Special programs for disadvantaged students and adult education are being cancelled. Tuition and other fees have soared. Because there is presently a great need for computer scientists and scientists of all kinds, the resources of the university are used to cater to corporations in this area. The more universities address business interests, the more corporations donate money for buildings or sports facilities. Often the humanities, education, and social sciences are looked upon with suspicious eyes, because they tend to foster critical thinking instead of what I call "functional thinking." In addition, a great deal of money is collected for sports programs to have stadiums and professional teams that become just as famous for their scandals as for their victories in the name of their alma mater. At my own university there have been at least five major sports scandals as well as two national medical scandals in the thirteen years I have taught there, and these scandals have cost the university millions of dollars, not to mention the preposterous salaries that the coaches, assistant coaches, and water boys draw. Indeed, we can rightly say that the university is modeling itself on the corporate world where corruption is part and parcel of daily business.

Universities are in the business of reproducing conditions in the socioeconomic system, either to stabilize it or to transform it and make it more effective. Professors who teach in higher education—including myself—further the interests of their universities by seeking to secure their own interests and mold students in their shape. Essentially, as the great French sociologist Pierre Bourdieu pointed out, there is essentially one shape, if you will, and that is the *homo academicus* and his or her habitus. Here I want to elaborate somewhat on Bourdieu's notion of habitus, for it is crucial for a critical understanding of the role or habitus of the storyteller.

In one of the more cogent studies of Bourdieu's works, Jen Webb, Tony Schirato, and Geoff Danaher commented, "Habitus can be understood as the values and dispositions gained from our cultural history that generally stay with us across contexts (they are durable and transposable). These values and dispositions allow us to respond to cultural rules and contexts in a variety of ways because they allow for improvisations, but the responses are always largely determined—regulated by where (and who) we have been in a culture."[5] Referring, in particular, to professors, they depicted academics as

> cloistered in their "ivory towers," who are disposed by their physical milieu (libraries, book-filled offices, lecture theatres) and spatial location (the university is a kind of "world within itself," set apart from the rest of society) to "bracket off" the rest of the world. This disposition manifests itself, however, not just in attitudes, approaches and values (real problems are made "academic," and treated as abstractions), but into terms of the production of an intellectual body. If you look at any number of jackets of academic books, you will find the author "arranged" and posed in particular ways (a sombre expression, hands on chin, wearing glasses) which are meant to connote, say, seriousness, or a contemplative state of mind.[6]

The habitus of a professor is not a static stereotype. There is a great range of types of professors and behaviors at the university. However, most professors are disposed to act and mold themselves in very particular ways if they want to attain a position and maintain it at the university. The habitus can be altered by the conflicts within the university and education, but there are very basic ways physically and mentally that professors, even though they may come from different fields of study, will comport themselves similarly to guarantee their authority and to reproduce facsimiles who can only gain membership in the "corporation" if they pass the proper tests, which means if they show that they have learned how to assume the habitus of a professor.

To be sure, there are professors who struggle against their very own habitus, and there are very different contesting positions at the university. There is also a hierarchy among professors and intense battles over the allocation of funds, the development of departments and programs, and education policies. Involved in struggles to protect and maintain their disciplines, professors lose sight of just how their behavior or habitus reproduces the same relations of production in the "outside" world that are based on exploitation and consumerism. Very few professors do community or outreach work, and if they do, they often consult or work to maintain the status quo, especially the professors in the fields of science and technology. This is not to say that the professors in the humanities and social sciences are "better" or more aware of how their conduct serves a cultural and systematic production of students who are being trained to dispose themselves in appropriate forms so they can market themselves for high prices and contribute to the economy. In some ways, they are more blind and at the same time more ambitious because they are generally lower in the hierarchy and are intent on building their departments and augmenting their power. Competition between departments and fields can become fierce at universities, and smart administrators must know how to keep this competition alive while maintaining good ties to the corporate world and state legislatures.

As I have already mentioned, there have been major studies about how the U.S. university has been incorporated into the corporate business world and is now unfortunately regarded as a new model to "save" education in Europe with grave consequences, for the emphasis is on cost efficiency and not on education. Given the excellent studies of higher education, I shall not expand my critique much longer except to comment on some of the negative tendencies that have affected folklore programs and storytelling at the universities.

Although folklore programs do not necessarily include storytelling as part of their curriculum, they generally do offer courses that involve or are related to storytelling. In fact, I would argue that every storyteller who takes his or her art seriously should have some basic knowledge about folklore, different narrative genres, and a comparative history of storytelling. Such a possibility for a student or storyteller has become more and more limited. When I began teaching some thirty-five years ago, there were large and thriving graduate programs at the universities of Indiana, Pennsylvania, Texas, Wisconsin, North Carolina, California–Los Angeles (UCLA), and California–Berkeley. UCLA and Texas have abandoned these programs, and the others have been greatly curtailed. Most universities and colleges in the United States do not have a folklore program, although they may have one folklorist or a professor interested in folklore in English, anthropology, and ethnology departments. There are many different factors that have contributed to the decline of folklore at the university. The most important one is elit-ism. From the very beginning, folklore was never popular at U.S. uni-versities, nor was popular culture. From the late nineteenth century through the post-1945 war period, there were very few courses offered on folklore, and popular culture was considered a vulgar topic. The uni-versity always regarded itself as a bastion of high culture, and though times have changed, the serious study of the people, the folk, and their lore is not a priority at the university. With the gradual rise of the styl-ish and flashy programs of cultural studies, now in vogue at U.S. univer-sities, and the gradual collapse of disciplines, at least in the humanities, the future of folklore looks bleak, and, thus, only in isolated places will students be able to attain a thorough knowledge of the history of folk-lore and popular narratives and the way common people have used sto-ries and storytelling for hundreds of years.

The situation is different at schools of education and library science, where folklore is rarely taught if ever but where storytelling is generally incorporated into the curriculum in some form or another. This is not to say that there are full-fledged courses that deal entirely with story-telling and how to use storytelling to enhance the basic skills of both educators and children. For instance, I have taught at the universities of Wisconsin (Milwaukee), Florida, and Minnesota, all very large state universities, and at New York University, and I cannot recollect any of these universities offering a course on storytelling per se. Even one of the most progressive schools of education, Bank Street, did not offer courses in storytelling until late in its development. Nina Jaffe recently commented, "Storytelling as part of teacher education has been included in graduate studies at Bank Street College since the 1970s, taught both by librarians and professional storytellers. A strong emphasis on narrative and folklore is included as well in courses in cur-riculum and children's literature. Storytelling and narrative as fields of interest have been occupying a growing number of scholars in the world of education."[7]

Note that Jaffe said that storytelling is part only of graduate studies and not of undergraduate studies, for there is no undergraduate curric-ulum at Bank Street. Moreover, the introduction of storytelling began in the 1970s, when the renaissance of storytelling began taking shape outside the university. It is my guess—and I can only speculate because

I don't think there has been a scholarly study on this subject—that more storytelling courses were gradually introduced into schools of education thanks to the formation of NAPPS, now known as the National Storytelling Network, and like-minded associations and the growth of interest in storytelling outside the university since the late 1980s, which Joseph Sobol documented so thoroughly in his book *The Storytellers' Journey: An American Revival*. In addition, only since the 1970s have important studies and handbooks of storytelling by such prominent advocates as Anne Pellowski, Vivian Paley, Margaret Mac-Donald, Kay Stone, Doug Lippman, Arthur Applebee, Jack Maguire, Bob Baron, David Booth, Rives Collins, Patsy Cooper, Kieran Egan, Frances Godforth, Carolyn Spillman, and others begun to have an impact at the university. Yet I would contend that there are still too few courses on storytelling taught at schools of education and at universities in general, and when they are taught, I wonder to what extent they contribute to the tendencies to make the university more a training place for the market and to reinforcing the habitus of the professor than anything else.

If I have already been too contentious in my critique of the university, I don't apologize. In fact, I want to be even more contentious when I discuss the role of storytelling, the storyteller, and the professor at the university. I want to begin with the premise, a very simplistic one, that even when universities and colleges cry poor and that they are being decimated because of the current economic crisis, they are still very rich and becoming richer through private donations. More and more state universities, which used to be affordable for most students, have become more expensive and are relying more and more on private industry and wealthy patrons to maintain themselves, or, to be more exact, to continue the development of the corporate university crowned by sports teams and their stadiums. For instance, my own university, a public institution, just completed a $1.656 billion capital drive fund[8] that will fill its coffers and support ongoing programs. The question we must always ask, however, is whether the universities are using their money wisely for the education of students or whether they are investing their money too much in sports, bureaucracy, business ventures, and programs that cater to the corporate world. After all, it does not cost very much to provide a room in which an average teacher with a moderate salary can teach his or her subject. Education need not be as expensive as it presently is. Whatever the case may be, universities are rich in money and resources, and though one could say they pay back society by providing students with the appropriate tools to function in our consumer society, I would argue that they deserve to be robbed by storytellers and academics—not to mention by students, who deserve free education—who, as *good thieves,* should take their money and resources to question the negative tendencies of consumerism, the market, and the excessive power of corporations. They, the professors as storytellers, must exploit the resources of the university to pay back the communities from which they come. Professors genuinely interested in storytelling, knowledge, and education must become good thieves and tricksters and infiltrate the university to challenge the very habitus they are expected to protect.

In no way do I mean that professors/storytellers must become subversive radicals or didactic ideologues who must be politically correct and deliver a critique of corporate capitalism in their classes. This is counterproductive. I am arguing for critical awareness, critical pedagogy, and critical literacy. Any professor/storyteller who introduces a course on storytelling into the university will by necessity have to become conscious of the condescending if not dismissive attitude toward the social role of storytelling in the hierarchy of values, especially if he or she is interested in critical pedagogy and critical literacy. Paradoxically, it is not too difficult to find a way to introduce such a course because it can be very popular and draw students, thus justifying its market value. Yet this market value may fluctuate. Anyway, it is not for its market value that I advise professors/storytellers to explore the potential of a storytelling course at the university, but for it to generate conditions for creating community.

Community is a term difficult to define today because it is used in so many different ways that it has lost much of its significant meaning. Some critics even claim that community no longer exists. For instance, the insightful and brilliant sociologist Zygmunt Bauman claimed, "We miss community because we miss security, a quality crucial to a happy life, but one which the world we inhabit is ever less able to offer and ever more reluctant to promise. But community remains stubbornly missing, eludes our grasp or keeps falling apart, because the way in which this world prompts us to go about fulfilling our dreams of a secure life does not bring us closer to their fulfillment; instead of being mitigated, our insecurity grows as we go, and so we go on dreaming, trying, and failing."[9] In keeping with Bauman's notion of community as a process that is never ending, we can modestly propose to create communities within schools that are related to the needs of the neighborhoods and areas from which children in a school come. In her cogent essay "Building Alliances, Building Community, Building Bridges through Literacy," Laurie Stowell maintained, "A first step for members of the potential community is to know one another and trust one another—that is, to build alliances. Customarily, community is applied to virtually any group—a neighborhood, town or city, school, church, or social club—even when the members may be total strangers. But community requires quality communication, not the mere exchange of words." Quoting M. S. Peck, Stowell continued, "Community is a way of being together with both individual authenticity and interpersonal harmony so that people become able to function with a collective energy even greater than the sum of their individual energies." Finally, she cited L. Christensen: "To become community, students must learn to live in someone else's skin, understand the parallels of hurt, struggle and joy across class and culture lines and work for change. For that to happen, students need more than an upbeat, supportive teacher; they need a curriculum that teaches them how to empathize with others."[10]

Communities can be created most anywhere as long as there is a group of people who learn to trust one another and share common values, ideas, and goals that they endeavor to implement in their everyday behavior and interaction with one another. A "concrete" community need not endure for more than an hour or two every day; it could, of course, last much longer if the community's customs take root. What is most important is that the formation of the community becomes a learning process of mutual respect. For youngsters it is crucial that this learning process take place within a structure that provides security so that the children can feel free to experiment and play freely with their ideas, test their ideas in actions, and even change the structure in which they are learning.

A classroom filled with a professor and students can become a community. A classroom filled with a professor who wants to teach a course on storytelling with students eager to learn about storytelling can become a community. A classroom filled with a professor who has a curriculum about teaching storytelling to create communities within schools to students eager to learn how storytelling can enable children to form their own communities and participate in their neighborhood communities can become a community. There are many different types of classes that one can offer on storytelling at the university that range from teaching the basic methods of selecting and performing tales to studying the therapeutic value of storytelling and using storytelling in different social institutions. For my purpose I want to reflect on several courses that I have taught during the summer under the auspices of the University of Minnesota, Hamline University, the Perpich Center for the Arts, and the Children's Theatre Company of Minneapolis at different times over the past seven years. I want to reflect on my work as critically as I can because my reflections may be useful for others interested in teaching storytelling related to building bridges between the university and the community. Let me say from the start that I am very much against platform storytelling in schools and that my course was and is not intended to further this type of storytelling. I am not dogmatically against platform storytelling in general, but I think young people see much too much of this kind of storytelling on television, on the stage, in the movies, and elsewhere, and the focus tends to be on the storyteller himself or herself. Moreover, such storytelling reproduces the very socioeconomic conditions of consumerism that, I believe, reduces children and stories to commodities and focuses too much emphasis on the storyteller as a star, who has magical powers and furthers notions of elitism. I am more interested in how storytelling can animate and enable children to become storytellers of their own lives.

From 1995 to the present, I have taught various courses on storytelling attended by teachers in k-12 education, professional storytellers, actors, and university students. Initially, the first course, which was held for about three to four hours every day for two weeks, was offered through the University of Minnesota to interest a general public of students in storytelling. When I began developing the storytelling program Neighborhood Bridges with the Children's Theatre Company of Minneapolis in 1996, my course also became a training ground for actors and teachers who would be implementing the program in the inner-city schools of Minneapolis and St. Paul. Though I did not want to make the course into a kind of service course for Neighborhood Bridges, there was a slight shift toward praxis within schools in the second week of the course, and the curriculum kept changing based on the needs of the participants and on what I learned from them.

The course description, which has constantly changed during the past seven years, read as follows: This course examines how storytelling and creative drama can be used as tools in developing students' critical literacy, and in making students more fluent readers and writers. Storytelling is a unique blend of performance, literature, and folklore. It engages personal and cultural identities, and it promotes creative thinking. Critical literacy is the ability to analyze the presentation of information and identify how the presentation influences listeners' and readers' understanding of the information. Writing, performing, and analyzing narratives are therefore powerful means of developing critical literacy. Key topics to be covered are (1) the historical background on fairy tales and oral traditions, (2) tools for developing a critical view of fairy tales, (3) practical instruction on how to use storytelling and story genres in the classroom to develop critical literacy, and (4) assessing storytelling work in the classroom. Given the focus on fairy tales, there are three goals:

1. To provide a historical background on fairy tales and oral traditions by examining the difference between an oral folktale and a literary fairy tale, studying the storytelling tradition of fairy tales, and exploring the historical interaction between folktales and fairy tales.

2. To provide tools for developing a critical view of fairy tales by investigating and challenging the canon of tales familiar to students and teachers. Are there new types of fairy tales? Can we create "countertales" that challenge preconceived notions of gender, class, and violence?

3. To provide practical instruction on how to use storytelling and story genres in the classroom to develop critical literacy. What are the basic principles of critical literacy? What are the particular creative drama techniques we can use to stimulate creativity and create both written and oral narrative in the classroom?

The purpose of the seminar is outlined as follows: to provide teachers and storytellers with some historical knowledge and a critical view of fairy tales and other folklore genres so that they can work with the tales in different ways to animate their students to become their own storytellers; that is, to develop their own creative and critical skills. Though most people think they know what a fairy tale is, and though they read and use fairy tales to socialize children, very few are aware of the distinction between the oral folktale and the literary fairy tale and the problematic aspects of fairy tales with regard to the socialization of children. Moreover, very few teachers are aware of the remarkable number of contemporary "revisionist" fairy tales that have been created and published to challenge the sexist and conservative ideologies embedded in the tales written by Charles Perrault, the Brothers Grimm, and Hans Christian Andersen. In fact, false notions and assumptions of fairy tales abound in the "real" world, and they limit our use of the tales in schools and communities. Consequently, this seminar endeavors to address mistaken ideas and mysteries on a historical and theoretical level and on a practical level: (1) it will provide a substantial historical understanding of the development of the oral folktale and literary fairy tale and how they intersect in our lives, and (2) it will demonstrate how fairy tales can be changed and used so that teachers and children can explore important social issues and aesthetic questions connected to literacy through fairy tales.

The important questions that I developed for the seminar concerned the following: What is the difference between an oral folktale and a literary fairy tale? When and where did the literary fairy tale originate? How do folktales and fairy tales continually interact? Who tells folktales and fairy tales? What is the storytelling tradition of fairy tales? What role do fairy tales play in the socialization of children? Do teachers and children know only a select canon of fairy tales? What is the impact of film on fairy tales? What types of fairy-tale plays are being produced? Are there new types of fairy tales? How can fairy tales be used in schools and communities to contribute to the creative development of children and adults alike? How do contemporary storytellers use fairy tales?

The requirements for the course were developed to cater to the needs of the participants. It is expected that all students are to participate fully in the storytelling activities and creative drama. Enrollment is limited to fifteen participants. During the second week each student is to conduct a two-hour storytelling class based on a tale taken from the Grimms' collection. The storytelling is to take place within a summer session of a public elementary school. Each student is also to write a five- to ten-page paper and outline a two-month storytelling program to be introduced into a school or community center where he or she works. This paper is to be submitted at the end of the course or during the week following the course, and the program is to demonstrate how the material and experiences of the course could serve the purposes of the participant/storyteller and the community in which he or she works.

The two required texts are *The Grammar of Fantasy*, by Gianni Rodari, and my book *Creative Storytelling: Building Community, Changing Lives*. I also produced a small reader consisting of fairy tales and articles or chapters from Ann Haas Dyson's *Writing Superheroes: Contemporary Childhood, Popular Culture, and Classroom Literacy*, Karl Kroeber's *Retelling/Rereading: The Fate of Storytelling in Modern Times*, and Colin Lanshear and Peter L. McLaren's *Critical Literacy: Policy, Praxis and the Postmodern*.

The first week of the course focuses on creating a community within the classroom in which the students can feel at ease to participate and use the various techniques of storytelling that I introduce and to articulate their opinions and criticisms of the readings, even if they might disagree with me or another member of the class. To give an idea of how each of my classes is structured, I want to recount how I generally teach the first meeting, which has the title "In Search of Genuine Storytelling."

After I briefly introduce myself and before I discuss the syllabus, I divide the class into pairs. Each pair is to find a space to talk privately with each other. Sometimes they just turn their chairs and face each other. Each partner has about five minutes to tell the other about her or his background: birth, childhood, schooling, profession, purpose for taking the course, and most exciting experience in life (including the most dramatic, traumatic, decisive, enlightening incident). In short, the participants are encouraged to tell each other about the most pivotal incident in his or her life. After each partner has had a turn, one partner will introduce the other to the group and is granted great poetic license to embellish the life story. I also participate in this introduction exercise and plant the notion of the tall tale, which we discuss later.

The purpose of this exchange is clear. I want the participants to become familiar with one another and to know something about each other's lives and outside community, while we begin to forge our own community. Moreover, I want them to relax and to want to observe their styles and skills. I have always been startled by teachers, some who have five to twenty years of teaching experience, who come to the course timidly without realizing that they are already remarkable story-tellers. I hope to instill confidence in all the participants and to dispel the notion that you have to be a "professional" and highly trained to be a storyteller or to work as a storyteller. Although I don't smash the aura of the storyteller, I certainly question it.

Some of the other questions I begin to introduce right away include the following: How is storytelling used today? What is storytelling? What is the history of storytelling, reading, and writing? How have forms changed? I put forward my notion of the skeptical storyteller who knows that folly generates wisdom and wisdom folly. I talk about my readings of Mario Vargas Llosa's *The Storyteller,* Walter Benjamin's "The Storyteller," and Karl Kroeber's *Retelling/Rereading* and the endeavors of Llosa, Benjamin, and Kroeber to define genuine storytell-ing that I have discussed in the previous chapter. After suggesting that there are many ways in which we genuinely share stories, I show how storytelling also has been used as a means of control, means of commu-nication, and means of subversion and liberation, as well as a means of personal quest for identity. I use the wonderful tale "The Forest Dweller" by Hermann Hesse as an example.

After the Hesse tale, I cover the following topics upon which I shall elaborate in the coming week: the history of storytelling in the United States involving creation and destruction—destruction of Native American, African American, and Mexican American traditions and creation of white American folklore; the growth of technology and print and its effect on oral storytelling; the importance of understand-ing the telephone, radio, film, video, and computer; the radical reaction to postmodern fragmentation and the renaissance of storytelling (the National Storytelling Network); the rise of cults and religious funda-mentalism; and the neglect of children—children as commodities; the reconfiguration of children within society; and the inability of children to articulate their position within changing configurations.

After approximately two and a half hours of lecturing with discussion, there is a break. I have asked the participants to read the four versions of "Puss in Boots" by Gian Francesco Straparola, Giambattista Basile, Charles Perrault, and the Brothers Grimm. I recommend that they review their readings during the break. When we return, I begin a discussion about the difference between oral and literary tales. Why were the oral tales changed? How? What was the audience? When did fairy tales become changed for children? After we discuss these questions, I divide the class into three groups and give each group about fifteen minutes to discuss the meaning of one of the "Puss in Boots" tales and then to improvise and change it. Depending on the time, one of the groups will perform their improvised skit in class. We then comment on the interpretation and why changes were made.

I conclude the first session by talking about the importance of creative drama and improvisation and storytelling theater initiated by Viola Spolin and Paul Sills.[11] The assignment for the next day is to design a contemporary version of "Puss in Boots" to be told in class. Some of the texts will be read the following day as an act of sharing. In fact, each day of the first week begins with some form of sharing and the demonstration of a particular method to animate storytelling in a class. The most important game is called the fantastic binominal, which involves bringing two disparate things, animals, or people together; that is, two nouns chosen arbitrarily, linking them with a preposition and creating a story through improvisation. This game (which I fully explain in chapter 5), which uses free association and sparks the imagination of the entire class, is a central part of the Neighborhood Bridges program.

By the end of the first intense week, all the participants are now prepared to conduct a storytelling session for two hours in an elementary classroom. Because we shall visit the school four days in a row, I divide the class into four groups, and the members of each group are assigned a particular tale type (fairy tale, folktale, fable, legend, myth, or family tale) that they will use as the basis for the storytelling session. Generally, I seek out a third-, fourth-, or fifth-grade class in a summer school and contact a teacher willing to collaborate with members of my class. To prepare the children of this class for the four days that we shall spend in their class, I visit the class a week in advance, introduce myself, explain what we shall be doing, and then demonstrate the fantastic binominal and animate them to tell some stories. In this way I am able to assess the atmosphere in the classroom and prepare the students for the arrival of about fifteen adults who will either be conducting the session or observing the session and taking notes. Later, I share my impressions of the students, teacher, and classroom ambience with my students.

After each two-hour session that we develop in the classroom, we leave the children and then move to another classroom or space in the school to discuss our work and try to analyze what was effective and why. What caused problems? What should we pursue the next day? We try to involve the teacher in these discussions if she or he is available. During one summer course, a student who was a media specialist taped all of our sessions so that we could watch and comment on specific incidents during the storytelling session. Our focus was generally on our interaction with the students and how our methods of storytelling, acting, and teaching enabled them to become more aware of their talents, their environment, and the importance of cooperation. Mutual support and trust are emphasized as we work with one another and with the children and teacher. We try to use all the arts in the classroom—writing, speaking, acting, drawing, and conceiving ideas and testing them out in play.

The last day of the course is spent reflecting on and reexamining our work during the past two weeks. I also address the problems of storytelling by discussing the use and abuse of children and fairy tales with a focus on the psychoanalytical and psychological approaches of Freud and Jung and the consequences of their work. I am particularly critical of the work of Bruno Bettelheim and C. G. Jung and other psychologists who have endeavored to take their theories and demonstrate how fairy tales can be used for prescriptive cures of social and individual "diseases." In addition I try to ask particular questions that will stimulate the participants to continue their own critical reflection. For instance, I ask the following questions: What relevance do fairy tales have for adults and children in today's postmodern electronic age? Is there something particularly utopian and beneficial in fairy tales that makes this genre a healthy antidote to the malaise of contemporary society? The purpose of this session is to make clear, from my point of view, that we should not deceive ourselves and pretend to have a therapeutic recipe for solving the daily problems of children and teachers at school. Nor should we pretend that story by itself can do this for the children. There is no doubt that literature and storytelling have a therapeutic value to a certain degree, but unless one is trained in psychology and early childhood education and does a thorough study in controlled experiments, we must be cautious when we talk about the therapeutic value of storytelling.

In my opinion it is easier to demonstrate how storytelling can help to form communities and develop a social conscience among all the participants, even though the community might be short lived. If children—and adults—learn on a consistent basis how story can enable them to think for themselves and to cooperate with others to produce an environment conducive to creativity and critical thinking, they will become more responsible citizens of the world. I say the world because the technological forces of globalization are shrinking the world and bringing us closer together. At the same time, as Zygmunt Bauman and others lament, the more we are connected, the more we become fragmented and isolated. To understand and perhaps undo this paradox is one way a storyteller as a good thief can pay back to society all that he or she has stolen and appropriated. After all, building bridges for community is the genuine pleasure of storytelling.

Neighborhood Bridges

Fig. 4.1 Student at Whittier School preparing a set.

4

THE NEIGHBORHOOD BRIDGES PROJECT

When I arrived in Minneapolis in 1990 to teach German literature at the University of Minnesota, I had every intention of continuing storytelling in the public school system as I had done in Milwaukee, Wisconsin, and Gainesville, Florida. As usual, I was fortunate to find teachers and friends who provided contacts to schools in which I began working and developing my own program that formed the basis of my book *Creative Storytelling: Building Community, Changing Lives*. However, despite some success in Pillsbury School with a teacher committed to innovative pedagogy, I was frustrated because I felt that our work had a limited impact in just one class, and I wanted to spread the word, so to speak, to demonstrate just how effective storytelling combined with creative drama could enable children to come into their own and develop their unique skills. So, I was dissatisfied with my work and was looking for more chances to experiment in depth, looking for the right moment when my work could have more of a social impact. Yet I had to wait several years before the right opportunity came along.

Seizing the Moment

Neighborhood Bridges was founded in a serendipitous moment during the fall of 1997 by Peter Brosius, artistic director of the Children's

Theatre Company of Minneapolis, and me. I say "serendipitous" because so much in life depends on chance and knowing intuitively when to seize the moment. Much of storytelling is about being opportunistic, about intuition and sensing when the opportunity is there and then grabbing it, even when you may not know the outcome. Serendipity depends on recognition, active intervention, and a certain amount of hard work and patience.

Brosius had arrived in the summer of 1997 from Hawaii to take over the Children's Theatre Company of Minneapolis. I had known him for twenty-some-odd years, and we always shared a great deal in common and often spoke about working together in some way, but we always lived hundreds of miles apart. Now he was in Minneapolis. At the same time, Herb Kohl, one of the most experimental and progressive educators in the United States, happened to show up in the Twin Cities that summer to talk about his new book at the Hungry Mind bookstore, now called The Ruminator. Kohl and I were good friends and had collaborated in different projects on various occasions during the past twenty years. Because Brosius had never met Kohl, I took him to the Hungry Mind to hear Kohl deliver an inspiring talk. Afterward we went to a bar and spent a few hours talking about children's theater, storytelling, and some projects that all three of us might develop together. As usual, Kohl was full of ideas and had soon persuaded Brosius to bring him to Minneapolis to produce contemporary Shakespeare plays with high school students. However, it was not to be.

Kohl had accepted a position on the humanities committee at George Soros's Open Foundation in New York, and this work consumed his time, but he was now in a position to support educational programs throughout the country, which he always wanted to do. He took advantage of this opportunity by contacting me and others involved in progressive education. In his typical frank and blunt manner, he said, "How'd you like a hundred thousand dollars to help your storytelling in the schools with that guy Brosius? If you get me a proposal in two weeks, I'll see what I can do."

For two weeks Brosius and I labored intensively, exchanging ideas and articulating our wildest dreams about a storytelling and creative drama program, not entirely sure of what might be possible but certain that the moment had come. By the middle of October, we sent Kohl our proposal, and by the beginning of January, we were informed that we received a grant from the Open Foundation to support our storytelling and creative drama program in the public schools of Minneapolis. And so, Neighborhood Bridges was born.

Brief History

Neighborhood Bridges is a comprehensive program of storytelling and creative drama for elementary and middle schools intended to develop the critical and cultural literacy of children and to transform them into storytellers of their own lives. Originally sponsored by a generous grant from the Open Foundation in New York, the syllabus was based on my book *Creative Storytelling* and on several years of my work in Minneapolis at different elementary schools with the help of Larry Johnson, a storyteller and media specialist. The initial purpose of Bridges was to set up a year-round program, with storytellers meeting two separate classes in two different elementary schools in Minneapolis—Whittier and Lucy Laney—for two hours a week. These two classes were to establish contact with one another during the course of the year, and in May, after exploring different genres of storytelling, writing, drawing, and improvisation for the theater, they would each present a play that they designed from their own storytelling and creative dramatic work to their own school and parents, then travel to the partner school, perform there, and finally join the other class in a festival at the Children's Theatre. In other words, there would be three productions that would create bridges within the school, community, and theater, with children, teachers, actors, relatives, and parents.

In the spring and summer of 1998, I trained eight actors in my methods and taught an intensive summer seminar for teachers and storytellers to prepare the teaching artists for the first year of Neighborhood Bridges. Our success in developing the talents and skills of more than one hundred students during the first two years in Whittier and Lucy Laney enabled us to obtain more support from other foundations and to expand our program so that, by the fall of 2003, Neighborhood Bridges had innovative programs in eight different inner-city elementary schools of Minneapolis and St. Paul—Whittier, Lucy Laney, Marcy Open, Powderhorn, Tuttle, Pratt, Sheridan, and Hayden Heights. More teaching artists have been trained in summer seminars that Maria Asp and I have taught in collaboration with the Perpich Center for the Arts, the University of Minnesota, and Hamline University. The program, now in its fifth year, involves eighteen classes with more than five hundred students participating in the program. There is extensive collaboration not only with numerous teachers in all the schools but also with the Minnesota Center for Book Arts and the College of Education at the University of Minnesota. The children form pen-pal relations with their friends at other schools and meet at the Children's Theatre in January to see performances and learn about the production of plays. As a celebration for their work during the school year, they perform their own plays on the main stage in school festivals in May, attended by friends, parents, relatives, and the general public.

Guiding Principles of Neighborhood Bridges

First, we believe that much harm has been done to children by the mass media and advertising in all its forms (from news broadcasts, commercials, and cartoons to violent and sexually prurient spectacles), and we view our creative work in part as a means to offset and question this influence. The overall tendency in the mass media and advertising is to make good consumers out of children. In contrast, we seek to enable children to take control of their own lives. Not that they won't consume. But they may reflect more about their own commodification. We do not, therefore, dismiss or denigrate popular culture. We try to use it against itself by exposing contradictions. We do not offer solutions or resolutions but alternative ways of thinking and acting.

There are other obstacles or forces against which we struggle: the testing mania of federal and state governments; lobby groups seeking to privatize and commercialize public education; the bad press given to teachers, principals, and administrators; and, at the same time, the misguided collaboration of school boards and administrators with groups that undermine public education and innovative programs that do not rely on so-called objectively measured test results.

Given the daily conflicts and battles over children's education in the United States, we view our work as part of a movement of progressive educators and in the context of these struggles. We deeply believe that the arts can offer unique opportunities for cooperative learning that bridges and brings together people from different walks of life.

Second, because we are not with the children all the time, we try to take a modest view of what we can accomplish in our year-long program. We know that we cannot fully change their lives, and we do not want to play the role of therapist. But we do know that we can touch their lives. We want to engage teachers and children to animate them, to set them on a path of self-discovery, to provide skills, to strengthen self-confidence. Without their desire and will, we cannot accomplish our goals. In the process, we learn as much about ourselves and our capabilities as they do about themselves and their capabilities.

Third, although we have focused on the elementary school, our work is not limited to a specific grade, level, or school. The techniques that we use to animate and to focus on storytelling as a means to enable people to become storytellers of their lives are flexible and can be used with children, students, and adults in preschools, high schools, universities, and other institutions. We do not believe in one-time workshops, seminars, or performances. They can perhaps be useful. Primarily, we seek to build community, which means that our work is long term and that we are concerned about involving children, parents, teachers, administrators, teaching artists, and friends in a creative process that at times may even test the conception and self-conception of the institutions within which we work. Our emphasis is on social and individual transformation and building bridges between people and communities through creative play.

Fourth, the heart of our program is centered on the transformation of the self through storytelling. When we state that our purpose is to make children narrators or storytellers of their own lives, we do not say this lightly. This purpose is based on the realization that all our selves—our identities—are contingent on narrative. We form and re-form ourselves through narratives. As Jerome Bruner remarked in his significant book *Making Stories*, "We constantly construct and reconstruct our selves to meet the needs of the situations we encounter, and we do so with the guidance of our memories of the past and our hopes and fears for the future. Telling oneself about oneself is like making up a story about who and what we are, what's happened, and why we're doing what we're doing."[1] He further stated, "Self-making is a narrative art,"[2] which recalls the great German poet Novalis's remark: "Menschwerden ist eine Kunst"—to become a human being in the truest sense demands art. The human being is a work of art, and art is not worth anything if it is not humane. Through our storytelling with children, we seek to explore how stories can assist each one of us to define what we mean to be in our communities.

Collaboration

From the beginning there was a danger—and there still is—that we would enter a classroom and impose our method and ideas on teachers and children. However, we have a slogan, borrowed from Bertolt Brecht, that keeps us fairly honest: We do our best to make ourselves dispensable. It is only the fearful individual who wants to retain power by keeping all his or her knowledge to him- or herself. By not sharing knowledge, the expert can pose as omniscient. In contrast, we want to show that we are all fortunately replaceable, different but replaceable, especially when it comes to sharing knowledge and skills. To this end, we make contact with all the schools, teachers, and administrators in the spring before we offer our program. We try to get to know the school environment and community to the best of our ability. We give them a printed syllabus for the year and discuss ways in which we can fit into their curriculum or how they can use our program to reinforce their teaching. We offer a summer workshop that all teachers can attend. We hold a one-hour preparatory meeting each week with the teachers in the school to discuss changes, problems, and new ideas. We hold three meetings a year with the teachers from all the schools in our program so that we can openly discuss problems and plans. One of the major problems that we have encountered pertains ironically to a conflict between our curriculum and their curriculum based on tests and state-based regulations. Teachers have found that our work makes the writing, reading, and learning that the children do more pleasurable and even more effective than the official programs do. This is a contradiction that we actually seek and seek to resolve through collaboration.

Our collaboration, however, involves not just the teachers, administrators, and teaching artists but also the staff at the Children's Theatre, parents, and university students and professors. At certain stages of our work, we called on their expertise, and we shared their knowledge. In the spring, each class has the opportunity to bring in musicians, set designers, costume makers, or dancers to help the children learn about different arts and crafts. The celebrations of their plays in May cannot be accomplished without an entire community of people working together. In short, our final celebration of nine months work with the children is a collaborative effort that expresses and articulates how the children see and imagine themselves in the world around them.

Transformation

The children in May are not the same children that we meet in September. Obviously they will have grown and changed because of all sorts of biological, psychological, and social factors. Viewed in light of our program, however, the children will have made individual and collective changes in varying degrees. We encourage and foster transformation in two primary ways: we are constantly changing the classroom environment and introducing the children to new environments and we use improvisation to change rules and regulations and to shift their expectations and audience expectations. Each session that we conduct is held within the school classroom, which we keep changing. For instance, after an initial game of the fantastic binominal that involves movement by the teaching artist, writing, and sharing of stories by the children in front of the other children, the chairs and tables are pushed to the side so that we have free space to create whatever environment we want. The children recognize that the classroom, which will often display their artwork, can be changed to their liking, and they will use found objects to create their plays and become something other than they normally are, just as the children will become other than what they think they are. Environmental change leads to personal change. Just as our initial game with the fantastic binominal animates the children to conceive stories in which two haphazard elements can be brought together through their imagination to form a story, so can our emphasis on movement and taking over terrain in the classroom for storytelling, discussion, games, rehearsal, and performance lead to an understanding of how appropriation can work.

As much as possible, we want to suggest to the children (and the teachers) that appropriation can enable them to express their desires and needs. We model change. We take risks. We show that we are not afraid to take risks even when we may make blunders. We adapt to constantly changing conditions in the classroom and in the school. We respond to parents who may not want their children to participate in our games because of religious reasons. We try to show how change may be linked to tolerance, and we form three groups of children within the classroom that stay together throughout the year. We hope that the formation of these groups will enable them to build their own little community and to cooperate with one another. We have learned that there are often conflicts within the groups, and sometimes changes have to be made. One of our goals is for students to learn how to collaborate with each other without the heavy hand of an intervening authority figure. Students are empowered to take on the role of negotiators and leaders. If the teaching artist and classroom teacher are always making decisions for the class, the students will not become autonomous and independent thinkers. Sometimes they cannot organize themselves to do a skit or presentation, but by allowing them to make errors, we encourage them to reflect on how they might do things differently so that they complete a task. In the end, when they do discover a way to work together, they become more respectful citizens. They learn that they or we may not always agree with the politics, religion, or lifestyle of their neighbors, but they can work, play, and live respectfully side by side. In short, we try to foster respect and understanding among the three groups that we have formed. Toward the end of the program, they will join together and become one large community to produce a play for other classes and schools.

With our emphasis on transformation, we have witnessed shy children stepping into spaces that they never entered before and fulfilling themselves. We have seen children who are unwilling to work with the teachers, or to read and write during the week, join with us to act, read, write, and express themselves as freely as they want. We have seen children conceive art, writing, and drama projects that represent their changes and reveal how much they are discovering about themselves and the world around them. Finally, we note changes in the teachers and ourselves—how more sensitive and responsive we are to the children's needs and our own needs and how we use conversation to do problem solving and to create projects that build on our social awareness and creative designs.

Creative and Critical Literacy

Our program is an explicit critique of functional literacy and how schools and politicians hinder learning by instituting programs that allegedly teach kids the basics and test their rote skills.

It is important to note that most people up until the end of the nineteenth century did not know how to read and write, and yet they were able to solve problems and demonstrate their intelligence and originality in their work and inventions. The oral form of transmitting and sharing knowledge was sufficient and in many cases still is sufficient for sparking an imagination and inspiring people to think critically about their circumstances. On the other hand, it is important to acknowledge that reading and writing have become more important skills in our advanced technological society and that they can enable a child to gain more meaningful pleasure out of life and to structure his or her existence in manifold ways. Therefore, we do not simply talk about learning how to read and write so that a child can function better within the society and can survive. We work toward helping children learn how to read and write so that they can better grasp who they are, why they are in a particular situation, and how they can discover their talents to develop and assume different roles in life. Without the requisite oral, literary, and dramatic skills, it is difficult to project oneself into the world and to narrate one's own life.

Implicit in all our work is a remark made by the renowned psychologist Jerome Bruner. This remark is one of our guiding principles:

> I conceive of schools and preschools as serving a renewed function within our changing societies. This entails building school cultures that operate as mutual communities of learners, involved jointly in solving problems with all contributing to the process of educating one another. Such groups provide not only a locus for instruction, but a focus for identity and mutual work. Let these schools be a place for the praxis (rather than the proclamation) of cultural mutuality—which means an increase in the awareness that children have of what they are doing, how they are doing it, and why. The balance between individuality and group effectiveness gets worked out within the culture of the group; so too the balancing of ethnic or racial identities and the sense of the larger community of which they are part.[3]

Bruner called for mutual learning that depends on collaboration, cooperation, and participation because it also enables the individual to develop his or her talents more deeply and more fully. The stories and plays that the children create from mutual learning in the Neighborhood Bridges program make the ordinary seem strange, and their strange and fantastic images and words reveal their hope for a better future. They demand close reading just as each child calls for close reading. The children in Neighborhood Bridges do not only become stimulating and demanding storytellers but also become risk takers, and they are willing to build and cross bridges to discover other worlds.

Summary of Activities

Neighborhood Bridges provides the following activities to all the schools in our program:

- two-hour sessions per week for thirty-one to thirty-four weeks, depending on any given academic year;
- one-hour meetings per week with teachers to prepare our common curriculum of cultural and critical literacy;
- complete Neighborhood Bridges curriculum with a section for teachers on follow-up work during the week;
- three dinner meetings of our general assembly (teachers, teaching artists, evaluators, administrators) per year that last about three hours and bring together everyone who is working together in the eight schools (Curriculum needs and methods as well as plans are discussed and implemented.);
- pen-pal exchanges between schools;
- Bridges Day, which is a meeting of all schools at a live performance at the Children's Theatre in January or February (Tickets are free. Children see a show and often get to meet their pen pals.);
- Festival of Family Stories, which is an optional event, but we help organize a potluck dinner at the school where the children and members of their families gather together to share family stories with other members of the community;

- collaboration with the Minnesota Center for Book Arts (Professional bookmakers visit schools.);
- collaboration with the set designers, musicians, and costume makers of the Children's Theatre Company who visit the schools;
- ongoing training of teachers throughout the year;
- Crossing Bridges Festival at the Children's Theatre Company in May (Classes perform original plays on the Children's Theatre Company main stage. There is a reception for students, families, and friends after the performances.);
- the Neighborhood Bridges Web site: http://www.neighborhood-bridges.org (This site is still being developed and will be designed to inform students, teachers, parents, actor/educators, and the general public of the Neighborhood Bridges program and all of the program components.); and
- an all-staff teacher training session in Bridges techniques in July or August.

Each participating school provides the following:

- financial and administrative support that is based on the school's budget,
- provision for weekly planning time between the classroom teacher and the teaching artist,
- support for the "bridge" portion of the project by facilitating the exchange of pen-pal letters and communication with other participating schools,
- transportation for Bridges Day and Crossing Bridges Festival at the Children's Theatre Company,
- bag lunches for students who participate in Bridges Day and at the Crossing Bridges Festival, and
- hosting and coordinating of optional events such as the Festival of Family Stories and dress rehearsal performances for other classes in the school.

Short Calendar

The following short calendar is an example of how we generally plan our year based on thirty-one weeks of work. The curriculum is always flexible, and we often change it during the course of a year if a particular class or group of classes has special needs. Often we encounter problems and obstacles that demand a shift in focus and themes. All changes are made with the consent and cooperation of the teachers and the students.

Short Calendar 2003–2004

August 25–Bridges introduction workshop for classroom teachers and teaching artist, 3:00 to 6:00 P.M. at Children's Theatre Company

September 2–First day of school grades 1 through 12; classroom teachers send home student permission slips and conduct preprogram survey

    8–Bridges meeting for classroom teachers and teaching artist, 4:30 to 7:30 P.M. at Children's Theatre Company; student permission slips, presurveys, and pen-pal forms due

    8–Week 1: Preliminary meetings; teaching artists generate first writing samples and students fill out pen-pal forms

    15–Week 2: Fairy tales: Red Riding Hood (Focus on character: Who)

    22–Week 3: Fairy tales: Frog King

    22–Teaching artist meeting, 1:00 to 3:00 P.M.; first writing sample due

    29–Week 4: Fairy tales: Cinderella; pen-pal exchange

October 6–Week 5: Fairy tales: Rumpelstiltskin; final draft week

    13–NO BRIDGES THIS WEEK

    16/17–NO SCHOOL

    20–Week 6: Animal tales and fables

    27–Week 7: Animal and trickster tales

    27–Teaching artist meeting, 1:00 to 3:00 P.M.

November (Focus on setting: Where)
  3–Week 8: Mixed fables
  3–NO SCHOOL
  4–General elections: Don't forget to vote!
  10–Week 9: Peace tales; final draft week
  14–NO SCHOOL
  17–Week 10: Peace tales
  17–Teaching artist meeting, 1:00 to 3:00 P.M.
  24–NO BRIDGES THIS WEEK
  26–28–NO SCHOOL—Thanksgiving break

December 1—Week 11: Preparation of peace tale skit
  8–Week 12: Preparation of peace tale skit
  15–Week 13: Performance of peace tale skit in schools
  22–NO BRIDGES THIS WEEK
  22–NO SCHOOL (January 4, 2004)
  29–NO BRIDGES THIS WEEK

January Minnesota Center for Book Arts will visit schools in January
    and February. Dates are to be announced.
  5–Week 14: Legends and myths: Pied Piper (Focus on action:
    What)
  12–Week 15: Legends and myths; pen-pal exchange, story swap
    week
  12–Bridges midyear meeting for classroom teachers and teaching
    artist, 5:30 P.M. at Children's Theatre Company
  16, 19–NO SCHOOL MINNEAPOLIS
  19, 23–NO SCHOOL ST. PAUL
  19–NO BRIDGES THIS WEEK
  26–Week 16: Myths; final draft week
  26–Teaching artist meeting, 1:00 to 3:00 P.M.

February 2–Week 17: Superheroes and myths
  9–Week 18: Repeat of superheroes
  16–NO SCHOOL
  16–Week 19: Tall tales

23–Week 20: Tall tales; final draft week

23–Teaching artist meeting, 1:00 to 3:00 P.M.

March Focus on movement

1–NO BRIDGES THIS WEEK

5–NO SCHOOL

8–Week 21: Tall tales; pen-pal exchange

15–Week 22: Family tales; preparations for interviewing family members and generating family stories

19–NO SCHOOL ST. PAUL

22–Week 23: Family tales

22–Teaching artist meeting, 1:00 to 3:00 P.M.

24–Bridges Day at Children's Theatre Company; students see main-stage show at 10:30 A.M. performance of SNAPSHOT (Powderhorn, Marcy Open, and Hayden Heights)

26–NO SCHOOL MINNEAPOLIS

26–NO SCHOOL (April 2, 2004)

29–NO BRIDGES THIS WEEK

April Focus on voice, sound, music

5–Week 24: Start final story prep: How Six Make Their Way in the World and Seven Brooms

6–Bridges Day at Children's Theatre Company; see main-stage show 10:30 A.M. performance of SNAPSHOT (Whittier, Lucy Laney, Pratt, and Sheridan)

5–CHILDREN'S THEATRE COMPANY VISUAL ARTIST VISITS BEGIN

12–Week 25: Final story rehearsal/visual artist visits

19–Week 26: Final story rehearsal/visual artist visits

26–Week 27: Final story rehearsal/visual artist visits

28–Teaching artist meeting, 8:00 A.M. All program material must be e-mailed to Gregory by this date: title of show, class list, teachers' and aides' names, and special helpers

May 3–Week 28: Dress rehearsal (schedule a performance at your own school) or final story/visual artist visits

10–Week 29: Dress rehearsal (schedule a performance at your own school)

10–Crossing Bridges Festival at Children's Theatre Company, 6:00 P.M. (Marcy Open)

13–Crossing Bridges Festival at 6:00 P.M. Children's Theatre Company (Powderhorn and Hayden Heights)

17–Crossing Bridges Festival at 6:00 P.M. Children's Theatre Company (Whittier, Pratt, Sheridan, and Lucy Laney)

17–Week 30: Evaluation
Postprogram survey
Final writing sample
Student evaluation
Classroom teacher evaluation
Teaching artist evaluation

24–Week 31: Evaluation or teachers' choice week

31–NO SCHOOL

June 1–Teaching artist meeting, 1:00 to 3:00 P.M.
1–Final Bridges meeting for classroom teachers and teaching artists, 5:30 P.M. at Children's Theatre Company
Evaluation of program; all paperwork due at this time

Teachers' Choice: Teaching artist and classroom teachers collaborate to select genres:
Pourquoi tales
Utopian tales
Science fiction
Tall tales
Family tales

Introductory Meeting

The teaching artists will have made contact with the teachers with whom they will work at a general meeting at the end of August. They plan their schedule together and discuss the curriculum, expectations, and conditions at the school. They will have ongoing meetings once a week.

We have discovered that the first meeting with the students, getting acquainted, is crucial for setting the tone for some of the themes during the year, especially conflict resolution, cooperation, and peace, and I suggest to the teaching artists that they tell a tale similar to "Building Bridges," which serves as the prologue to this book. Otherwise, they are free to choose a similar tale from our collection of reading material. This tale is followed up with games that enable the teaching artist to become acquainted with the students.

We have used the following games:

- Bring in a large bag (the Get-to-Know-Me Bag) filled with items that have some meaning for you like a doll, stuffed animal, old favorite hat, sneaker, tennis ball. Ask the students to fish into the bag and pull out an item. Each time an item is drawn from the bag, you are to tell them a story about the meaning it has for your life. After about five items have been pulled and you have told them something about your life, ask them to give you the names of their favorite items. Write them on the board. Then ask them to share stories about these items and their meanings for them.
- Tell students stories about the worst thing that has ever happened to you. Ask for worst stories from students.
- Tell students about the best thing that has ever happened to you. Ask students for their best stories.
- Theater game using a circle: Have each student say his or her name proudly by stepping forward into the middle of the circle. Do a second round in which the student says his or her name, and then says, "When I grow up, I want to be …" The student must then show through a gesture, mime, or speech what it would be like to be the person he or she wants to be.

It is be advisable to have students wear name tags the first day. The most important purpose is to form a contact with students and to try to get a sense of their desires. In addition, there will always be obstacles to overcome. The teacher will always know best which students might cause some difficulty or may be having problems at home or in the community. We always take our cue from the teachers. Here is a sample outline of the introductory session:

- Move all the chairs into a circle.
- The teaching artist introduces herself and writes her name on the board. She asks whether anyone has heard of the Children's Theatre Company before. If any students raise their hands, she asks them what they know about Children's Theatre Company or what plays they might have seen there. At the end of the discussion, she tells them that she works at Children's Theatre Company.
- She asks whether anyone has ever heard of the Neighborhood Bridges program. Has anyone had brothers, sisters, or cousins who participated in this program before? Did anyone see the Crossing Bridges Festival last year? What do they remember?
- The teaching artist tells the "Building Bridges Tall Tale," and at the end, she asks them whether they think the story is true.
- Play the Get-to-Know-Me Bag game.
- All stand and play the movement name game with each student introducing her- or himself.
- Everyone remains standing, and the teaching artist asks them to tell her something they did over the summer. She suggests a few ideas and shows with movement what she did during the summer. She explains that in the theater it is often important that actors show, not tell, us what they are doing. She asks the students to show what they have done, and they go around the circle taking turns showing something without words. The students must guess what it is that the student shows.
- Everyone sits. The teaching artist explains to them that they are one of eighteen classrooms in Minneapolis and St. Paul that will be participating in the Neighborhood Bridges program. She explains what a typical session will be and provides an overview of the events for the coming year: performing peace plays in December, writing to pen pals, making a book with people from the Minneapolis Center for Book Arts, attending a play at the Children's Theatre, creating a play and performing it on the main stage of the Children's Theatre.
- Optional—Community- or team-building game called the Human Knot. This can be played in one big circle or three little circles. Each student is asked to reach across the circle and grab

hold of someone else's hand with his or her right hand, then reach across again and grab some else's hand with his or her left hand. From there, the participants of each group must discuss how the Human Knot can be untangled while still holding hands. Once a decision is reached, the students gradually try to untangle the knot. A discussion follows: When did this activity work well? When did it fall apart? What skills did the students have to use to make the game successful? How do those skills apply to working with other people? The teaching artist should make clear that these skills are some of the same skills that we shall be using to create scenes and plays.

- The classroom teacher and teaching artist divide the class into three groups of students who will be working together throughout the year. They are asked to name their own group by consensus, but before they choose a name, the teaching artist asks them whether they watch TV. If so, how much? Do they watch commercials? Does anyone have a favorite commercial? Usually some one or several students will begin to sing an entire retrospective of summer commercials. The teaching artist explains that these commercials are ministories, and she tells them that each group is to come up with a name for its group and then make a commercial that highlights the group name. The teaching artist demonstrates the process with three volunteers.

- The teaching artist sets a model with the volunteers. First she brainstorms ideas by going around and asking each volunteer for an idea to name the group. The next step is to decide on the name of the group by voting. Once the name is chosen, the group begins to brainstorm ideas for an opening frame, middle frame, and closing frame. Once the frames are clarified, the students rehearse them through improvisation.

- Each group is now asked to move to a different part of the room and to brainstorm a name and rehearse a commercial for the group's name. The students have ten minutes to do this. The teaching artist and teacher roam the room and provide guidance and suggest ideas to help the students.

- Chairs are set up for an audience. Each group performs for the other two groups, who form the audience.
- The classroom is reassembled with desks and chairs in their usual places.
- The teaching artist passes out notebooks that the students will use for the entire year to write and illustrate stories. Students are encouraged to decorate the covers of their notebooks.
- The teaching artist tells the students about the other schools that will be part of the Neighborhood Bridges program and that they will have pen pals. She passes out the pen-pal forms that will be sent to the other schools. Finally she tells them when she will see them the following week.

It is important that the pen-pal project should begin during the first week. Students are to be informed that other students at a different school are also involved in a storytelling project. Matches are to be established by teachers and storytellers. By the middle of October we want to begin the first exchange of letters. If possible, it might be a good idea to have students send either photos or self-portraits (drawings) of themselves to the other students. In fact, every effort should be made to have students draw self-portraits and to write a few words about themselves as a way of introduction. The teachers and storytellers should also try to find a way to set up a meeting of pen pals in January or February.

As an experiment in the 2002–2003 school year, we encouraged teachers and teaching artists to create a video that introduces the class to another class in another school. The video should be created with the students and can take many different forms. For instance, the video could depict the school itself, the building, the neighborhood, and the classroom and activities. Or, it could be a film that features each child in the class who introduces him- or herself and says something about family and interests. The production of the video should be in keeping with the Neighborhood Bridges program: it should be a project that the students conceive and create with the guidance of the teacher and teaching artist. As many of their ideas as possible should be incorporated, and the film should be a means to create understanding between the classes. If the first exchange is successful, a second exchange should be developed to depict the "everyday" life of a particular class or to show a field trip or special project or even work that is done in the Neighborhood Bridges program.

We urge teachers and teaching artists to keep a journal about the weekly sessions, although this can be very difficult. What works? What does not work? Observations. Innovations. Suggestions. Journal records are discussed at monthly meetings of the teaching artists. We also try to find a way to share these records with teachers and everyone involved in our project because they have generally been used to change and improve our program.

Future Plans

Given the success of Neighborhood Bridges, we are seeking to strengthen and expand our work on different fronts. Though it is very difficult to find funding for all the projects that we want to develop, we never abandon hope, and we are constantly conceiving new plans to make our program stronger and more effective.

- Provided that we are successful in obtaining funding, we hope to include more schools in the Minneapolis and St. Paul public school systems. Our goal is to try to establish a core of schools in Minneapolis and St. Paul that would be willing to commit to our program, and we would dedicate ourselves to developing a curriculum to further the aims of the schools, using the arts as a means to develop critical and creative literacy.
- To make our work more accessible, we would like to create a two-hour videotape that demonstrates how our methods can be incorporated in classrooms and why we use particular techniques to cultivate the critical and cultural literacy of children. In addition we want to publish a booklet that would accompany the tape and help explain and illustrate how our program works. Finally, we want to distribute the tape nationally and possibly send teaching artists to schools that would have an actual workshop.
- To assist our work, we want to form a small theater group called "Gorilla Theater," which would produce plays relevant to our work and issues that schools are addressing. We are currently

planning to produce plays about literacy, coexistence, and tolerance that can easily be performed in schools. The performance would be followed by a workshop organized by the students to discuss how we use our storytelling and creative drama methods to cultivate critical literacy.

- We have established a Web site for Neighborhood Bridges, but we need to design it so that we can have interactive programs that connect the children as pen pals in the different schools in which we work. In this way, children can share their stories and send stories through the Internet. We can also reach schools beyond those in the Twin Cities.

- We want to explore a high school program based on our work in elementary and middle schools. To this end, we are seeking collaboration with the different high schools.

- We are hoping to write a grant to create a documentary about our work that might be useful for storytellers, theaters, and schools that might want to develop their own programs.

- We want to videotape the stories that the children produce and eventually create a CD with their stories.

- We are planning to regulate the training of all the teaching artists throughout the year so that we can assist them in their work. This training has already begun. We are observing and videotaping the teaching artists during their sessions, and we shall use these tapes to discuss ways in which we can improve their work.

- We intend to increase the summer workshops from two to three weeks, and we plan to keep the summer workshops open to teachers and artists in the Minneapolis and St. Paul areas. Aside from recruiting teaching artists from the workshop to collaborate with us during the year, we want to train teachers and artists to develop our program on their own in their schools.

Fig. 5.1 Student at Whittier School reading a story based on the fantastic binominal.

5

A Typical Bridges Session with Untypical Games and Learning

The Bridges storytelling program is unthinkable without creative drama and the introduction of specifically designed games that enhance the writing, reading, drawing, and thinking of the children. Though our work has primarily involved grades two through six, our program and techniques can easily be adapted to the needs and skills of three-year-olds to ninety-year-olds. I have traveled throughout the United States and given workshops for all levels of students, including university students and adults, who attend special programs at community or cultural centers. They had no difficulty exploring, changing, and then using our methods and games to suit their purposes. Our storytelling and theater games have been created so that they foster the cognitive development and cooperation of all the participants: the teaching artist, the teacher, the students, and anyone else who participates in a given session. Everyone undergoes changes in our program. Each session has a set structure that provides the students with a secure and flexible framework within which they work and play. They are constantly challenged by variations and unexpected tasks, new twists and turns that form the roadways of their lives. As they navigate through our two-hour session, they learn the importance of narrating their own lives with found objects and through improvisation.

There are four movements in the process of a typical Bridges session:

1. the fantastic binominal,
2. the transformation of the classroom into a setting for storytelling and the implementation of the chair game,
3. creative drama exercises and skits, and
4. the retransformation of the classroom for writing games.

The Fantastic Binominal

As a stimulus for storytelling and writing, the fantastic binominal, which I borrowed and developed from Gianni Rodari's *Grammar of Fantasy*, plays an essential role in initiating every session. It starts the thinking and imagining of the teaching artist and listeners through free association. It is possible to bring together any two arbitrarily chosen objects in narrative form, especially if there is cooperation and collaboration between the animator and the audience. Every failure and blunder is productive. Discoveries are made at every turn of the process. The stages of this cooperative work lead into creative drama and the production of a play. Each story written by a student provides material to be refined during the week. It is important that the teacher encourages the students to revise their stories, to illustrate them, and to keep them in a folder. It is imperative that each one of our sessions begins with some form of the fantastic binominal and that we animate the students to develop dramatic skills in presenting their stories before the other students in the class, to encourage them to write and draw as best they can, and to cooperate with each other in the writing and performing of their stories.

We use the fantastic binominal in stages, each time adding new components and variations throughout the thirty-one weeks of our residency. The teaching artists generally begin developing the activity, and gradually they involve the teacher and students, who can take over the game at the prompting of the teaching artist. The following is an outline of how we incorporate the fantastic binominal in the first three months.

1. The teaching artist asks the students whether they know what a preposition or "linking word" is. After discussing the nature of a preposition and how it helps link words or phrases together, the teaching artists asks for examples from the students and writes prepositions on the board.

about	between	over
above	beyond	through
across	by	throughout
after	during	to
against	for	toward
along	from	under
amid	in	underneath
around	inside	until
at	into	unto
before	of	up
behind	off	upon
below	on	with
beneath	onto	within
beside	outside	without

Once a list has been established by the students, the teacher will later be asked to create a paper roll list of the prepositions with the students that is to be hung on the wall or next to the blackboard for each Bridges session. Now that there is a list on the board, the teaching artist asks for two nouns to be quickly thrown at her. For our pedagogical purposes, we might limit the choice of nouns by connecting it with the themes of the day. For instance, if we are working with "Little Red Riding Hood," we might ask for names of predatory animals and get lions, leopards, dragons, sharks, and so forth. We might then ask for articles with colors such as blue dress, pink pants, or red car. We take what we get. The actor/educator writes down the nouns and asks the audience for their choice of a linking word. She then tells a story such as "the panther in pink pants" or "the shark below the red car" with the help of the audience. For instance, I was once given the two nouns "penguin" and "Australia" by two third-grade students, and I told the following tale, which I rewrote and developed a few days after the session.

The Penguin in Australia

There once was this penguin in Australia. He hated it. Penguins don't normally live in Australia. It's too hot. Much too hot. Dripping hot. Sweltering hot. Steamy hot. And this penguin kept sweating so much that he decided to head inland and see if he could find a barbershop and have his fur trimmed in an air-conditioned beauty salon. Maybe, he thought, he'd stand the heat better with a lighter coat of fur.

Just as he got to the outskirts of a town, he noticed a restaurant with a huge sign that read CHARLEY'S CHICKEN COOP and underneath it said "All You Can Eat in Cool Comfort." Now the penguin wasn't really hungry, but when he read "cool comfort," he went straight to the front door, but unfortunately it was locked. The penguin hadn't realized that it was six in the morning, and not a creature was stirring. What was stirring, however, was the air conditioner, and so the penguin looked for a way to enter the restaurant. He circled the small building until he found a back door that was open, and he entered right into the kitchen.

"Hallo!" he cried.

No answer.

"Hallo!" he cried again.

No answer. Only the rumbling of the air conditioner. It was so cool, so very cool, that the penguin decided he would make himself at home until the owner arrived. So he began to poke around in the large kitchen until he found the door to a gigantic freezer. When he opened it, he felt a blast of freezing cold air. "Ahh, just what I needed!" he said, and he decided to step inside for a moment. But that was a mistake. Just as he entered, the door slammed behind him, and he couldn't get out. Now the penguin had more than he had wished for. He began to tremble. It was freezing and dark inside. He shivered and shivered until his beak turned blue and he could no longer move. Soon he was nothing but a block of ice.

Three hours went by, and Charley and his cook, named Max, arrived to prepare the food for the luncheon specials. Charley was a mountain of a man and used to be a cowboy. Max was as wide as Charley was tall. He was from Paris—you all know where Paris is, don't you?—and was known to make the best sauces in all of Australia, and that's probably why he was so round. He loved to taste everything he made.

"Today, I shall make schicken à la peenappel," Max told Charley as he put on his chef's cap and apron.

"You mean, chicken with pineapples," Charley corrected Max, who still had a strong French accent even though he had been living in Australia for ten years.

"Fetch me a beeg schicken from the freezer," Max commanded.

Charley went to the freezer, opened the door, and grabbed the first big chicken in sight, which happened to be the penguin.

"Hey, this is a giant one!" Charley cried out. "Come and help me."

Max ran over to the freezer door and helped Charley carry the frozen penguin to the large chopping block in the middle of the kitchen. The penguin had become a strange block of ice, and because Max was nearsighted and Charley was color-blind, neither one of them realized that there was a penguin in the block of ice.

"Let it defrost a while," Charley said. "I'll get the tables set, and you get the potatoes."

Charley went through a revolving door into the restaurant and began setting the tables while Max ran out the back door, jumped into a small truck, and drove to the market where he picked up three huge sacks of fresh potatoes. In the meantime, the penguin felt the ice melt, ounce by ounce, inch by inch, drip by drop. Soon he could move his beak, and just as he began to flap his flippers and stretch his webbed feet, Max entered the kitchen carrying one of his sacks. The penguin was frightened and jumped off the chopping block.

"Schicken!" yelled Max. "What are you doing?"

"I'm not a chick-chick-chicken," the penguin replied, but he could barely say chicken because he was still shivering and his beak rattled.

"You are my schicken!" Max claimed, "And I neet you for lunch."

"I'm not anyone's lunch," the penguin said, "and I'm not your schicken, whatever that is."

The penguin had never heard a Frenchman speak English before.

"Sharley!" Max screamed. "Our schicken is on ze loose!"

The penguin became frightened and began waddling away from Max, who was blocking the back door. Just then Charley came through the revolving door. Max picked up a huge carving knife and locked the back door.

"Oh, oh, this does not look good," the penguin peeped. "From the freezer into the frying pan. That's not what I wanted."

"What the devil!" Charley shouted. "What's going on here?"

"Our schicken!" Max pointed.

Well, because Charley couldn't tell the difference between a chicken and a walrus, and Max was nearsighted, they were both convinced that the penguin was a chicken.

"I'm not a chicken!" the penguin insisted.

"Get the bird!" Max told Charley.

Charley lunged, but the penguin sidestepped him and ran through the revolving door followed by Max waving his knife and Charley, who had picked up a broom.

"I'm not a chicken!" the penguin shouted as he headed toward the front door of the restaurant, but it was locked.

"You're our chicken, and we've got you now!" Charley said.

"We've got you cornered, schicken. Geeve up!" Max added.

But the penguin was smart and dove between Charley's legs and slid to the opposite wall, knocking over tables and chairs. Max and Charley began chasing the penguin all over the room.

"Schicken, come to roost!"

"I'm a penguin, not a chicken! Besides, you shouldn't be killing anyone or anything," the penguin answered. "Try eating vegetables or fruit! They're good for you!"

"We only keel schickens becauze we love zem."

"You two are mad," the penguin said. He was getting anxious as he scooted from the restaurant back into the kitchen followed by Charley and Max. But when Max ran through, the revolving door whacked him on his back and his knife plunged into Charley's rear end.

"Owww!" yelled Charley, who fell on his stomach, while Max tumbled to the ground.

The penguin saw his opportunity and turned around and grabbed the knife stuck in Charley's rear. Some blood began to splatter from Charley's wound, but it wasn't serious. After all, Charley was a mountain of a man.

"Now who's going to kill who?" the penguin cried out.

Charley couldn't move, and Max was frightened.

"Schicken, we were only keeding."

"You wouldn't take advantage of a wounded cowboy, would you?" Charley pleaded.

"How'd you like it if I had you for my lunch?" the penguin began waving the knife.

"Hey, that's not fair," Charley said.

"Life's not fair," the penguin replied, "but I'll give you a chance if you agree to my terms."

"We av no choice, Charley," Max was whimpering. "Geeve heem what e wants."

Charley threw up his hands. He was resigned and entered into negotiations with the penguin. Well, the next day, there was a different sign over the restaurant, and it read

CHARLEY'S VEGGIE TAVERN

and underneath it said

> The best vegetable and fruit dishes in all of Australia.
> Penguin pool performances free.

It was true. Max still made the best sauces in all of Australia. Charley was still a mountain of a man with a patch on his rear. And the penguin waited on the tables and took dips in the pool that Charley built for him. And he performed for the customers as well. The penguin never did get his fur trimmed, but at night he slept next to the freezer in cool comfort.

As I told this tale, which was originally much shorter, I asked the students to help me at various points in the narrative by asking such questions as, What did the penguin do next? Where should the penguin hide? How do the French speak? Why do Max and Charley want to eat the penguin? What do you know about penguins? It is important that the children become cocreators of the tale, no matter what a storyteller may make of it later. It is also important that the storyteller model the telling of a tale as improvisation.

After this first stage is completed, the teaching artist asks for two volunteers to come to the board and write two more nouns. They are to cover their nouns until both students are ready to reveal them at the same time. Once revealed, the words are to stimulate the students to write and illustrate very short stories by using the two nouns with a preposition. The teaching artist gives the students about five minutes to write a story based on the nouns and a preposition linking the nouns. The teacher and the teaching artist circulate among the students to help them with spelling and writing and to prompt them if they are having difficulty. When the time is up, three or four volunteers are asked to come to the front and read their stories. Before they read their stories, they are requested first to read the stories to themselves to make sure that they understand what they have written. Sometimes they have problems reading their own handwriting. The students read the stories and are coached by the teaching artist to use gestures freely and to modulate their voices. Their written stories are placed in their folders and serve as the basis for further work during the week, with the teacher helping the students hone their stories and draw pictures. There is at least one story produced each week, if not two, that is placed in the student's folder. These stories are to be revised and illustrated during the week. One story will eventually be reproduced in the class anthology that is generally completed during the month of December. Each student contributes to the anthology and helps design the book.

2. *This is a repetition of the first session, with one big exception.* The teaching artist will no longer model the tale telling in an oral interaction. The students know the game and are prompted immediately to enter the writing part of the game. Here again, the teaching artist might suggest animals and sports objects if the tale is "The Frog King." For instance, there might be snakes, ants, bears, or elephants and basketballs, hockey sticks, bats, or helmets. The students might choose to write a tale about "the elephant in the basketball" or "the basketball in the elephant." The students who come to the front are asked to read their stories to themselves. Then they are asked to put their sheets of paper on the floor and to tell their stories in their own words to the audience. This is the first step toward developing their memories and animating them to go beyond the written word and use their imaginations. The text is a kind of safety net. They know what they have written. They should be somewhat secure in knowing a general narrative. Often I ask a student to repeat the tale and to add gestures and to make eye contact with the audience.

3. *This session begins with the teaching artist asking the students to generate a list of prepositions, which she writes on the board.* Then she invites a student to come up front and write on the board two nouns presented

by the class. Any two nouns will do. For the title of their story the student will link the nouns with one of the prepositions. In other words, the student and the teaching artist will work together to tell a story, passing the narrative back and forth to one another and taking suggestions from the other students in the class. Once the teaching artist and the student have finished, they will have set a framework of themes for the writing exercise that follows immediately after the oral storytelling. Instead of asking for any kind of noun, the teaching artist now says that she wants nouns that have something to do with place: forest, airport, neighborhood, house, department store, school, mall, sports arena, and so forth. The student, who has remained with the teaching artist, asks for a particular type of noun. The student writes the nouns on the board, and then the writing and telling of the stories follow.

4. *To make sure that the game of the fantastic binominal is taking root, we repeat the previous session, and another student is requested to help lead the game.* This is also a good time for the teacher to lead the game with the student.

5. *Now the teaching artist asks for two students to come up front, and he fades out of the initial fantastic binominal game.* The two students take over and ask the other students to suggest nouns. When they are finished, telling a story based on the fantastic binominal, the teaching artist suggests a theme for the writing game, which involves two new nouns and a preposition. When the students are finished writing, the teaching artist now begins to work on narrative voice, gestures, movement, and eye contact when the students come up front to read their stories. For example, after students read their stories, they are asked to set their paper down and to tell their stories in the first-person narrative or third-person narrative. Or, the student will be asked to tell the story in the voice of a grandmother or grandfather, truck driver, soprano, bass, angry person, sad person, and so forth. The student will be asked to tell the story in dialect, street talk, formal language, foreign language, and so forth. This exercise is very important and should continue in various ways until the end of the year. From this point on, we try to give the students a sense of different narrative perspectives and voices to show them how they can play different roles and how these differences can alter the storytelling.

6. The teaching artist can either have oral stories told and lead into a writing game or move immediately into a writing game and ask for two nouns related to the theme of the day. By the end of the second month or the beginning of the third month, the students are well aware of the structure of the fantastic binominal game and how it can be varied. It is not necessary to start with an oral tale because the students will be telling tales based on the fantastic binominal after they write their stories. Now once the student comes to the front of the classroom, he or she will be asked to imagine a situation in which the story is being told: family kitchen table, stranded island, airplane, campfire, locker room, lunchroom, street. What effect does a place have on the telling of a story? The setting, context, or environment of the storytelling plays a crucial role in the delivery of the story and its meaning, and we try to make the students aware of the conditions that determine the narrative.

7. Variety session. This session can be developed initially in any way. But the second part, the written exercise, is to take the following form. After the teaching artist and students tell the first story, the teaching artist will distribute blank pieces of paper and suggest a topic. All the students are to write two nouns on their pieces of paper with their names written on the bottom. The teaching artist collects the pieces and shuffles them. Then she redistributes the pieces of paper and asks the students to use the two nouns to develop a story. The stories are then read, and they can be read in the traditional manner, or, depending on the stage of development of the class, they can be enacted or performed without a reading of the text. During the first time using this type of game, it is a good idea to have five or ten students share their versions with the rest of the class because there will be so many differences.

8. Variety session. The teaching artist brings a huge hat or bag to the classroom. She then asks students to take small pieces of paper, write a noun, and put the pieces of papers in the hat or bag. Then two students come to the front and choose pieces of paper and write the nouns on the board. These nouns will be the basis for their stories.

9. Variety session. When working with popular culture or a particular topic, it is a good idea to have the students list five to ten names on the board. For instance, if working with superheroes in popular culture, the teaching artist might get a list with names, such as

Buffy the Vampire Slayer
Jackie Chan
Superman
Batman
Hercules
Xena
Wolverine
Pokémon
Supergirl
Spiderman

After the list is formed, the teaching artist asks the students to provide a second noun (object or place). Then she tells a model story with the superhero. The modeling should serve as a counter to expectations of students. Thus, if a hero is known for violent acts, we try to find a way to introduce peaceful solutions without demeaning the superhero's character. The purpose of the counternarrative is not to mock or belittle superheroes or popular culture but to demonstrate that these admirable heroes can use their extraordinary powers to bring about peace and justice, and they can do this without killing or destroying people, animals, or places. After the story is told by the teaching artist, two students are asked to come to the board to write the names of another two superheroes on the board that will serve as the nouns for everyone's story. Students are encouraged to invent other superheroes and to bring them into play in their stories.

This particular game can be repeated a few times, especially when the teaching artist is working on legends, myths, and superhero stories.

10. Variety session. Once the stories are written, perhaps based on the theme of the day, three pairs of students are asked to come forward with their fantastic binominal stories. After one student reads his or her story, the partner will take the story and read it in any way he or she desires. There should be a fourfold storytelling here. The first student reads his or her story from the paper. Then the partner reads it from the paper. Then the first student, who has been listening, tells the tale again without looking at the paper and can change it any way he or she wants. Finally, the partner tells the tale for the final time without looking at the paper. Once this cycle is completed, the partner reads his or her original tale, and the cycle begins again. There should be no more than three couples chosen for this game.

11. Let us say that the class is working with "Little Red Riding Hood" and wants to explore how words can be used like rocks thrown into a pond, causing waves and vibrations that lead to associations, meanings, images, and memories. There are several games introduced by Gianni Rodari in his book *The Grammar of Fantasy,* and I want to suggest that the teaching artist use these games as means to animate students to write and act out their stories. Similar to the fantastic binominal, these games challenge the students to use their imaginations with real words and invent stories in free by improvising and working freely off given or "found" objects.

Take the color red, for example. The teaching artist asks the students to

1. form words that begin with the letter *r* but that are not followed by an *e,* such as row, rat, rind, rock, rude;
2. form words that begin with *re,* such as rest, reed, rent, reel, read;
3. form words that rhyme with *ed,* such as bed, lead, bread, head, dead, fed;
4. form words that are associated with *red* in meaning, such as violet, blush, apple, beet; and
5. form a story using all the words that rhyme with *red* or form a story with all the word associations. The words should be written on the board, and the students must include all the words in their story.

For instance, a student might tell the following story:

> Millie wanted to go to bed with lead instead of bread and she ate the lead instead of the bread. Then she placed her head on the bed and felt as if she were really dead. But then she fed herself with bread and placed the lead beneath the bed. It was the last time she ever took some lead to bed.

12. The teaching artist asks a student to come to the board and write a noun vertically, such as

p
h
o
n
e

The teaching artist asks the students the following questions: What do they associate with a phone? How do they use it? How long do they talk? Is a phone important? What kinds of phones do they have? When was the phone invented? After many questions about the phone are raised, she asks the students to write an association next to each letter. For instance,

p—park
h—house
o—owner
n—nose
e—egg

Can we create either a poem or a nonsense story out of these words?

The park was dark,
the house was bright;
the owner did not want a light.
He showed his nose
to all the crows who laid an egg right on his nose.

or

Deep in a park there was a house, and the owner never showed his nose. The kids in the park knew that something was wrong and wondered why the owner never showed his nose. They thought he might be a wizard or a thief. So, one night they gathered together in the park and decided to creep up to the house and look for the owner. When they looked through the window, they did not see anything except a huge painted egg on top of the table. "Maybe," they said to each other, "it's an Easter egg, and a rabbit will come hopping out if we crack it."

"And maybe," said a huge monster standing behind them, "I'll crack your skulls for looking through my window!"

"Help," yelled the kids.

Just then a big rainbow rabbit popped out of the egg and chased the nasty owner away. From then on, all the kids could play in that house whenever they wanted, and they brought tons of grass for the rabbit to eat.

13. Another game Rodari suggested is the arbitrary prefix game. Words are formed as the students add unusual prefixes. For instance, the teaching artist sets up a list of prefixes in one column and nouns in another to form new words. The original word is deformed, but a new image is created and can be used for starting a story featuring this word.

semi-ice cream
mini-bear
tri-picture
inter-store
bi-dog
pre-car
pseudo-professor

The prefix and noun can serve as the title of the story, such as "The Minibear," and the students can write about a minibear, who perhaps has difficulties with the big bears or perhaps is ashamed because it is so tiny. The new combination of prefix and noun prompts the students to think differently to explore the possible meanings of the new composite noun. The students read and share their stories in front of the class.

In addition to the prefix game, the class can use the suffix game:

-ism—ageism or school-ism
-ist—sexist or traveler-ist
-ette—runner-ette
-ian—cat-ian

Once again, it is the unusual combination of a suffix with a noun that can spark an idea for a story. For example, "school-ism" could prompt a story about the head of a company who hates anyone who has been to school and won't give a job to anyone who has studied and is smart. Why? Is he afraid of schools and students?

14. Montage. The teaching artist brings in some old magazines, news-papers, and tabloids. The students are asked to cut out two headlines from any of the stories and paste them on top of a sheet of paper. Then they use the headlines to tell a story that incorporates the headlines into their own stories. These stories are then read and shared in front of the class.

The Transformation of the Classroom into a Setting for Storytelling and the Implementation of the Chair Game

Once the fantastic binominal game has been played and completed, the students are asked to move all the chairs and desks to the side, as care-fully as possible, so that there is room for storytelling and acting. The transformation of the classroom is important because we want to emphasize change and re-creation. We suggest each week that different pictures and stories created by the children be hung up on the walls of the room and that books bearing on the particular theme of the week are made available to the students. After the chairs and desks are pushed to a side, the teaching artist, teacher, and children sit down on the floor in a circle. Depending on what narrative genre is to be introduced and what the theme is, the teaching artist will tell two tales, often two different versions of the same tale or tales related to each other.

It is important that the teaching artist does not intimidate the students or the teacher. Most of the teaching artists in our program are either professionally trained actors or professional storytellers, and they are very gifted performers. Therefore, we try to walk a fine line of telling all the tales with great gusto and skill, but we do not want to awe the audience. We provide an example—something we call modeling a tale—to show one possible way to tell a tale. We try to alter our styles and modify them each week. We never tell the same tale the same way twice. We never memorize a tale. Instead, in my training sessions I ask participants to read a story a couple of times and to remember the major turning points of a tale and major pedagogical points, the meaning we want to bring out. In other words, we "point" a tale, rehearse it, and then discuss the different ways a tale can be presented and why. We want to show how we can be used as models, imitated, and then replaced. The teacher will gradually be incorporated into the program as storyteller, and the students are incorporated the very first day through the fantastic binominal and then through our chair game.

The students' playing the chair game produces the third tale of the storytelling phase. Before the program has even begun, the teaching artist has asked the teacher to divide the class into three equally talented groups that will remain together throughout the academic year. We are constantly emphasizing cooperation and community. For us, there are several important communities: the class community, the three groups of approximately eight students, the school community, and the neighborhood community. We have found that working in small groups within the class enables better concentration and cooperation on the part of the students. Sometimes there may be conflicts within one group, and so we are not rigid and sometimes we change the composition of the groups to bring about conflict resolution. We try to guide and coach the members of a group to make their own decisions and to develop their own skits and means of working together.

Two of the groups will enact the versions of the stories they hear from the teaching artist. The third group in the chair game invents the third story. There are two ways of playing this game: (1) Each member of the group takes a chair and sits down in it in a row facing the other students, who form the audience. The participants are on stage, so to speak. (2) Each member of the group takes a chair and sits down in a circle in the middle of the room. The other students are sitting in a circle on the ground and form an audience. The teaching artist begins by explaining that she will "feed" one of the students two or three lines to begin a story. The student must repeat these lines and add no more than two sentences to the story and then pass the lines on to the next student, who must repeat in his or her own words what the previous student said, add two more sentences, and pass them on to the next student. This process goes on until the last student receives the unfinished story, which he or she must bring to an end in any way she or he decides.

For instance, if I worked with "Little Red Riding Hood" on a particular day, I might throw out this beginning: "One day Little Red Riding Hood was eating a sandwich for lunch at home. The phone rang. It was her grandmother who yelled, 'Help! Help! Two nasty hunters have shot a poor wolf cub in my backyard. Come and help me!'"

Or I might want to shift the voice and perspective and begin with "I went fishing one day, and as I was fishing, a gigantic fish pulled me into the lake and dragged me deep down to an underwater cave and said, 'How would you like it if people came after you with a hook?' "

We always try to contrive situations that upset the expectations of the students and that raise social issues. They are encouraged to run with the story as they see fit. If the game is played in a circle, the first student does not have to follow the sequence of the students sitting in a row in front of the class. Instead, he or she can choose another participant in the inner circle, who then can choose another until all the participants in the circle have been called on. Of course, the last student must try to end the story in some manner or form.

The students can become very inventive and often will test the teaching artist and teacher by turning vulgar or saying something atrocious. For the most part, however, the game is challenging because it involves memory, imagination, quick thinking, and articulation. Once the story is finished it is the group's story, which the members will enact in a skit. The first two groups will each be assigned one of the stories that have already been told.

Each of the groups will move into a separate corner of the room to discuss their tales, change them, and decide on who will act out a particular role. But before we go into our rehearsal mode, we generally introduce theater games and techniques that will provide the students with the skills, knowledge, and confidence to produce their own skits throughout the year, but especially at the end of the year at the Bridges Festival in May or June. Our emphasis is never on the final production or on a production per se but on the process. We are not interested in a finished product but in the manner in which the students relate to the materials we present, to one another, and to us. We seek to animate them to bring out all the talents they possess so they can better express their desires and needs.

Creative Drama Exercises and Skits

Because creative drama is fundamental for our work, Maria Asp and I have outlined some basic games and methods that we use throughout the year. We are constantly adding new exercises, and the following games are used at the teaching artist's discretion. Because our session is intense and involves key steps, we do not spend more than ten or fifteen minutes exploring the basics of creative drama. We have time in March, April, and May to devote more attention to theater.

Movement Games

1. *Statue game.* All the students sit on the ground and face the front of the class which is envisioned as a stage, which we often mark with duct tape. One group of students is requested to come up front to the stage. They are asked to move around the stage area among themselves and to weave slowly in and out. The speed can be changed. At one point the animator asks them to be a specific person or thing. Generally, it is a good idea to connect the persons and things to the stories that are to be told during the day. So, for instance, with "Little Red Riding Hood," the students are asked to act out any of the following roles: mother, girl going on a picnic, hunter, wolf, or grandmother. Then they are asked to be other animals or things associated with woods: a rabbit, a fox, a gardener, and so forth. As the students create the person and setting, the animator yells "Freeze!" The students must hold their poses, and then the teaching artist as animator asks the audience whether the students look the roles they have been asked to play. If they say "no," the students must redo the characters. If they say "yes," the teaching artist moves on to another role.

   This game also can be used to introduce particular atmospheres: people caught in a thunderstorm, people starving on an island, people looking for a lost item, people flying a plane, people on strike and marching in a protest, people basking in the sun, people shoveling a sidewalk. The purpose of this game is to get the energy flowing, to develop a sense for characterization and setting, and to focus on movement without words. After one group has performed the game for several minutes, a second group is asked to come on stage.

2. *Charade.* Students are asked to act out a person or animal in a particular situation. The teaching artist begins by modeling a situation and plays a truck driver who has a flat tire. Once the teaching artist is finished acting a character and situation, she asks the class to guess what the role was. Whoever guesses comes up front to act out a role. The purpose of this game is to develop characterization and situation.

3. *Mirror games.* A traditional mirror game can be played with students pairing off and facing each other. The students are either A or B, and the animator

asks A to begin an action in slow motion which student B is to follow. Then the teaching artist calls out "switch!" and B takes the lead. The object of the game is to develop concentration and movement in slow motion.

An interesting variation can be created by the students' forming a circle. A student is sent outside, and then one person in the circle is chosen to lead in the movement of the entire group. The student, who was outside, comes back into the middle of the circle and must guess who is leading the movements that all the students are following.

Conflict Resolution Skits

These skits are to enhance the cooperation among the members of a group, to develop their improvisation skills, to provide them with a sense of staging, and to incorporate the other skills they are learning: movement, voice, and characterization.

1. Group A is asked to set up a table with three chairs, while the other groups form an audience. The animator explains to them that they are to act out a story in which three customers have difficulty with a waiter. For instance, the waiter is rude or spills a pizza on one of the customers, and they start arguing with the waiter. Then they call the owner, who calls a policeman, and they must resolve the conflict. The students must first perform all this without saying a word. Then they are to use gibberish. Finally, they are to use language and appropriate gestures. Found objects in the classroom can be used for props.

   After Group A sets an example, so to speak, I sometimes ask all three groups to huddle together and to conceive their own conflict situation. They perform their situations for another. The first time they perform their skit without language, the audience is asked to guess what they have enacted and to make suggestions to improve the skit. After they perform the skit without language, they are then asked to perform it a second time with language and to take into consideration changes suggested by the audience.

2. The students in each group are given slips of paper with the following written on them:

   a. A landlord wants to throw out a family from their home because they can't pay the rent. Is there a way that the neighbors can help out the family? What do the neighbors do? How is everything solved?

b. Some farmers are planting their crops when a cyclone hits. Their crops are destroyed. Their homes are wrecked. How can they be helped? How can they save their farms?

c. A general makes his people work in factories and fight a war so he can become rich. The people become poor and starve. Finally, they realize they must do something to drive out the general. What do they do? How are they going to live when the general is gone?

The students are asked to discuss the situation and form a brief skit that represents the situation and how they might solve the situation. This task is somewhat difficult because the students are not given a narrative to enact. Instead, they must discuss the situation and then form their own narrative. The following are other suggestions:

a. Three children are walking along the street, and a stranger approaches and offers them each one hundred dollars if they help him steal things from a supermarket. Do they accept the money? What do they do?

b. Three workers go on strike because their boss won't pay them enough money for the work they do in a restaurant. He tries to bribe one of them or to bring in other workers so that he can keep control of the restaurant. What do the workers do?

c. Three space people are sent to the moon, and they meet a monster who tells them he will eat their spacecraft and they will never be able to return to the earth unless they become his slaves for ten years. What do they do?

3. Stories to enact. The groups are each given a slip of paper with a short story about a common event. They tell the story among themselves. Each one takes a turn looking at the paper and telling the story to the rest of the group in his or her own words. They are encouraged to add and change elements of the story after they have read the story. Once they each tell the story in their own words, they are to discuss how they might make more changes and perform the story as a skit.

a. There was once a farmer who went to pull out a gigantic carrot in his garden. Try as he may, he could not do it. So he went to one neighbor for help. Together they tried, but they couldn't do it. Then they went to another and another neighbor, but no one could do it. But once all the neighbors were gathered, they held onto each other and pulled. They managed to pull out the gigantic carrot, and they then shared it together for dinner.

b. There was once a poor old man walking along the street, and a robber came and tried to steal his money. Some people walked by and didn't help him. They were afraid of the robber. But three good friends saw what was happening and stopped the robber and brought him to the police.

c. There was once a messenger who had to deliver an important package to a city across the country. As he was driving, his car broke down, and nobody would stop on the highway to help him. One car did stop, but the man demanded a thousand dollars to help him. The messenger did not have the money, and the man drove off. Then three young friends who were driving on their vacation from school saw the messenger in tears, and they gave up their vacation to take him to the city.

The point of all these skits is to bring about a sense of cooperation and mutual support. By having the students work through the skits without words and then with words, they can work through the problems in different modes. It is also a good idea for them to switch roles and see how someone else might perform the role or estimate the situation.

4. Where did you get that? What happened to you? The teaching artist leaves the classroom for a minute and then reenters with a bandage on her head or her arm in a sling. The children will undoubtedly become curious and ask what happened. She invents an outrageous story, such as she bumped into an elephant in the corridor. The children don't believe her. Then she invents another story. The principal was having fun and tripped her in the corridor. And so on. The teaching artist tells a tall tale each time she is asked what happened to her. She can prompt them not to believe her, or she can tell the story so that it seems believable. The students are then divided into groups, and the students take turns traveling to another group. Along the way, before they enter the middle of the group, they must pretend to be hurt or to have had an accident. When the student arrives in the middle of the group, the others ask, "Where did you get that? What happened to you?" The student is to make up a story and has a minute to try to get them to believe the story.

In this game we try to bring out the inventiveness of the students and demonstrate the importance of improvisation. Many of the students use these stories in their daily lives—white lies, excuses they tell their parents or teachers, boastful stories, and exaggerated family stories. When we observe their tales, we discuss them later and try to make distinctions to discuss the nature of different genres or kinds of storytelling.

Preparation Games and Exercises for Theater

We divide the thirty-one weeks that we spend with the students into four phases that will prepare them for acting with a focus on Who? Where? What? How? In each phase of approximately eight weeks, the teaching artist will introduce terms and focus on aspects of storytelling and acting that involve characterization, place, event, and action. The theater games that we use can be complemented with games developed by Viola Spolin in *Improvisation for the Theater* and *Theater Games for the Classroom*. There are also several other books such as Cecily O'Neill and Alan Lambert's *Drama Structures,* Jonothan Neelands and Tony Goode's n*Structuring Drama Work,* Ruth Heinig's *Improvisation with Favorite Tales,* and Norah Morgan and Juliana Saxton's *Teaching Questioning and Learning,* which provide useful ideas to incorporate creative drama in the classroom.

Retransformation of the Classroom for Writing Games

After the students have participated in the theater games and have acted out their skits, we ask them to retransform the play area into their classroom and to take their seats. Their adrenalin has been flowing, and we want to make use of their "juices" in a final writing game. We also want to wind down in a calm moment to enable them to concentrate and develop their ideas on paper. In other words, we bracket the entire session with two writing games, always beginning with the fantastic binominal and ending with a writing exercise closely connected to the theme of the day.

What If Game

For instance, we often use the What If game throughout the year. Let us suppose that we have been telling "Hansel and Gretel." The teaching artist or teacher stands in front of the room and asks some questions, such as the following:

> What if Hansel and Gretel did not become lost in the woods, but their father did?
> What if the witch was a kind and lovely lady with a lot of money who adopted Hansel and Gretel?

What if Hansel and Gretel robbed the witch, who was a kind old woman?

What if the stepmother fought with the father to keep Hansel and Gretel at home against the father's will?

After the teaching artist proposes these questions, she asks the students for more what if questions pertaining to "Hansel and Gretel," and she writes their suggestions on the board. After she has five or six what if questions, she asks the students to choose any one of them on the board or to think of a new question and to use it as the title of their stories. Then they have between five and ten minutes to write and illustrate a story. At the end, if there is still time, the teaching artist asks three students to come up to the front of the class and share their stories with the rest of the students. These stories are not acted out. They are placed in the students' folders, and during the week the teacher can work with the students and help them revise their stories. One of these stories can become part of the anthology that the students will create in November or December.

The What If game can be used with any theme or genre. For instance, when we work with superheroes and introduce Superman or Supergirl in a story, we might ask,

What if Superman lost all his powers for good?

What if Supergirl discovered that Superman was evil?

What if Clark Kent was not Superman but Lois Lane was Supergirl?

Any story or character can be altered. We want to prompt the students to become editors and creators of their own stories involving tales they have read, heard, or seen.

The Mixed Salad Game

If we have been working on myths and superheroes over a period of two or three weeks, we might ask the students to suggest the names of the heroes, such as

Spiderman

Buffy the Vampire Slayer

The Incredible Hulk
Wolverine
Batman
Wonder Woman
Jackie Chan
Hercules
Venus
Mercury
Xena
Zeus
Diana

Then we ask them to take three or four nouns, such as

bus
forest
restaurant
knife

Then we tell them to mix all these characters and nouns in a story. Each one has to be used. For instance,

> One day Diana happened to meet Wolverine and Wonder Woman in a Chinese restaurant, when all of a sudden Jackie Chan appeared, and started yelling that someone had kidnapped the cook. There would be no food until the cook could be found. Immediately, Wolverine called Mercury to come and help them. When he arrived, he told them that the cook had been kidnapped by Zeus and Venus and had been taken to the forest to prepare a special banquet.

The salad game is similar to the fantastic binominal insofar as the characters will bring up associations, and they are brought together arbitrarily to challenge the students to create connections in a plot of their own making.

Writing Tall Tales and Rumors

This writing game can be played after a session dealing with tall tales, legends, superheroes, and family tales. It can be played in different ways. For instance, the students are asked to "throw" the name of a famous or popular person, dead or alive, at the teaching artist, who immediately tells a tall tale or a rumor. For instance, let us suppose the name is Michael Jordan, and the teaching artist begins, "Did you hear that Michael Jordan is now going to play football for the New York Giants. He signed a contract. …" Or, "Did you hear that when Michael Jordan was only five-years-old, he could dunk the ball, dribble between his legs, and shoot with his left and right hand. Well, let me tell you about the time he was in a game on a playground when he was only six. …"

After the teaching artist models the storytelling, the students are asked to write down on a slip of paper the name of a famous or popular person. The teaching artist collects the slips in a hat or a bag and then mixes them. Then she goes around the room and asks the students to take a slip of paper that they will use to write their own rumor or tall tale. It is important that the teaching artist explains the difference between a rumor, a story—often negative or sensational—spread to warn, scare, or delight the hearers, and a tall tale, which is often based on some truth and is an exaggeration or a lie to demonstrate the prowess of an individual. In a brief discussion with the students, the teaching artist asks for their definitions and writes them on the board. In the discussion with the students, we often try to ascertain whether rumors and tall tales are harmful. How are they used? Why? Who spreads the tales?

Sharing the Stories

The end of the session is a time of sharing stories. It is very important that the students listen and show respect to their classmates. Throughout the two hours that we spend in the classroom, we emphasize that listening is just as important as speaking and acting. The audience is just as important as the actors. Some of the students may finish writing their stories sooner than their classmates, and this is why we always have drawing paper and colored pencils or crayons available. We encourage the students to illustrate all their stories, whether they do this during our session or later during the week. We keep a record of which students have come up before the class to read their stories so that everyone has a chance. Although some students will be timid at the beginning of our program and refuse to read before the class, we have found that, over the course of time, everyone grows confident and wants to participate in all our activities.

Spreading Tales, Opening Minds—Sample Sessions

Fig. 6.1 Students at Lucy Laney School carrying a set in to the school.

6

FAIRY TALES, ANIMAL FABLES, TRICKSTER STORIES, AND PEACE TALES

The curriculum of Neighborhood Bridges changes from year to year, and it is essentially set up so that we can explore the basic short narrative genres of storytelling and expose the children to them. We teach through modeling the art of storytelling, animation, coaching, and discussion. We use traditional and untraditional stories to give the students a knowledge of the canonical tales, and throughout the course of an academic year, we animate them to write, read, draw, and produce their own tales and skits. Because our curriculum is large and extensive, I focus on several key sessions in this chapter and the next to demonstrate how we use the tales within the flexible structure that we have developed. Our structure allows for substitution of different tales and exercises. Teaching artists and teachers in our program are given free rein to experiment as they see fit.

The Importance of Working with Canonical Fairy Tales

During weeks two through five we introduce such tales as "Little Red Riding Hood," "Hansel and Gretel," "Puss in Boots," "Rapunzel," "The Frog King," "Jack and the Beanstalk," "Cinderella," and "Beauty and the Beast," with the intention of exploring why the tales have become canonical.

Fairy tales constantly seep into our lives without our realizing how deeply they infiltrate our bodies. Some linguists and biologists argue that we are actually born with a capacity to grasp language and grammar through genetic evolution. We seem to be disposed to learn and pass on certain narrative forms with ease, as though they were part of our nature. Perhaps this is why fairy tales flourish in all kinds of forms. They are not just tales for children, never were, and never will be. They are relevant metaphorical means of communication in which we discuss and debate social, political, and cultural problems such as the formation of gender roles, sibling rivalry, social class conflicts, revolution, social codification through dress, and so on. As a genre, the fairy tale has cultivated specific recognizable conventions and motifs for narrating important messages that have a bearing on our lives. Consequently, we are more apt to remember and recall a fairy tale than other generic forms because this specific genre has provided us with an effective linguistic mode to deal with what is relevant and special in our lives and is with us practically from birth to death.

The fairy tale is not just an oral or written narrative. Today it can be a TV commercial, a poster, a napkin, a T-shirt, a videocassette, a postcard, a film, a play, a musical, and so on. It has been condensed and expanded through mass media and technology. It rarely assumes the same form twice, although there are basic constellations in the canonical tales that recur constantly. These canonical tales, largely disseminated through the works of Charles Perrault, Jacob and Wilhelm Grimm, and Hansel Christian Andersen and established in the nineteenth century by all kinds of cultural institutions, are now known throughout the world. Though "impregnated" with codes of Western civilization, the tales such as "Little Red Riding Hood," "Cinderella," "Sleeping Beauty," "Rapunzel," "Rumpelstiltskin," "Tom Thumb," "Hansel and Gretel," "Bluebeard," "The Frog King," "Puss in Boots," "The Ugly Duckling," "Beauty and the Beast," "The Emperor's New Clothes," "The Little Mermaid," "The Red Shoes," and so on have become globalized and are distributed throughout the world in different forms by cultural conglomerates such as the Disney Corporation, which has played a major role in leaving its imprint on specific fairy

tales, including ones that originated in Asia. In many instances, there
are local versions that contend with the mass-marketed products, and
artists who have a more contemporary if not progressive perspective on
social relations often contest the meanings of the canonical tales.

I specifically use the word *progressive* in an ideological sense because
most of the canonical fairy tales tend to be sexist and conservative in
their approach to topics of gender, justice, and government. Although
they are narratives of hope and reveal the triumph of the oppressed,
the happy ending of the tales generally involves a restoration of the
status quo with power largely in the hands of men. This critical comment is intended not to dismiss the tales but to reflect on the fact that
they were institutionalized in Western civilization in the nineteenth
and early twentieth centuries when our attitudes toward sex and government were less democratic. Thus, the canonical tales and their off-
shoots represent the spirit of their times; these narratives became very
much contested in the 1970s and continue to be questioned and challenged today.

For children, not to mention adults, it is socially important to be
familiar with the canonical fairy tales to understand interliterary and
intercultural references. This does not mean we need to valorize canonical literature as superior to popular culture or other noncanonical
works. It simply means that it is important to be knowledgeable about
icons and social codes to navigate one's way through institutions of all
kinds and to be able to use them to one's pleasure or advantage. In part,
to become the storyteller of one's life means that a young person must
learn how to use, manipulate, and exploit social and cultural codes,
especially linguistic and semantic ones, so that she or he will be able to
contend with the constant bombardment of signs, often commercial
and propagandistic, that occur every day. To know how to cope with a
fairy tale is the first step of coping with one's desires in relation to other
human beings in a social context fraught with conflict.

In the Neighborhood Bridges program we always begin with "Little
Red Riding Hood," because I claim it is probably the most popular and
well-known fairy tale in the world and because I am in some strange
way obsessed with this tale. In 1982 I published a book titled *The Trials
and Tribulations of Little Red Riding Hood* to counter the misleading
and formulaic interpretations of fairy tales in Bruno Bettelheim's book

The Uses of Enchantment: The Meaning and Importance of Fairy Tales. I endeavored to demonstrate that an oral tale that dealt with the initiation of a clever and brave young girl in an agrarian, sewing society was transformed into a tale about violence, if not rape, by Perrault and the Grimms in which the girl called Little Red Cap was held responsible for her violation by a wolf/man. There are, of course, many ways to interpret and illustrate "Little Red Riding Hood," but I want at the very least to show that if we look at the tale in a historical sociocultural context, we can see that the conflict centers on the desire of a predatory male, who wants to eat a gullible cute female, and she, in turn, is blamed for her tragic end, especially in the first literary version by Perrault in 1697. Perrault made it seem either that the girl wanted to be eaten or that she somehow contributed to her violation. Soon after my book appeared I was flooded with all sorts of new literary and oral versions, and the scholarly debate about the meaning of this tale continued in full force as well. By 1993 I published a second edition of *The Trials and Tribulations of Little Red Riding Hood* with more tales and critical commentary to document once again how relevant this tale had become with regard to questions of rape and violence throughout the world. There is no end to the spread of this tale in manifold versions. In some ways the best contemporary critical comment on the plot is the superb film *Freeway* (1998), directed by Matt Bright, which is a fascinating study of a rebellious teenager who refuses to assume the role of the gullible Red Riding Hood. But I should also mention three books—*Recycling Red Riding Hood* by Sandra Beckett, *Little Red Riding Hood Uncloaked: Sex, Morality, and the Evolution of a Fairy Tale* by Catherine Orenstein, and *Language and Gender in the Fairy Tale Tradition: A Linguistic Analysis of Old and New Story Telling* by Alessandra Levorato—because they bring the developments concerning the "fate" of Little Red Riding Hood up to date.

In short, each canonical fairy tale is invested with deep historical and cultural meaning that we want to mine and undermine in our sessions. We always tell a canonical version first, discuss it with the students without imposing an interpretation. Then we tell a countertale, such as "Polly and the Stupid Wolf," followed by questions and answers. Finally we set up a third tale with our "Chair Game," which will produce a third version of the tale.

Finding Canonical and Noncanonical Tales

Because it is important to have a large repertoire of canonical and noncanonical tales, I want to introduce a short list of the books we use. There are many other useful anthologies to be found in my general bibliography.

Canonical Tales

Andersen, Hans Christian. 1974. *The Complete Firy Tales and Stories.* Translated by Erik Christian Haugaard. New York: Doubleday.

Grimm, Jacob, and Wilhelm Grimm. 2003. *The Complete Fairy Tales of the Brothers Grimm.* Edited and translated by Jack Zipes. 3rd expanded ed. New York: Bantam.

Tatar, Maria, ed. 1999. *The Classic Fairy Tales.* New York: W. W. Norton. (Also contains countertales.)

Zipes, Jack, ed. 1989. *Beauties, Beasts, and Enchantment: French Classical Fairy Tales.* New York: New American Library. (Contains the complete tales by Charles Perrault.)

Noncanonical Tales

Attic Press. 1985. *Rapunzel's Revenge.* Dublin: Author.

Attic Press. 1989. *Sweeping Beauties.* Dublin: Author.

Carter, Angela, ed. 1990. *The Virago Book of Fairy Tales.* Illustrated by Corinna Sargood. London: Virago.

Carter, Angela, ed. 1993. *Strange Things Sometimes Still Happen: Fairy Tales from around the World.* London: Faber and Faber.

Hearne, Betsy, ed. 1993. *Beauties and Beasts.* Illustrated by Joanne Caroselli. Phoenix, Ariz.: Oryx Press.

Lurie, Alison, ed. 1980. *Clever Gretchen and Other Forgotten Folktales.* New York: Corwell.

MacDonald, Margaret Read, ed. 1993. *Tom Thumb.* Illustrated by Joanne Caroselli. Phoenix, Ariz.: Oryx Press.

Minard, Rosemary, ed. 1975. *Womenfolk and Fairy Tales.* Boston: Houghton Mifflin.

Phelps, Ethel Johnston, ed. 1978. *Tatterhood and Other Tales.* Old Westbury, N.Y.: Feminist Press.

Phelps, Ethel Johnston, ed. 1981. *The Maid of the North: Feminist Folk Tales from around the World.* New York: Holt, Rinehart & Winston.

Pogrebin, Letty Cottin, ed. 1982. *Stories for Free Children.* New York: McGraw-Hill.

Ragan, Kathleen, ed. 1998. *Fearless Girls, Wise Women, and Beloved Sisters: Heroines in Folktales from around the World.* New York: Norton.

Sierra, Judy, ed. 1992. *Cinderella.* Phoenix, Ariz.: Oryx Press.

Web Sites

Ashliman, D. L. "Folklore and Mythology Electronic Texts," http://www.pitt.edu/~dash/folktexts.html.

"The Cinderella Project," http://www.usm.edu/english/fairytales/cinderella/cinderella.html.

"Marvels & Tales," http://www.langlab.wayne.edu/MarvelsHome/Marvels_Tales.html.

Peck, Russell, "The Cinderella Bibliography," http://www.lib.rochester.edu/camelot/cindere/cinitr.html.

"SurLaLune Fairy Tale Pages," http://surlalunefairytales.com/.

Vandergrift, Kay. "Kay Vandergrift's Snow White Page," http://www/scils.rutgers.edu/~kvander/snow white.html.

Windling, Terri, "The Endicott Studio of Mythic Arts," http://www.endicott-studio.com/.

Fairy Tales

We begin each fairy-tale session by asking the students if any of them know the tale, and the teaching artist goes around the circle asking the students to retell the tale. Inevitably there are gaps and disputes among the students who retell the tale. All the better, because we want to show that there is no such thing as a definitive version. The introduction of the canonical version is intended to make students aware that there is a literary tradition in which particular versions become canonized because they are regarded as most representative of particular aesthetic and ideological standards.

Little Red Riding Hood

Instructions to teaching artists: Bear in mind the social and political ramifications of this particular tale that deals with violence and rape. These issues should rise to the fore in the telling and games. The purpose of this session is to encourage children to seek nonviolent solutions to predicaments confronted by the characters. The emphasis in the improvisational skits is on character: Who is your character? Why does your character act and behave a certain way?

Basic Structure of the Session

Fantastic binominal: Try to link the fantastic binominal to the theme of the day. For instance, ask for specific nouns such as clothes (relating to Red Riding Hood's hood and cloak) and the names of animals that are predators. What clothes do people wear today? What do clothes symbolize? What clothes are worn in the country? In the city? What are predators? What do animals prey upon? Do humans prey? Once the nouns are listed on the board, ask for prepositions to link the nouns.

Retelling of the key canonical tale by Charles Perrault: It is very important that this version be told, not read. To begin with, ask how many of the students know the tale and let them go around and offer their versions. They will contradict each other and have completely different notions about the tale. This is fine. Once they are done, proceed by announcing that you will be telling the first literary version of "Little Red Riding Hood" by Charles Perrault.

Little Red Riding Hood

Once upon a time there was a little village girl, the prettiest that had ever been seen. Her mother doted on her, and her grandmother doted on her even more. This good woman made the little girl a little red hood, which suited her so well that she was called Little Red Riding Hood wherever she went.

One day, after her mother had baked some biscuits, she said to Little Red Riding Hood, "Go see how your grandmother's feeling. I've heard that she's sick. You can take her some biscuits and this small pot of butter."

Little Red Riding Hood departed at once to visit her grandmother, who lived in another village. In passing through the forest she met old neighbor wolf, who had a great desire to eat her. But he did not dare because of some woodcutters who were in the forest. He asked her where she was going, and the poor child, who did not know that it is dangerous to stop and listen to a wolf, said to him, "I'm going to see my grandmother, and I'm bringing her some biscuits with a small pot of butter that my mother's sending her."

"Does she live far from here?" the wolf asked.

"Oh, yes!" Little Red Riding Hood said. "You've got to go by the mill, which you can see right over there, and hers is the first house in the village."

"Well, then," said the wolf, "I'll go and see her, too. You take that path there, and I'll take this path here, and we'll see who'll get there first."

The wolf began to run as fast as he could on the path that was shorter, and the little girl took the longer path, and she enjoyed herself by gathering nuts, running after butterflies, and making bouquets of small flowers that she found along the way. It did not take the wolf long to arrive at the grandmother's house, and he knocked.

"Tic, toc."

"Who's there?"

"It's your granddaughter, Little Red Riding Hood," the wolf said, disguising his voice. "I've brought you some biscuits and a little pot of butter that my mother's sent for you."

The good grandmother, who was in her bed because she was not feeling well, cried out to him, "Pull the bobbin, and the latch will fall."

The wolf pulled the bobbin, and the door opened. He pounced on the good woman and devoured her quicker than a wink, for it had been more than three days since he had eaten last. After that he closed the door and lay down in the grandmother's bed to wait for Little Red Riding Hood, who after awhile came knocking at the door.

"Tic, toc."

"Who's there?"

When she heard the gruff voice of the wolf, Little Red Riding Hood was scared at first, but she thought her grandmother had a cold and responded, "It's your granddaughter, Little Red Riding Hood. I've brought you some biscuits and a little pot of butter that my mother's sent for you."

The wolf softened his voice and cried out to her, "Pull the bobbin, and the latch will fall."

Little Red Riding Hood pulled the bobbin, and the door opened.

Upon seeing her enter, the wolf hid himself under the bedcovers and said to her, "Put the biscuits and the pot of butter on the bin and come lie down beside me."

Little Red Riding Hood undressed and went to get into bed, where she was quite astonished to see the way her grandmother was dressed in her nightgown, and she said to her, "What big arms you have, grandmother!"

"The better to hug you with, my child."

"What big legs you have, grandmother!"

"The better to run with, my child."

"What big ears you have, grandmother!"

"The better to hear you with, my child."

"What big eyes you have, grandmother!"

"The better to see you with, my child."

"What big teeth you have, grandmother!"

"The better to eat you with."

And upon saying these words, the wicked wolf pounced on Little Red Riding Hood and ate her up.

Moral

One sees here that young children,
Especially pretty girls,
Polite, well-taught, and pure as pearls,
Should stay on guard against all sorts of men.
For if one fails to stay alert, it won't be strange
To see one eaten by a wolf enraged.
I say a wolf since not all types are wild,
Or can be said to be the same in kind.
Some are winning and have sharp minds.
Some are loud or smooth or mild.
Others appear just kind and unriled.
They follow young ladies wherever they go,
Right into the halls of their very own homes.

Alas for those who've refused the truth:
Sweetest tongue has the sharpest tooth.

Discussion: It is important that the moral is not told. After you say, "the wicked wolf pounced on Little Red Riding Hood and ate her up," pause. Generally, the students will be startled. Then say, "Did you expect a hunter? Did you think the tale ended differently?" Then reveal what Perrault's moral was: "Little girls who invite wolves into their parlors deserve what they get." Ask whether they think this is fair. Was the ending strange? Is the moral by Perrault a good one? Are girls stupid? Do they deserve to be eaten by wolves? Should children talk to wolves?

Countertale: Tell the tale "Little Polly and the Stupid Wolf," by Catherine Storr.

Little Polly and the Stupid Wolf

Once every two weeks Polly went over to the other side of the town to see her grandmother. Sometimes she took a small present, and sometimes she came back with a small present for herself. Sometimes all the rest of the family went too, and sometimes Polly went alone.

One day, when she was going by herself, she had hardly got down the front door steps when she saw the wolf.

"Good afternoon, Polly," said the wolf. "Where are you going, may I ask?"

"Certainly," said Polly. "I'm going to see my grandma."

"I thought so!" said the wolf, looking very much pleased. "I've been reading about a girl who went to visit her grandmother and it's a very good story."

" 'Little Red Riding Hood'?" suggested Polly.

"That's it!" cried the wolf. "I read it out loud to myself as a bedtime story. I did enjoy it. The wolf eats up the grandmother and Little Red Riding Hood. It's almost the only story where a wolf really gets anything to eat," he added sadly.

"But in my book he doesn't get Red Riding Hood," said Polly.

"Her father comes in just in time to save her."

"Oh, he doesn't in my book!" said the wolf. "I expect mine is the true story, and yours is just invented. Anyway, it seems a good idea."

"What is a good idea?"

"To catch little girls on their way to their grandmothers' cottages," said the wolf. "Now where had I got to?"

"I don't know what you mean," said Polly.

"Well, I'd said, 'Where are you going to?'" said the wolf. "Oh yes. Now I must say, 'Where does she live?' Where does your grandmother live, Polly Riding Hood?"

"Over on the other side of town," answered Polly.

The wolf frowned.

"It ought to be 'Through the Wood,'" he said. "But perhaps town will do. How do you get there, Polly Riding Hood?"

"First I take a train and then I take a bus," said Polly.

The wolf stamped his foot.

"No, no, no, no!" he shouted. "That's all wrong. You can't say that. You've got to say, 'By the path winding through the trees,' or something like that. You can't go by trains and buses and things. It isn't fair."

"Well, I could say that," said Polly, "but it wouldn't be true. I do have to go by bus and train to see my grandma, so what's the good of saying I don't?"

"But then it won't work," said the wolf impatiently. "How can I get there first and gobble her up and get all dressed up to trick you into believing I am her, if we've got a great train journey to do? And anyhow I haven't any money on me, so I can't even take a ticket. You just can't say that!"

"All right, I won't say it," said Polly agreeably. "But it's true all the same. Now just excuse me, Wolf, I've got to get down to the station because I am going to visit my grandma even if you aren't."

The wolf slunk along behind Polly, growling to himself. He stood just behind her at the booking office and heard her ask for her ticket, but he could not go any further. Polly got into a train and was carried away, and the wolf went sadly home.

But just two weeks later the wolf was waiting outside Polly's house again. This time he had plenty of change in his pocket. He even had a book tucked under his front leg to read in the train. He partly hid himself behind a corner of brick wall and watched to see Polly come out on her way to her grandmother's house. But Polly did not come out alone, as she had before. This time the whole family appeared, Polly's father and mother too. They got into the car, which was waiting in the road, and Polly's father started the engine.

The wolf ran from behind his brick wall as fast as he could and was just in time to get out into the road ahead of the car and to stand waving his paws as if he wanted a lift as the car came up.

Polly's father slowed down, and Polly's mother put her head out of the window.

"Where do you want to go?" she asked.

"I want to go to Polly's grandmother's house," the wolf answered. His eyes glistened as he looked at the family of plump little girls in the back of the car.

"That's where we are going," said her mother, surprised. "Do you know her then?"

"Oh no," said the wolf. "But you see, I want to get there very quickly and eat her up and then I can put on her clothes and wait for Polly, and eat her up too."

"Good heavens!" said Polly's father. "What a horrible idea! We certainly shan't give you a lift if that is what you are planning to do."

Polly's mother screwed up the window again and Polly's father drove quickly on. The wolf was left standing miserably in the road.

"Bother!" he said to himself angrily. "It's gone wrong again. I can't think why it can't be the same again as the Little Red Riding Hood story. It's all these buses and cars and trains that make it go wrong."

But the wolf was determined to get Polly, and when she was due to visit her grandmother again, a fortnight later, he went down and took a ticket for the station he had heard Polly ask for. When he got out of the train, he climbed on a bus, and soon he was walking down the road where Polly's grandmother lived.

"Aha!" he said to himself. "This time I shall get them both. First the grandma, then Polly."

He unlatched the gate into the garden, and strolled up the path to Polly's grandmother's front door. He rapped sharply with the knocker.

"Who's there?" called a voice from inside the house.

The wolf was very much pleased. This was going just as it had in the story. This time there would be no mistakes.

"Little Polly Riding Hood," he said in a squeaky voice. "Come to see her dear grandmother, with a little present of butter and eggs and—er—cake!"

There was a long pause. Then the voice said doubtfully, "Who did you say it was?"

"Little Polly Riding Hood," said the wolf in a great hurry, quite forgetting to disguise his voice this time. "Come to eat up her dear grandmother with butter and eggs!"

There was an even longer pause. Then Polly's grandmother put her head out of a window and looked down at the wolf.

"I beg your pardon?" she said.

"I am Polly," said the wolf firmly.

"Oh," said Polly's grandmother. She appeared to be thinking hard. "Good afternoon, Polly. Do you know if anyone else happens to be coming to see me today? A wolf, for instance?"

"No. Yes," said the wolf in great confusion. "I met a Polly as I was coming here—I mean, I, Polly, met a wolf on my way here, but she can't have got here yet because I started specially early."

"That's very queer," said the grandma. "Are you quite sure you are Polly?"

"Quite sure," said the wolf.

"Well, then, I don't know who it is who is here already," said Polly's grandma. "She said she was Polly. But if you are Polly then I think this other person must be a wolf."

"No, no, I am Polly," said the wolf. "And, anyhow, you ought not to say all that. You ought to say 'Lift the latch and come in.'"

"I don't think I'll do that," said Polly's grandma. "Because I don't want my nice little Polly eaten up by a wolf, and if you come in now the wolf who is here already might eat you up."

Another head looked out of another window. It was Polly's.

"Bad luck, Wolf," she said. "You didn't know that I was coming to lunch and tea today instead of just tea as I generally do—so I got here first. And as you are Polly, as you've just said, I must be the wolf, and you'd better run away quickly before I gobble you up, hadn't you?"

"Bother, bother, bother, and bother!" said the wolf. "It hasn't worked out right this time either. And I did just what it said in the book. Why can't I ever get you, Polly, when that other wolf managed to get his little girl?"

"Because this isn't a fairy story," said Polly, "and I'm not Little Red Riding Hood, I am Polly and I can always escape from you, Wolf, however much you try to catch me."

"Clever Polly," said Polly's grandma. And the wolf went growling away.

Discussion: What is different in this tale? Where does it take place? Are girls different nowadays than during the times of Charles Perrault? Why is Polly so smart? Why is the wolf stupid? Both seem to have read "Little Red Riding Hood." Why are their interpretations of the tale so different?

Third version invented by the students: The students sit on chairs and are fed a line such as "Little Red Riding Hood was home eating a sandwich when the phone rang. It was her grandmother who said, 'Help! Help! Two nasty hunters shot the poor wolf, and he is wounded and lying on the ground. Come help!' "

Theater games and improvisation led by the teaching artist: Ask the class what a character is. Every time they give an answer, summarize what they say and add one idea. For example, the students state that a character is a person in a show. Then ask, "Can a character be a wolf?" Each time expand the definition. Each time the students suggest something, expand on their definition. Eventually you may come up with the following: a character is a person, an animal, or a thing that is real or imagined. Next ask them, "Who were the characters in today's stories?" and have the class stand and practice showing the physical characteristics of some of the characters. Then tell them to "Freeze!" and point out the students who have creatively captured the features. Tell the students to keep their frozen position and point out what makes their frozen positions so interesting so that the other students can see and use their ideas and integrate them into their own. This game also can be done by having the students walk in slow motion as mothers, grandmothers, wolves, hunters, and so on. Ask the students to freeze at different times and prompt them to develop certain gestures.

Skits: It is important to stress to the students that they should try to find a nonviolent solution to the conflicts in their tales. Because the tale is about violence, the students are apt to introduce other violent incidents. If so, they should be questioned about this, not censured, and they should be asked to try to find a peaceful solution to the problems of the girl and the wolf.

Writing game: Ask the students "What if?" questions.

What if the wolf were a vegetarian?
What if Little Red Riding Hood were a boy?
What if Little Red Riding Hood knew karate?
What if granny hypnotized the wolf?
What if the wolf were a policeman?

Hansel and Gretel

We use the Grimms' "Hansel and Gretel" and my adaptation of a French tale "Bernard and Bernadette" as a countertale. The history of the Grimms' text reveals how assiduously the Grimms, particularly Wilhelm, sought to influence our notions of socialization and the rearing of children through the constant revision of a fairy tale. In essence, his story seeks to apologize for the abandonment of the children (as do many others), and it depicts women as threatening figures while it apologizes for the father's behavior. There has always been a close connection between the rationalization process of writing and the reception of fairy tales. In the case of "Hansel and Gretel," Wilhelm heard the story from Dortchen Wild, daughter of a pharmacist in Kassel in about 1809. The Grimms indicated in their notes that they knew Charles Perrault's "Le Petit Poucet" ("Little Tom Thumb," 1697), which has a similar plot, as well as other folk versions. By the time Wilhelm wrote the next version for the second edition in 1819, he also was familiar with Giambattista Basile's "Ninnillo and Nennella" (1634). Wilhelm constantly revised the tale in each edition, making it more Christian in tone and placing greater blame on a stepmother for the abandonment.

The popularity and importance of similar tales that can be found throughout Europe in the oral and literary tradition are due to the theme of child abandonment and abuse. Although it is difficult to estimate how widespread child abandonment was, it is clear that famines, poor living conditions, and lack of birth control led to the birth of many unwanted children. In the Middle Ages it was common to abandon children who could not be nourished in front of churches, in special places of village squares, or in the forest. Sometimes the abandonment or abuse, or both, was due to the remarriage of a man or woman who could not tolerate the children from a previous marriage. When the children are abandoned in the fairy tales, they do not always have an encounter with a witch, but they do encounter a dangerous character who threatens their lives, and they must use their wits to find a way to return home.

The central focus here is on child abandonment and abuse. The Grimms tend to rationalize the behavior of the parents, especially the father, by bringing about a happy end. We want to explore the reasons for such behavior and the alternatives for the children in the telling of the tale and its enactment.

Rapunzel

The incarceration of a young woman in a tower (often to protect her chastity during puberty) was a common motif in various European myths and became part of the standard repertoire of medieval tales, lais, and romances throughout Europe and Asia. In addition, the motif of a pregnant woman who has a strong craving for an extravagant dish or extraordinary food is very important. In many peasant societies people believed that it was necessary to fulfill the longings of a pregnant woman, otherwise something evil like a miscarriage or bad luck might occur. Therefore, it was incumbent on the husband and other friends and relatives to use spells or charms or other means to fulfill the cravings. However, the fulfillment of the craving or desire generally involves breaking a taboo or a trespass that must be atoned. The witch, fairy, godmother, or wise woman is generally depicted as both cruel and kind; she is the female authoritarian figure who guards the young female against the outside world. When she is cast as a witch or sorceress, as is the case in the Grimms' tale, she appears in a negative light. There were, however, many oral and literary versions that preceded the Grimms' work, and they reveal that the older woman is more complex than we are led to believe. We retell the Grimms' "Rapunzel" and use "Angiola" in *Beautiful Angiola: The Great Treasury of Sicilian Folk and Fairy Tales Collected by Laura Gonzenbach* as the countertale.

Jack and the Bean Stalk

Jack, the little cunning hero who often bumbles at first before accomplishing a great feat, is related internationally to a number of bumbling heroes in Europe and the Middle East: Pierre (France), Hansel (Germany), Pietro (Italy), Giufà (Sicily and Middle East), and Ivan (Russia). In each country there is also a particular cultural history about the peculiar hero. For instance, in England the tale developed during the eighteenth century and generally portrayed the hero as the smart son of a Cornish farmer who encounters giants and obtains their wealth and marries a noble wife. This tale was mixed with many different literary motifs, and Jack often was portrayed as serving King Arthur. In one of the more popular eighteenth-century versions in which Jack faces the two-headed Welsh giant Thunderel, the giant utters the famous verse,

Fee, fau, fum,
I smell the blood of an *English* man,
Be he alive, or be he dead,
I'll grind his bones to make my bread.

But it is Jack who defeats the giant using a magic cloak, cap, and shoes, all traditional fairy-tale motifs. To emphasize his prowess, Jack chops off the giant's heads and sends them to King Arthur.

The Jack tales were extremely popular and published as chapbooks, broadsides, and illustrated books for children in the late eighteenth and nineteenth centuries. Gradually, however, Jack's character changed so that he was more like a simple farm boy. No longer did he serve King Arthur. Rather, he became more concerned with basic living conditions and survival. This transformation of Jack may have been due to the influence of the oral tradition and a shift in English sensibilities. Jack is generally poor, and though smart, he is clumsy. He does not necessarily marry a wealthy princess, but he does defeat a powerful giant or ogre in some unearthly realm and brings back a fortune to his mother. In the United States, the Jack tales became well-known in the southern Appalachians; here, too, Jack underwent a transformation to become a loveable, lazy scoundrel, and he combined features of the English and continental tradition to demonstrate how a small cunning hero can always find ways to rise in society and obtain wealth or simply survive against the odds.

The focus in our retelling is on poverty, greed, and violence. Both stories deal with poor people who must find a way to survive. These tales continue some of the themes raised in "Hansel and Gretel." Here, however, we have a young man who manages to succeed after making a mistake by selling the cow for the beans or selling a cow for a pot. The heroes and their mothers are poor and "small people." Their situation is not unlike the situation of many single mothers and their children throughout the world. Their triumph represents the triumph of small people who are constantly fighting unfair odds. We use the canonical version "Jack and the Beanstalk" adapted from *English Fairy Tales* by Joseph Jacobs and a complementary tale, "The Miraculous Pot," which I adapted for the curriculum.

Optional Tales

In our work over the past five years, we have sometimes returned to a fourth-fifth- or fifth-sixth-grade classroom in which some of the children have already participated in our program. Therefore, we vary our curriculum with other tales while keeping the basic structure. It does not matter that some of the students know the methods and games we use. In fact, it is often useful because the students with experience help mentor those who are new to the program. Moreover, our program is never the same each year. The teaching artist or classroom teacher may change. Certainly the interpersonal relationships are different, and there will always be a different approach each year to our repertoire of tales, which we keep expanding. The following tales can be substituted for any of those discussed previously.

The Frog King

It is significant that the Brothers Grimm always included this tale as the first one in their *Children and Household Tales* because they believed it offered a charming, didactic lesson about humility and responsibility. At the same time, as part of the oral beast-bridegroom tradition, it also has a certain erotic dimension and involves an initiation into sex. In the German version most people forget that the princess throws the frog against the wall, and this violent act breaks the magic spell that had changed the prince into the frog. We do not know who cast the spell and why it had been cast on the prince. Most of the other versions—and there are thousands—depict the princess kissing the frog, then the prince appearing. The motif of the kiss can be traced back to the Middle Ages, and in many adaptations of the Grimms' tale, the kiss has been substituted for the violent rejection of the frog. Whether the key motif is a kiss or violent act, it has always been clear to listeners and readers that the frog's intrusion has something to do with sexual initiation, and the hundreds if not thousands of variations in comics, cartoons, films, and books play on the princess's aversion or desire to learn more about the "phallic" identity of the frog. In his book *Tradition and Innovation in Folk Literature* Wolfgang Mieder made the point that the fairy tale has become a major product of the mass media and commercialism, and he provided the background story for a proverb known throughout the world: "You have to kiss a lot of toads before you meet your handsome prince." However, many critics do not pay attention to the blackmailing and humiliation of the princess and the arbitrary way her father treats her. Not every king is judicious, and not every frog will become a prince. The constant humiliation of the princess in the classical tale is important to stress. This story is similar to "King Thrushbeard," which formed the basis of Shakespeare's *The Taming of the Shrew*. The girl is shamed into realizing that she should do what the king—her father—and the prince want her to do. As countertale, I think "Mathilde" in *Creative Storytelling* is appropriate. It has the sports element to it, but see also "The Marvelous Sea Frog" in the appendix to *Creative Storytelling*. This is also an effective and humorous countertale.

Cinderella

There are thousands of oral and literary versions of "Cinderella," one of the most popular fairy tales in the world. There are indications that the tale may have originated in ancient China or Egypt. The shoe or slipper test may have been connected to a marriage custom in which the bridegroom takes off the bride's old shoes and replaces them with new ones. But this thesis has never been completely verified, and shoes are used in many different ways in marriage celebrations, depending on the society and its customs. In the various literary versions, the shoes are leather, gold, silver, and glass. Perrault invented the glass slippers most likely as an ironic joke because a glass slipper was likely to break if it were to fall off a foot. What most of the tales, oral and literary, have in common is the conflict between a young girl and her stepmother and stepsiblings about her legacy. Cinderella must prove that she is the rightful successor in a house in which she has been deprived of her rights. She receives help from her dead mother in the guise of doves, fairies, and godmothers. Belief in the regeneration of the dead who can help the living in the form of plants or animals underlies one of the key motifs of the fairy tale. Many different literary and oral tales fostered a huge Cinderella cycle in the East and the West. Alan Dundes's *Cinderella: A Casebook* provides valuable background information and discussions about the cycle and different interpretations. The early literary work of Basile, Madame d'Aulnoy, and the Grimms certainly played a role in the creation of nineteenth-century plays and musical adaptations, such as Nicolas Isouard's popular fairy opera *Cendrillon* (1810), as well as in the equally successful opera *La Cenerentola* (1817) by Gioacchino Antonio Rossini. In the twentieth century there have been numerous Cinderella musicals, films, and videocassettes.

There are additional background materials in *Creative Storytelling*. As a possible countertale, the film *Ever After* provides some interesting transformations and character development that can be adapted for storytelling. It is important to tell the Perrault version of "Cinderella," not the Grimms' version. Perrault's tale has more magical qualities and is more anachronistic. The Disney version is closer to Perrault's story. All the more reason to tell it. The emphasis should be on jealousy and competition. Cinderella is also exploited. "The Indian Cinderella" works nicely as a countertale, but there are other possibilities, such as Jane Yolen's "The Yellow Ribbon."

Rumpelstiltskin

The importance of spinning in the economy of Europe from the medieval period to the end of the nineteenth century can be documented in the thousands of folktales and fairy tales that were disseminated by word of mouth and through print. The most popular tale about spinning is, of course, "Rumpelstiltskin," and like many tales about spinning, it reveals how important spinning can be for women: a good spinner can rise in social status and find a husband who will reward her efforts. Indeed, there are different perspectives about the value of spinning for women in thousands of tales, and many of them, which were probably originally told by women in spinning rooms, reveal how the spinners would actually like not to spin anymore but use their spinning to entangle a man and to weave the threads and narrative strands of their own lives. The origins of the figure and the names "Ricdin-Ricdon," "Rumpelstiltskin," "Tom Tit Tot," and others have never been conclusively determined. Sometimes the character is a demonic figure; sometimes a magical gnome, dwarf, or spirit. In the English tradition, Rumpelstiltskin generally goes by the name of Tom Tit Tot, and there are hundreds of different versions of this tale in Great Britain, as the English folklorist Edward Clodd showed in his book *Tom Tit Tot: An Essay of Savage Philosophy* in 1898. Joseph Jacobs published one of the best texts of "Tom Tit Tot" in *English Fairy Tales* in 1890.

The two best tales to use are the Grimms' "Rumpelstiltskin" and "The Three Spinners." Both tales can be told with a great deal of gusto, with a focus on the blackmailing and oppression of a young woman who does not want to spin. But why is spinning so important? This is also a major theme of the tale: the industry of a young woman and spinning as a means to demonstrate one's industry. Joseph Jacobs's British version of "Tom Tit Tot" is also a good tale to tell, but it should be countered by a version in which the maiden picks up the threads of her own life and spins her own tale.

Beauty and the Beast

Most scholars generally agree that the literary development of the children's fairy tale "Beauty and the Beast," conceived by Madame Leprince de Beaumont in 1756 as part of *Le Magasin des Enfants*, translated into English in 1761 as *The Young Misses Magazine Containing Dialogues between a Governess and Several Young Ladies of Quality, Her Scholars*, owes its origins to the Roman writer Apuleius, who published the tale of "Cupid and Psyche" in *The Golden Ass* in the middle of the second century A.D. It is also clear that the oral folktale type 425A, the beast bridegroom, played a major role in the literary development. By the end of the seventeenth century, the Cupid and Psyche tradition was revived in France, especially by Madame d'Aulnoy, who was evidently familiar with different types of beast-bridegroom folktales. Her two most important versions are "The Ram" (1697) and "The Green Serpent" (1698). The issues at hand in both narratives are fidelity and sincerity, or the qualities that make for tenderness, a topic of interest to women at that time. Interestingly, in Madame d'Aulnoy's two tales, the focus of the discourse is on the two princesses, who break their promises and learn that they will cause havoc and destruction if they do not keep their word. On the other hand, the men have been punished because they refused to marry old and ugly fairies and they sought a more natural love. In other words, Madame d'Aulnoy sets conditions for both men and women that demand sincerity of feeling and constancy if they are to achieve true and happy love. Her tales may have had an influence on Madame Gabrielle de Villeneuve, who published her highly unique version of "Beauty and the Beast" in *La Jeune Amériquaine et les contes marins* in 1740, which became the classic model for most of the Beauty and the Beast versions that followed in the eighteenth century. Indeed, it served as the basis for Madame Leprince de Beaumont's most famous tale in 1756. Most significant is the fact that Madame de Villeneuve wrote a tale more than two hundred pages in length for an educated reading public. Like Madame d'Aulnoy, Madame de Villeneuve was concerned with the self-realization of a young woman, and, like Madame d'Aulnoy's lesson, Madame de Villeneuve's message for women is ambivalent. Although all the rules and codes in her fairy tale are set by women—there are numerous parallel stories that involve a fairy kingdom and the laws of the fairies—Beauty is praised most for her submissiveness, docility, and earnestness.

With Madame de Villeneuve's projection of Beauty, the person as an embodiment of the virtue self-denial, the ground was prepared for a children's version of the Beauty and the Beast tale, and Madame Leprince de Beaumont did an excellent job of condensing and altering the tale in 1756 to address a group of young misses, who were supposed to learn how to become ladies and that virtue meant denying themselves. In effect, the code of the tale was to delude the young misses into believing that they would be realizing their goals in life by denying themselves.

By the time the Grimms wrote their version of "The Singing, Springing Lark," there were hundreds if not thousands of oral and literary versions that incorporated motifs from the oral beast-bride-groom cycle and the literary tradition of "Cupid and Psyche" and "Beauty and the Beast." For instance, even before the publication of the Grimms' tale, Charles Lamb wrote the long poem *Beauty and the Beast: Or a Rough Outside with a Gentle Heart* in 1811, and there were impor-tant versions by Ludwig Bechstein, Walter Crane, and Andrew Lang in the nineteenth century. The proliferation of these tales up to the present has been strengthened by the classical film *La Belle et la Bête* in 1946 by Jean Cocteau and later by the Walt Disney Corporation's pro-duction of *Beauty and the Beast* in 1993. Betsy Hearne provided a com-prehensive picture of the different versions of this tale type in *Beauty and the Beast: Visions and Revisions of an Old Tale.*

This tale is related to "The Frog King." It is part of the beast-bride-groom cycle. Again we have a situation in which a young woman is asked to sacrifice herself for her father and to live with or marry a beast (an ugly man). There are hundreds if not thousands of oral versions, but our students will probably know the Disney film version. Therefore we begin with the most classical tale by Madame Leprince de Beau-mont and then move to an interesting Grimms' version as a countertale in which the young woman demonstrates great bravery and courage.

From Animal Fables to Peace Tales

From week six to week fifteen we cover mixed narratives (a mixture of the animal fable and fairy tale), trickster tales, and peace tales. From the fairy tale we move on to other genres and make the transition to animal fables by introducing a mixed tale. We explain to the students that an animal fable is generally an allegorical narrative that chiefly uses ani-mals as characters to represent human beings and to illustrate a moral or political message. In addition, fables also personify the elements such as the winds and seas, inanimate objects, and other natural objects and may include humans and gods to teach a principle of behavior and practical lesson. A fable also can be based on a proverb such as "The grass is always greener on the other side." This broad definition enables us to show connections between different subgenres and to show how genres can be mixed. We discuss the characteristics of certain animals such as the lion as king, the fox as cunning thief or rogue, the wolf as predator, or the rabbit as coward. We ask the students to provide a list of animals, which we write on the board, and to try to identify either with an adjective or with a phrase. What is the meaning of such phrases as "scared as a chicken," "stubborn as a mule," or "silly as a goose"? What is the difference between the characteristics that we give to animals and our own characteristics? Are they true? The students are asked whether they can recall any stories that involve animals as human beings, and we recall that some stories, like "Little Red Riding Hood," use an animal to portray a predatory human being. In fact, "Little Red Riding Hood" is not a "pure" fairy tale, if there is such a thing as a pure fairy tale. It is a mixed narrative that employs an animal, and in Perrault's literary version, it even has a moral. The Grimms' version also has a second narrative that serves as a moral. Not all fairy tales, we make clear, have morals, but most fables do have morals, and we introduce a mixed tale such as "Puss in Boots," because it makes use of animals and human beings to form a moral and raises many interesting questions. It is also significant because the cat, as a fairy or magical helper, is a trickster figure that plays an important part in animal tales, and we shall discuss the nature of animal tales with tricksters in the next few weeks.

Puss in Boots

This tale is perhaps one of the most popular in the world and is circulated in many different oral traditions. Cats are not always the magic helpers in the literary and oral versions; there are foxes, jackals, fairies, dead people, and trees that help a commoner rise in society to become a rich nobleman. The theme of "clothes make the person" is very important, and the helper is sometimes depicted as the protagonist's alter ego. What is most interesting in the early literary versions of Giovan Francesco Straparola and Giambattista Basile, which preceded the canonical tale written by Perrault, is that the cats are female and that the peasant protagonists need the feminine intelligence and guidance to rise in society. Moreover, the end of Basile's narrative "Cagliuso," presented below, reveals how ungrateful the peasant is and how the cat rejects his society. Perrault changed the gender of the cat; he is clearly the protagonist of the tale as master cat, who uses his wits not only to help his master and to survive but also to climb the social ladder himself. Perrault's tale was reprinted and spread through chapbooks during the eighteenth century and had a profound influence on most of the literary and oral versions that circulated during that time and later. Ludwig Tieck, the gifted German romantic writer, used Perrault's version as the basis of his play *Der gestiefelte Kater* (*Puss in Boots*, 1797), and his play had, in turn, an effect on Wilhelm Grimm, who published his version of this tale in the 1812 edition of the *Children and Household Tales*. However, he removed it in the second edition because it was so closely related to Perrault's French text.

Basic Structure of the Session
Retelling of Charles Perrault's "Puss in Boots": Whatever version is told, it is important to include Perrault's two morals that can be summarized in prose so that the students can discuss the importance of the morals.

Moral

Although the advantage may be great
When one inherits a grand estate
Passed on from father to son,
Young men often find their industry,
Combined with ingenuity,
Leads to greater prosperity.

Another Moral

If the miller's son did quickly gain
The heart of a princess whose eyes he tamed,
When he turned on the charm in a remarkable way,
It's due to good manners, looks, and dress
That inspired her deepest tenderness
And always help to win the day.

Retelling of Giambattista Basile's "Cagliuso"
There was once an old man who was totally impoverished. He was a wretched beggar without a penny to his name and nothing in his pockets. Indeed, he went about as naked as a louse. When the time of his death approached, he called his two sons, Luigi and Cagliuso, to his

side and said, "My time has come, my dear sons, and though I have not been very successful in life, I want to leave you with some sign of my love at my death. Luigi, you who are my firstborn, take that hoe which is hanging on the wall. It will be your means to earn a living. And you, Cagliuso, you who are my little one, you are to take the cat. And may both of you remember your father."

After he said this, his sons burst into tears, and a few hours later, the father uttered his last words, "Good-bye. It is night."

Luigi buried his father with help from charity, and then he took the hoe and went to work here and there. And the more he used his hoe, the more he earned. Meanwhile, Cagliuso took the cat with him and said, "Look at what a poor legacy my father has left me! I have nothing to eat for myself, and now I have to feed two mouths. What a burden this inheritance is! It would have been better not to have received it."

When the cat heard this, she said, "Stop complaining so much! You have more luck than you realize. I can make you very rich if I put my mind to it."

As soon as Cagliuso heard that he had a talking cat, he was overjoyed because he was now hopeful she would bring him some luck. He thanked the cat, stroked her back three or four times, and placed himself in her charge. Indeed, the cat felt sorry for the unfortunate Cagliuso, and every morning, as soon as she spotted some fine goldfish, the cat would catch the fish and carry it to the king, saying, "My Lord Cagliuso, a humble servant of your highness, sends this fish to pay homage to you and says, 'There is no gift large enough for a great king.' "

The king's face broke into a pleasant smile and answered, "Tell this lord, whom I do not know, that I thank him very much."

Another time the cat ran to a place known for hunting. It was in the marshes, and when the hunters shot an oriole, blackbird, or pheasant, she would pick them up and take them to the king with the same message. She repeated this trick many times until, one morning, the king said to her, "I feel myself greatly obliged to your Lord Cagliuso, and I should like to make his acquaintance so that I may repay the affection that he has shown me."

"Lord Cagliuso's desire," the cat responded, "is to place his life and blood at the service of your throne. Tomorrow, without fail, he will come to pay homage to you at sunset."

When morning came, however, the cat went to the king and said, "Sire, the Lord Cagliuso sends his apologies. He cannot come because last night some of his servants stole everything and left him without even a shirt to his back."

Upon hearing this, the king immediately ordered some clothes and linen to be taken from his wardrobe and had them sent to Cagliuso. Even though Cagliuso preferred his old rags to the new clothes, he put them on and looked just like a grand duke. Within two hours, Cagliuso arrived at the palace accompanied by the cat, and once there, the king gave him a thousand compliments and asked him to sit down beside him. Then the king had a splendid banquet prepared for Cagliuso. While they were eating, however, Cagliuso kept turning to the cat and saying, "Make sure, puss, that those great rags of mine don't get lost. I feel so uncomfortable in these royal clothes."

"Oh, shut up," replied the cat. "Don't you have any sense? Hold your tongue, and don't talk about those miserable things."

Now the king asked whether the cat desired anything, and she responded that she would like to have a small lemon. So the king sent his servants at once to the garden and ordered them to fetch a whole basketful. Shortly after, Cagliuso turned again to pipe the same tune about his rags and tatters, and the cat told him again to shut his mouth. In turn, the king inquired once more whether the cat wanted anything. This time she had an excuse ready to cover up Cagliuso's poor manners.

At last, after they had finished eating and had chatted at length about this and that, Cagliuso took his leave. Meanwhile the cat remained with the king, describing the courage, talents, and wisdom of Cagliuso and, above all, the great wealth that he had on his estates in Rome. Indeed, the cat suggested, it was because of this that Cagliuso deserved to marry the daughter of a king. In response, the king inquired how much Cagliuso owned, and the cat answered that it was impossible to give an account of the properties and treasure of her rich lord because he himself did not know how much he possessed. Nevertheless, the cat responded, "Your majesty, if you want to obtain information for your-self, you can send some of your people around the region with me. Then they would be able to determine that there was no one in the world as rich as my master."

The king immediately called some of his trusty men and ordered them to follow the cat and gather detailed information about Cagliuso. But the cat used the excuse that she had to find refreshments for them along the road and went out before them. No sooner was she outside the kingdom than she ran ahead. Wherever she encountered flocks of sheep, herds of cows, troops of horses, and droves of pigs, she would say to the shepherds and keepers, "Ho there, pay attention! There's a band of robbers ransacking everything they come across in this district. If you want to escape their fury and protect your homes and property, you must say that everything belongs to Lord Cagliuso, and they won't touch a hair of your heads."

And she continued to say the same thing at all the farms that she passed so that wherever the king's men went, they heard the same music, like bagpipes. Indeed, everyone kept telling them that everything they saw belonged to the Lord Cagliuso. Exhausted from asking the same question over and over again, they returned to the king and told him about the immense riches of Lord Cagliuso. When the king heard all this, he promised a good reward to the cat if she could manage to bring off this marriage. In turn, the cat pretended to shuttle back and forth between the king and Cagliuso until she, at last, arranged the affair.

When Cagliuso came to court, the king gave him a large dowry of gold and his daughter in marriage. After a month of festivities, Cagliuso told the king that he wanted to take his bride to his territories. The king accompanied them to the borders. Then they went onward toward Rome where Cagliuso acted upon the cat's advice and bought land and property with the king's own gold and became a baron.

Seeing himself now so tremendously rich, Cagliuso could not thank the cat enough, saying that he owed his life and his greatness to her because of her services and that the tricks of a cat had brought him greater benefits than the cleverness of his father. Therefore, she could do whatever she pleased with the things at his castle. He promised that when she died, even in a hundred years, he would have her body placed in a golden cage and kept in his own room so as to have the memory of her always before his eyes.

Sensing that this was a boast, the cat pretended three days later to be dead, and she lay stretched out at full length on the ground. When

Cagliuso's wife saw her, she cried out, "Oh my husband, what a great misfortune! The cat has died."

"May she take all bad luck with her," Cagliuso answered. "Better her than us!"

"What shall we do with her?" asked the wife.

"Take hold of a paw, and we'll throw her out the window," he said.

When the cat heard this gratitude, something that she had never imagined, she started screaming, "So, this is the reward that I get for helping you rise in society! These are the thousand thanks for ridding you of the rags from your back that were dirty and filthy! This is what I get in exchange for having worked like a busy spider to clothe you so elegantly and to feed you when you were famished! You miserable creature! You're nothing but a tattered, ragged, deceitful wretch! What a fine golden cage you've prepared for me!"

Upon saying this and shaking her head, the cat jumped up and departed, and no matter how Cagliuso tried to calm her down by calling out sweet things to her, there was no way the cat would come back. Instead, she kept on running and repeating,

> Beware of the poor turned rich and greedy,
> They'll act like boors, so you'd better leave quickly.

Discussion: How is this tale different from Perrault's "Puss in Boots"? Is Cagliuso smart? Why does he want to keep his rags? Does he understand what the cat is doing for him? Who is the cat? Why are females often identified with cats? What is the meaning of the word *catty*? What do we mean by "cat fight" or "they fight like cats"? Is the cat in this tale treated kindly by Cagliuso? Did she really have to leave him for good at the end?

Chair game: There was once a butcher who died. He left his shop to the oldest son, his butcher's knife to the second son, and his old floppy-eared dog to his youngest daughter. "What good is this floppy-eared dog to me?" asked the daughter.

Improvisation and theater games led by the teaching artist: The focus is on clothes and the topic "clothes make the people." Have students walk around the stage space and pretend that they are dressed up for a visit to a king or a president. Call out, "Freeze!" Then tell the students to keep walking, but this time they are all to pretend they are wearing pants and have realized that there is a big hole in them. Keep repeating this formula, but change the conditions of their clothes. For example, tell the students they are each wearing a brand new coat and they should show it off while they walk. Or tell them they are wearing very high heels or their shoes are too small. New running shoes. A sweater they do not like that was knit by a grandmother.

Three "Puss in Boots" skits: Have the students perform three skits.

Writing game: Invent a tale in which an animal becomes human and does not know what the world is like and is not familiar with trains, bikes, cars, and so on. Another possibility is to invent a tale in which a human becomes an animal and tries to explain to other animals that he or she is really a human. Begin the game by writing a list of animals on the board and discuss their characteristics with the students.

Themes for follow-up discussion:

1. What is an inheritance? How should we cherish an inheritance even if it is small?
2. How do bonds of loyalty form?
3. Do clothes make the person? Why are clothes so important as markers of distinction?

Fables

Most fables tend to represent the moral perspective of the underdog or the oppressed. As we know, Aesop was a slave, who told his tales to criticize and warn his listeners about the injustices he witnessed in ancient Greek society. Yet some of his tales are pessimistic and show how people never learn lessons from experience. Some are even questionable today in their treatment of gender roles or even the roles of animals, for nobody in Aesop's times thought women, slaves, or animals had rights.

In moving to fables, it is important to bear in mind that countertales exist. For instance, we often move from the fairy-tale and countertale structure to show that there are countertales in the fables by questioning so-called archetypical features of animals. Do certain animals always have to be pitted against one another? Can they learn to cooperate? Implicit in our questions is how human beings are depicted as traditional antagonists (men against women) or how human beings can achieve solidarity.

In the Grimms' collection, there is the wonderful tale about "The Companionship of the Cat and the Mouse," which plays out the traditional antagonistic roles of cat and mouse. This tale can be countered by telling another animal tale, such as "The Bremen Town Musicians," which is also about how society discards old people when they are no longer useful. It is also a tale about cooperation and solidarity in contrast to the antagonism played out in "The Companionship of the Cat and the Mouse." We also work with morals and proverbs during the next two or three sessions that often accompany fables.

Trickster Tales

If the wolf is often deceitful, it is not because he is a rogue or a rascal. He is generally a predatory animal in folklore, and, more often than not, because he is smart, he kills his prey. Only in certain instances can he be likened to a trickster, who is one of the most notorious figures in folklore throughout the world. The trickster is a shifty character who assumes many forms, depending on the culture in which he originates, and he can be a con man who is an animal or a human. Most of all he is amoral, and he behaves in ways that draw mixed reactions from characters in the tales and from listeners themselves. He is a survivor, and sometimes he is a she, as in the case of many cats and foxes. Yet traditionally the trickster has been a male character who, I believe, fascinates us because we admire his raw energy and zest for life. He is pure libido. Kathleen L. Nichols gave one of the best succinct descriptions of his character: "Trickster alternately scandalizes, disgusts, amuses, disrupts, chastises, and humiliates (or is humiliated by) the animal-like proto-people of pre-history, yet he is also a creative force transforming their world, sometimes in bizarre and outrageous ways, with his instinctive energies and cunning. Eternally scavenging for food, he represents the most basic instincts, but in other narratives, he is also the father of the Indian people and a potent conductor of spiritual forces in the form of sacred dreams."[1]

There are literally hundreds if not thousands of trickster figures throughout the world. For instance, it is possible to associate many of the Greek gods such as Hermes or the titan Prometheus with the trickster figure, not to mention Zeus. Even Odysseus has something of the trickster in him. Others tricksters in Europe include Loki, Puck, and

Renard the Fox. In fact, foxes are important figures in Japan, China, South America, and Eastern Europe. In Africa the trickster is often associated with the spider Ananse, and in North and Latin America, the Native American tribes have created numerous unusual rascals who are called Hare, Bluejay, Rabbit, or Mink. Perhaps the most popular trickster figure is Coyote, who eventually became a major figure named Wile E. Coyote in the animated cartoon *The Roadrunner*. Given their popularity, we work with two classic Coyote tales, which have many different versions, because they are closely related to the Greek myths that deal with creation and the origins of fire, which we introduce later.

Basic Structure of the Session Fantastic binominal: Call for an animal and another noun. Model a story that deals with a shape shifter or trickster. Ask the students to suggest other animals that can change their shape. Write them on the board and ask for a noun. Then have the students write a tale about how the animal uses its cunning to get its way.

Tell a story: Tell the students the tale "The Spirit Names the Animal People," which is adapted from a story by Mourning Dove in *Coyote Tales*.

The Spirit Names the Animal People

Once the Great Spirit called all his people together. They came from all parts of the world. Then the Spirit Chief told them that there was to be a change, that a new kind of people was coming to live on earth.

"All of you Animal People must have names," the Spirit Chief said. "Some of you have names now. Some of you haven't. But tomorrow all will have names that shall be kept by you and your descendants forever. In the morning, as the first light of day shows in the sky, come to my lodge and choose your names. The first to come may choose any name that he or she wants. The next person may take any other name. That is the way it will go until all the names are taken. And to each person I will give work to do."

The Animal People became very excited. Each wanted a proud name and the power to rule some tribe or some part of the world, and everyone determined to get up early and hurry to the Spirit Chief's lodge.

Coyote boasted that no one would be ahead of him. He walked among the people and told them that he would be the first. Coyote did not like his name Imitator; he wanted another. Nobody respected his name, but it fit him. He was called Coyote because he liked to imitate people. He thought that he could do anything that other persons did, and he pretended to know everything. He would ask a question, and when the answer was given, he would say, "I knew that already. I didn't have to be told."

Such smart talk did not make friends for Coyote. Nor did he make friends by the foolish things he did and the rude tricks he played on people.

"I shall have my choice of the three biggest names," he boasted. "Those names are the Mountain Person—Grizzly Bear—who will rule the four-footed people; Eagle, who will rule the birds; and the Good Swimmer—Salmon—who will be the chief of all the fish that the New People use for food."

Coyote's twin brother, Fox, who at the next sun took the name Soft Fur, laughed. "Don't be so sure, Coyote," said Fox. "Maybe you will have to keep the name you have. People despise that name. No one wants it."

"I am tired of that name," Coyote said in an angry voice. "Let some-one else carry it. Let some old person take it—someone who cannot win in war. I am going to be a great warrior. My smart brother, I will make you beg things from me when I am called Grizzly Bear, Eagle, or Salmon."

"Your strong words mean nothing," scolded Fox. "Better go to your tepee and get some sleep, or you will not wake up in time to choose any name."

Coyote stalked off to his tepee. He told himself that he would not sleep a wink that night. He would stay wide awake. He entered the lodge, and his three sons called together as if one voice, "Father!"

They were hungry, but Coyote had brought them nothing to eat. Their mother, who after the naming day was known as Mole, the Mound Differ, sat on her foot at one side of the doorway. Mole was a good woman, always loyal to her husband in spite of his mean ways, his mischief making, and his foolishness. She was never jealous, never talked back, never replied to his words of abuse. She looked up and said, "Have you no food for the children? They are starving. I can find no roots to dig."

"Eh-ha!" Coyote grunted. "I am no common person to be addressed in that manner. I am going to be a great chief tomorrow. Did you know that? I will have a new name. I will be Grizzly Bear. Then I can devour my enemies with ease. And I shall need you no longer. You are growing too old and homely to be the wife of a great warrior and chief."

Mole said nothing. She turned to her corner of the lodge and collected a few old bones, which she put into a cooking basket. With two sticks she lifted hot stones from the fire and dropped them into the basket. Soon the water boiled, and there was weak soup for the hungry children.

"Gather plenty of wood for the fire," Coyote ordered. "I am going to sit up all night."

Mole obeyed. Then she and the children went to bed.

Coyote sat watching the fire. Half of the night passed. He got sleepy. His eyes grew heavy. So he picked up two little sticks and braced his eyelids apart. "Now I can stay awake," he thought, but before long he was fast asleep, although his eyes were wide open. The sun was high in the sky when Coyote awoke. If it had not been for Mole, he would not have awakened. Mole called to him. She called him after she returned with her name from the Spirit Chief's lodge. Mole loved her husband. She did not want him to have a big name and be a powerful chief. For then, she feared, he would leave her. This is why she did not arouse him at daybreak, and she kept quiet about this. Only half awake and thinking it was early morning, Coyote jumped at the sound of Mole's voice and ran to the lodge of the Spirit Chief. None of the other animals were there. Coyote laughed. Blinking his sleepy eyes, he walked into the lodge. "I am going to be Grizzly Bear," he announced in a strong voice. "That will be my name."

"The name Grizzly Bear was taken at dawn," the Spirit Chief answered.

"Then I shall be Eagle," said Coyote, and his voice was not so loud.

"Eagle flew away at sunrise," the other replied.

"Well, I shall be called Salmon," Coyote said in a voice that was not loud at all.

"The name Salmon has also been taken," explained the Spirit Chief. "All the names except your own have been taken. No one wished to steal your name."

Poor Coyote's knees grew weak. He sat down beside the fire that blazed in the great tepee, and the heart of the Spirit Chief was touched.

"Coyote," the Chief said, "you must keep your name. It is a good name for you. You slept long because I wanted you to be the last one here. I have important work for you, much for you to do before the New People come. You are to be chief of all the tribes. Many bad creatures inhabit the earth. They bother and kill people, and the tribes cannot increase as I wish. These People-Devouring Monsters cannot keep on like that. They must be stopped. It is for you to conquer them. For doing that, for all the good things you do, you will be honored and praised by the people who are here now and who come afterward. But, for the foolish and mean things you do, you will be laughed at and despised. You cannot help this. It is your way.

"To make your work easier, I shall give you *squas-tenk*, a special magic power. No one else shall ever have it. When you are in danger, whenever you need help, call upon your power. It will do much for you, and with it you can change yourself into any form, into anything you wish. To your twin brother, Fox, and to others, I have given *shoo'-mesh*. It is a strong power. With that power Fox can restore your life, if you should be killed. Your bones may be scattered, but if there is one hair of your body left, Fox can make you live again. Others of the people can do the same with their *shoo'-mesh*. Now, go, Coyote! Begin the work laid out for your trail."

Well, Coyote was a chief after all, and he felt good again. After that day his eyes were different. They grew slanted from being propped open that night while he sat by his fire. The New People, the Indians, got their slightly slanted eyes from Coyote.

After Coyote had gone, the Spirit Chief thought it would be nice for the Animal People and the coming New People to have the benefit of the spiritual sweat house. But all of the Animal People had names, and there was no one to take the name of Sweat House, the Warmer. So the wife of the Spirit Chief took the name. She wanted the people to have the sweat house, for she pitied them. She wanted them to have a place to go to purify themselves, a place where they could pray for strength and good luck and strong medicine power, and where they could fight sickness and get relief from their troubles.

The ribs, the frame poles, of the sweat house represent the wife of the Spirit Chief. As she is a spirit, she cannot be seen, but she always is near. Songs to her are sung by the present generation. She hears them. She hears what her people say, and in her heart there is love and pity.

Discussion: What do you like about Coyote? What don't you like? Have you ever seen a real coyote? Why does this Coyote want a new name? Is he ashamed of his name and his character? All children are given names when they are born. Do they always like their names? Do they change them to suit their character? Why doesn't the Spirit Chief want to change Coyote's name? Does his wife accept Coyote as he is? Why? Do you think Coyote will accept himself the way the Spirit Chief's wife, the Warmer, accepts herself?

How Coyote Stole Fire (adapted from a Karok tale)

Long ago, when man was newly come into the world, there were days when he was the happiest creature of all. Those were the days when spring brushed across the willow tails, or when his children ripened with the blueberries in the sun of summer, or when the goldenrod bloomed in the autumn haze.

But always the mists of autumn evenings grew more chilly, and the sun's strokes grew shorter. The man saw winter moving near, and he became fearful and unhappy. He was afraid for his children, and for the grandfathers and grandmothers who carried in their heads the sacred tales of the tribe. Many of these, young and old, would die in the long, icy, bitter month of winter.

Coyote, like the rest of the People, had no need for fire. So he seldom concerned himself with it, until one spring day when he was passing a human village. There the women were singing a song of mourning for the babies and the old ones who had died in the winter. Their voices moaned like the west wind through a buffalo skull, prickling the hairs on Coyote's neck.

"Feel how the sun is now warm on our backs," one of the men was saying. "Feel how it warms the earth and makes these stones hot to the touch. If only we could have a small piece of the sun in our tepees during the winter."

Coyote, overhearing this, felt sorry for the men and women. He also felt that there was something he could do to help them. He knew of a faraway mountaintop where the three Fire Beings lived. These Beings kept fire to themselves, guarding it carefully for fear that man might somehow acquire it and become as strong as they. Coyote saw that he could do a good turn for man at the expense of these selfish Fire Beings.

So Coyote went to the mountain of the Fire Beings and crept to its top. He watched the way that the Beings guarded their fire. As he approached, the Beings leaped to their feet and gazed searchingly around their camp. Their eyes glinted like bloodstones, and their hands were clawed like the talons of the great black vulture.

"What's that? What's that I hear?" hissed one of the Beings.

"A thief, skulking in the bushes!" screeched another.

The third looked more closely and saw Coyote. But he had gone to the mountaintop on all fours so the Being thought she saw only an ordinary coyote slinking among the trees.

"It is no one, it is nothing!" she cried, and the other two looked where she pointed and also saw only a gray coyote. They sat down again by their fire and paid Coyote no more attention.

So he watched all day and night as the Fire Beings guarded their fire. He saw how they fed it pinecones and dry branches from the sycamore trees. He saw how they stamped furiously on runaway rivulets of flame that sometimes nibbled outward on edges of dry grass. He saw also how, at night, the Beings took turns to sit by the fire. Two would sleep while one was on guard, and at certain times the Being by the fire would get up and go into the teepee and another would come out to sit by the fire.

Coyote saw that the Beings were always jealously watchful of their fire except during one part of the day. That was in the earliest morning, when the first winds of dawn arose on the mountains. Then the Being by the fire would hurry, shivering, into the teepee calling, "Sister, sister, go out and watch the fire." But the next Being would always be slow to go out for her turn, her head spinning with sleep and the thin dreams of dawn.

Coyote, seeing all this, went down the mountain and spoke to his friends among the People. He told them of hairless man, fearing the cold and death of winter. And he told them of the Fire Beings, and the warmth and brightness of the flame. They all agreed that man should have fire, and they all promised to help Coyote's undertaking.

Then Coyote sped again to the mountaintop. Again the Fire Beings leaped up when he came close, and one cried out, "What's that? A thief, a thief!"

But again the others looked closely, and saw only a gray coyote hunting among the bushes. So they sat down again and paid him no more attention.

Coyote waited through the day and watched as night fell and two of the Beings went off to the tepee to sleep. He watched all night long as they changed over at certain times, until at last the dawn winds rose.

Then the Being on guard called, "Sister, sister, get up and watch the fire."

And the Being whose turn it was climbed slow and sleepy from her bed, saying, "Yes, yes, I am coming. Don't shout so loudly."

But before she could come out of the tepee. Coyote lunged from the bushes, snatched up a glowing portion of fire, and sprang away down the mountainside.

Screaming, the Fire Beings flew after him. Swift as Coyote ran, they still managed to catch up with him, and one of them reached out a clutching hand. Her fingers touched only the tip of the tail, but the touch was enough to turn the hairs white. Coyote tail tips are white still today. Coyote shouted and flung the fire away from him. But the others of the People had gathered at the foot of the mountain. Squirrel saw the fire falling and caught it, putting it on her back and fleeing away through the treetops. The fire scorched her back so painfully that her tail curled up and back, as squirrels' tails still do today.

The Fire Beings then pursued Squirrel, who threw the fire to Chipmunk. Chattering with fear, Chipmunk stood still as if rooted until the Beings were almost upon her. Then, as she turned to run, one Being clawed at her, tearing down the length of her back and leaving there three stripes, which are seen on chipmunks' backs today. Chipmunk threw the fire to Frog, and the Beings turned toward him. One of the Beings grabbed his tail, but Frog gave a mighty leap and tore himself free, leaving his tail behind him in the Being's hand, which is why frogs have no tails.

As the Beings came after him again, Frog flung the fire to Wood. And Wood swallowed it.

The Fire Beings gathered round, but they did not know how to get the fire out of Wood. They promised it gifts, sang to it, and shouted at it. They twisted it and stuck it and tore it with their knives. But Wood did not give up the fire. In the end, defeated, the Beings went back to their mountaintop and left the People alone.

But Coyote knew how to get fire out of Wood, and he went to the village of men and showed them how. He showed them the trick of rubbing two dry sticks together, and the trick of spinning a sharpened stick in a hole made in another piece of wood. So man was from then on warm and safe through the killing cold of winter.

Discussion: Why do you think fire is so helpful? Doesn't fire destroy forests and homes? How have human beings put fire to good use? Why don't the Fire Beings want humans to be as powerful as they are? Why does Coyote need the help of other small animals and of wood? Do you think the humans are grateful for what Coyote has done for them? How do the tales reveal how animals got their characteristics?

Other retellings: Depending on the demographics of the school and class, the teaching artist can introduce other sets of trickster tales from other parts of the United States or the world. For instance, there are several collections of Ananse tales that might replace the Coyote tales. Consider also the Brer Rabbit tales in Joel Chandler Harris's collection, or Richard Chase's *The Jack Tales,* in which Jack often appears as a trickster. A good example of a classical fairy tale that also can be regarded as a trickster tale is "The Brave Little Tailor" in *The Complete Fairy Tales of the Brothers Grimm.*

Chair game: One day Coyote, who could change himself into many different forms, went walking into the woods, and he found himself trapped by hunters who wanted to capture him and sell him to the zoo. "Stop, Coyote, and don't try any of your tricks on us!"

Improvisation and theater games led by the teaching artist: Aside from focusing on place, try to introduce shape-shifting characters. Do the characters change with the place?

Ask the students, "How do you know where you are?" The students are to be specific. Ask them the difference between a beach and a park with a pool. Each place is to be described in detail. Come up with a class definition about place. For instance, you know where you are by the objects around you and your relationship to them. You know a place by its people, the way they dress, their language, and their architecture. Have students divide into small groups and pick a place. They are to choose four defining objects that are found in this place. Each group acts and uses the four objects to give the audience a sense of place. The audience is to guess where the place is.

Three trickster skits: Have the students perform three trickster skits.

Writing game: Choose a shape shifter or trickster. Imagine what you yourself would like to change into and write a story about how your shape shifter or trickster becomes this other person or thing. Ask for examples of what students would like to become, and write them on board.

Fables about Loyalty, Conflict, and Survival

Many fables and animal tales concern themes dealing with questions of loyalty and survival, sometimes pitting humans against animals, sometimes pitting animals against other animals. In a world that often reflects some of the worst aspects of survival of the fittest, we want to raise questions that involve loyalty and cooperation. Just as the Coyote depends on the loyalty and cooperation of other animals to provide humans with means to warm themselves and to cook, other animals will face bitter conflicts that necessitate the use of force in desperate situations. Can violence be avoided? What brings about violent reactions? We retell "The Faithful Sparrow" in *The Complete Fairy Tales of the Brothers Grimm* and endeavor to examine different forms of conflicts and possible alternative solutions. There are many other stories in *Aesop's Fables*, which we use to illustrate the notion of survival of the fittest.

Peace Tales

The next two weeks of storytelling and creative drama are intended to encourage and stimulate the students to produce their own play about the causes of war and the possibilities for peace. It is important that we precede the sessions with a frank discussion about war and peace and that all the word and theater games somehow focus on the theme of peace. It is also important that we do not intimidate the students or overwhelm them with problems. Though we may have very specific opinions about which side has caused a specific war or whether we (the United States) are supporting the wrong war or the wrong side, it is best not to address the present situation (which is in constant flux and will change in the coming months and years). We can best address the present by talking about the past or future; that is, by using stories about war, conflict, and peace. I think that we are probably all in agreement that war is devastating and terrible for all concerned, particularly for the common people, who are the average workers in U.S. society, struggling to make ends meet. Their lives are anything but privileged. If there is a theme that we might want to stress, it is the powerlessness of the common people and children and how we can empower the common people and children to understand the causes of war and to resolve conflicts. When I use the word *powerlessness,* I do so discreetly, for the purpose of telling tales about war and peace is not to discourage the students and make them feel helpless. On the contrary, we want to empower them so they can do something to stop conflicts and wars, as can we. But we do not want to mislead the young. It is not easy to stop violence and conflicts. We do not want to give our students a false sense of empowerment. Rather, we hope to develop their self-confidence and thinking so that they will grasp why disputes arise and how they can resolve them in peaceful and humane ways. By using metaphors that can be applied to the conflicts surrounding their lives, we want to open the eyes of our students to all the conditions that contribute to war and to engender hope so that they can play some sort of role to preventing wars through nonviolent action. This kind of action is a negotiation and an exchange of ideas, teaches respect for different opinions and cooperation, and develops ways to share with and help one's neighbor.

Because we have been working on fables and animal stories, we can lead into the theme of war and peace by discussing how and why animals fight. What is a predatory animal? Is there a hierarchy among animals? Why do we think of the lion as the king of animals? Does he really govern all the animals? How do animals get along? Do they have natural enemies? What makes human beings different from animals? Why do we use animals in stories? Do they reflect the way animals are or the way human beings are?

Basic Structure of the Session Fantastic binominal
Select animals that are predatory. Ask students for names of animals
that live off other animals. Explain what predatory means. Form a list
on the board with names of animals given by students. If the animal is
nonpredatory, explain why. Place prepositions on the board. Ask students for names of animals that are either nonpredatory or vegetarian.
Form a list on the board. Ask students to link a nonpredatory animal
with a predatory animal. For instance, rabbit on tiger, tiger on rabbit,
tiger with rabbit, tiger under rabbit, and so on. Ask students to write a
story about how the animals work out their differences.

To make the transition to peace tales, which will mainly involve
humans in "fantastic" situations, we begin with a fable about oppression
and conflict. The first fable is "The Lion and the Jackal with Weapons," a late-nineteenth-century story from North India.

The Lion and the Jackal with Weapons

A lion, who lived with his wife in a cave, used to leave her and go hunting every day to look for food for their family. One day, a jackal arrived
at the cave while the lion was gone. He was riding a fox and carrying a
bow and arrow and some other weapons.

"Where is that wretched husband of yours?" the jackal asked the
lioness.

"What do you want with him?" she responded.

"Don't you know that I have taken over this jungle with my weapons. I am now your lord, and your husband must now pay house taxes.
This cave is large and expensive. If he doesn't pay me soon, tell him
that I'll kill him!"

Seeing the jackal's weapons, the lioness was afraid to make a move,
and to pacify him she gave the jackal some of the meat stored for the
use of her family.

After this happened, the jackal knew exactly when the lion would
leave the cave, and he would come every day to threaten the lioness
with his weapons and get some meat. Because she was so worried and
bothered, the lioness grew quite lean until the lion noticed and asked
her, "Why have you become so thin when I bring so much meat home
every day?"

Then she told him of the jackal's visits and threats. When he heard it all, the lion became enraged. The next morning, instead of going out to hunt, he lay down in ambush close to the cave. Soon the jackal arrived and began to abuse and threaten the lioness. Then the lion attacked him, and the jackal managed to scamper away as fast as he could, with the lion at his heels. He ran for his life and scrambled under the pillar shoots of a banyan tree and pushed himself through them, but the lion was too large and got stuck between two branches. Try as he might, he could not escape, and his roars could not be heard by his wife because he was so far away. In a few days he died of hunger and thirst.

Some time later, the jackal cautiously returned to the place, and when he saw that the lion was dead, he was delighted and decided to pay a visit to the lioness.

"It's not good for any female to stay a widow. You must come and live with me as my wife," the jackal said, and he flashed his weapons. Seeing that she had no choice, the lioness went with him to his den. Now the lioness was about to have cubs right before the lion died, and soon after she went to live with the jackal, she gave birth to three healthy cubs and pretended that they were the jackal's sons because she was afraid of angering the jackal. When her cubs were six months old and already quite powerful, they went to her and asked her who their father was because they looked so different from the jackal. However, she told them that the jackal was their father, and if they didn't believe her, they should go and demand proof from the jackal.

Then the cubs went to him and said, "Father, teach us the language you speak."

"I can't teach you my language because, if you learned it, you would become masters of the jungle, and you are too young to understand how to use power the way I do."

But at last they persuaded him to teach them, and when he gave one whining howl and could not roar, they knew that he was only a pitiful jackal after all. So they fell upon him and tore him to pieces. From that day forward, nobody had to pay house taxes in the jungle, and all the animals began to roam more freely.

Discussion: What is a jackal? What kind of a character is a jackal? Why does he carry weapons? Why is the lioness afraid of him? What lesson do the lion cubs learn? Should they have killed the jackal?

"The Missiles of Peace," adapted from a tale by Gianni Rodari: This tale is to be told as a participatory tale. The class is to be divided into two. One side will be asked to sing out "Ding dong, ding dong" on cue; the other side will be asked to sing out "Ding dong dell, ding dong dell" on cue.

The Missiles of Peace

Many years ago there was a war to end all wars. Nobody knew how it had started or why. On one side was General Bing Bombardy, who was so enormous that he made elephants seem small. Wherever he walked, the ground trembled. Whenever he gave orders, his voice blared like a tuba. On the other side was General P. Pike, a tiny slim man with a crooked smile. When he walked, he was so close to the ground that he slithered like a snake. Nobody ever knew where he was or when he might attack with his poisonous fangs.

Both generals had secret police, who spied on everyone and anyone, and special agents, who spied on the secret police, and undercover cops, who spied on the special agents, who spied on the undercover cops, so that no one was safe from spying or suspicion.

"There is evil all around us!" declared General Bombardy.

"There is evil in us!" General Pike insisted.

"The barbarians are on our doorsteps," General Bombardy said, frightening his people.

"General Bombardy will make us slaves!" General Pike cried out.

But General Bombardy was quick to respond that General Pike and his followers had sharp teeth, big ears, and hairy bodies and he showed ugly pictures of them on TV, even though he didn't know what they really looked like. He told his people that General Pike and his followers believed in strange gods and that they would be killed if they did not worship General Pike's gods. He rallied his people around the flag of the nation. So, the war went on for many years. Both countries became poorer and poorer. Thousands of people died. There was little to eat. Nothing to enjoy. And the children of his country had nothing to look forward to.

In the meantime General Bombardy kept talking about how war was good for their souls.

"What's more," he announced, "we must cleanse the souls of our enemies!"

But conditions became so bad that his factories eventually ran out of steel and iron, and no more weapons could be made.

What to do?

Well, our General Bombardy was no dunce. He ordered the people of his country to collect all the bells of all the churches, schools, city halls, and colleges. Even the bells on children's bikes and doorbells were taken. And these bells—there were thousands of them—were brought to the capital of the country. There they were melted down in a huge furnace that spit gigantic flames. Once all the iron and steel were melted, General Bombardy ordered his engineers to build a gigantic missile. The task was so great, however, that it took them three years to build this monstrous missile. When it was finished, it was as high as the Eiffel Tower and wider than five football fields put together. Inside it carried one hundred bombs to match the one hundred workers whose lives were lost building the missile. When it was finished, General Bombardy commanded his officers and soldiers to bring it to the front line of the war. But, given the size of this humongous missile, they needed to construct a truck that was larger than five football fields and had a thousand wheels.

"Do it!" yelled General Bombardy. "Do it soon, or else!"

Though the soldiers and workers were starving, they did it because the secret police had taken away their families and threatened their lives. They had no choice, and they worked until they managed to bring the missile to the front line of the war to end all wars.

Once it was positioned and pointed toward the enemy, General Bombardy laughed so loud that the surrounding mountains shuddered.

"I'm going to shoot them to the moon!" he exclaimed. Then he ordered his chief officer to get ready to push the gigantic button that would fire the missile. Once it was shot, the missile would fly through the air and destroy the enemy.

"Get ready!" General Bombardy shouted, and all the soldiers and officers put cotton in their ears and wore sunglasses, for they were petrified by the missile and all the bombs inside it.

"When I count to three, you fire!" ordered the general, and the chief officer nodded sadly, for he was reluctant to kill thousands of people.

"One, two, three, fire!"

The chief officer pushed the button, and everyone waited for the huge explosion, but after waiting one minute in eager anticipation, all they could hear was

Ding Dong! Ding Dong! Ding Dong!

Astonished, everyone took the cotton out of their ears and took off their sunglasses.

"You fool!" screamed General Bombardy. "You must have pushed the wrong button. Get ready to do it again!"

The chief officer got set, and everyone put the cotton back into their ears and put on their sunglasses.

"One, two, three, fire!" the General shouted.

Again the chief officer pushed the button and again all the soldiers could hear was

Ding Dong! Ding Dong! Ding Dong!

General Bombardy turned red with rage. He huffed and he puffed, and he almost blew the missile down with spitting words.

"You numbskull! You ignoramus! I'll have you court martialed and shot! You bumbling stiff!" The General went on and on, and finally he screeched, "This is your last chance! If the missile doesn't work, I'll stuff you inside it and shoot it myself!"

The chief officer fainted when he heard those words, and the General ordered him to be replaced by his colonel, who also feared for his life.

"Get ready!" shouted General Bombardy. "One, two, three, fire!"

Frightened, the colonel pushed the button, and again all that could be heard was

Ding Dong! Ding Dong! Ding Dong!

The General took a pistol out of his belt and took aim at his colonel. Then all of a sudden a strange sound could be heard from across the front:

Ding Dong Dell! Ding Dong Dell! Ding Dong Dell!

What was going on? Everyone was puzzled.

Well, it seems that General Pike had also run out of steel and iron, and that he, too, had ordered all the bells of his country to be melted down to build a gigantic missile stuffed with bombs. And he had it brought to the front and pointed at General Bombardy's troops. When he had given the order to fire, all he could hear was

Ding Dong Dell! Ding Dong Dell! Ding Dong Dell!

"Impossible!" screamed General Pike. "The missile's got to work."

"Impossible!" yelled General Bombardy. "I'll blow them to the skies!"

The two generals had blood in their eyes. They would not give up, and they ordered more officers to get ready to fire once more.

"One, two, three, fire!" they shouted.

This time beautiful chimes could be heard all across the front:

Ding Dong! Ding Dong Dell! Ding Dong! Ding Dong Dell! Ding Dong! Ding Dong Dell!

It was like magic, and when the soldiers on both sides heard the heavenly music coming from the missiles, they thought they were hearing the bells of peace. They threw down their arms and ran across the fields to embrace one another. Joy was written all over their faces. Tears rolled down their cheeks. They had suffered much too long.

The missiles kept chiming.

Ding Dong! Ding Dong Dell! Ding Dong! Ding Dong Dell!

Soon all the people from both countries came running from the towns and cities and were hugging each other and dancing in the fields to celebrate the peace. There was nothing the secret police could do to stop them.

When General Bombardy and General Pike saw this, they were outraged. What could they do without a war? What if the people found out that there was no need for war? They stood alone and began fearing for their lives. The people might attack them, they thought. They might place them on trial.

So General Bombardy ran to his car, and General Pike raced to his limousine. They jumped in and sped away in different directions, driving one hundred miles an hour, hoping to forget the terrible end to their war. But, strange to say, they could not forget. The missiles of peace kept ringing in their ears.

Ding Dong! Ding Dong Dell! Ding Dong! Ding Dong Dell!

Everywhere they went, their ears were filled by the music of peace. And though the missiles were eventually melted down to make new tools and machines, the people of the two countries continued to hear the music that was soothing to their ears, and they never went to war again.

Discussion: Why do the generals love war? Why do the people follow the generals? What effect does the war have on the people? Why don't the people rebel against their generals? Is war necessary?

Chair game: Lead with a few sentences similar to these: "There was once a mouse who decided that he was sick and tired of being hunted by cats. So he went to a big bulldog and told him he would give the dog a thousand dollars if he would get rid of all the cats in the neighborhood."

Improvisation and theater games led by teaching artist: These games should focus on the representation of animals and their characteristics. The games could be charades or the statue game, or the circle game, where a student is sent outside the circle while one student leads a silent game of movement of different animals. The student outside the circle returns and must guess who is leading the movement.

The following are ideas for improvised skits:

Animals in a zoo are sick and tired of being imprisoned, and they decide to rebel and break out of the zoo. How will they break out of the zoo? Where will they go? What type of society will they establish?

Animals on a farm are tired of being force fed and slaughtered. They get together and decide to revolt. How will they overcome the farmers? Are there really farmers at the farm or business executives? What will they do once they take control?

Animals in a forest up north are tired of hunting season. They steal the weapons of the hunters and herd them into a corral. Will the animals hunt them? What will they do to prevent the hunting and slaughtering of animals? What peaceful resolution can they find?

Skits: Have the students act out two stories and the chair game story. Emphasize peaceful resolution of conflict.

Writing game: Ask students to think of their favorite animal. Once they have chosen their favorite animal, ask them to think of who the animal's "natural" enemy is. Is there such a thing as a natural enemy? Once they have discovered or created an enemy, ask the students to write a story of how their favorite animal and the animal's natural enemy resolve their differences. What do they fight about? Why don't they like each other? How can they come to like each other?

More Peace Tales

We now move away from the fables and focus entirely on fantasy stories that are intended to animate the students to think about war and peace. The shift in this session is to human beings and to problematic situations that involve violence, conflict, and miraculous transformations. The emphasis is on conflict resolution: alternatives to violent behavior. Recommended books for this session are as follows:

Brody, Ed, Jay Goldspinner, Katie Green, Rona Leventhal, and John Porcino, eds. 2002. *Spinning Tales, Weaving Hope: Stories of Peace, Justice and the Environment.* 2nd ed. Philadelphia: New Society Publishers.

Hart, Carole, Letty Cottin Pogrebin, Mary Rodgers, and Marlo Thomas, eds. 1974. *Free to Be ... You And Me.* New York: McGraw-Hill.

MacDonald, Margaret Read, ed. 1992. *Peace tales: World Folktales to Talk About.* Hamden, Conn.: Linnet Books.

Pogrebin, Letty Cottin, ed. 1982. *Stories for Free Children.* New York: McGraw-Hill.

Once we have told two peace tales, we ask the students to choose one of them, which we begin to adapt as a skit in which the entire class will participate. Through discussion and improvisation during the month of December, we create a short play that is generally performed with costumes and sets for other classes in the school. It is extraordinary to see how quickly the students can create their own play and are willing to share their talents and ideas with students from other classes. Because the play is performed during the month of December, it is usually a festive occasion in which peace is celebrated.

Fig. 7.1 Student at Whittier School writing a legend.

7

LEGENDS, MYTHS, SUPERHERO STORIES, TALL TALES, FAMILY STORIES, AND UTOPIAN TALES

There are very clear distinctions to be made between the legends, myths, and stories about superheroes that we cover from the sixteenth to the twenty-first week in our program. Obviously, they are related to one another in many ways, and though the more contemporary superhero stories, comics, novels, and films often blur the distinctions, it is important to offer definitions to the students that they can modify as they realize how precise and relative a definition may be.

We generally operate with the following definitions as starting points.

1. Originally a legend was a short story that recounted the life of a saint. By the end of the Middle Ages, the legend came to be regarded as an improbable if not unreliable story about a real person or event generally involving famous saints, rulers, heroes, and villains. Although the legend is clearly fictitious, large numbers of people believed and still believe that there is a certain amount of truth to any given legend. Because of the seemingly real and somewhat truthful elements of the narrative, the legend can be distinguished from the fairy tale and myth, which are clearly and totally based on

fiction. Interestingly, the legend employs motifs, characters, and conventions of the fairy tale and myth to celebrate a person and event and convince readers or listeners that the heroes lived and the events actually happened. More than any of the other short narrative genres, the legend was and is constantly used locally and nationally to reflect on notable people and events in families, communities, religions, and nations. Some of the feats attributed to people and some of the descriptions of events border on the supernatural, and thus the legend is often associated with the extraordinary and the fantastic in real life. Finally, there are many legends about common people who have extraordinary talents and use them to benefit society.

2. A myth is a story that generally explains the creation of the world and the powers of the gods who rule the world. Because there were and still are hundreds of religions and cultures, there are hundreds of myths about the gods and their exploits. Many religions such as those of the Greeks, Egyptians, and Romans are ancient and are no longer followed in our day. They have lost their "truth" validity and are regarded as fictitious, just as many religions today contend for the truth and must constantly seek validation. The older religions of the Greeks and Romans had a great appeal and following more than two thousand years ago, and there are many similarities between their gods and the gods of other ancient religions in North and South America, Asia, and Africa.

3. A superhero story is a fantastic narrative about human beings endowed with extraordinary powers. Generally speaking, the original superheroes such as Superman, Batman, Supergirl, Captain Marvel, Flash Gordon, and so on cannot entirely explain how they acquired their super powers. Sometimes their powers are caused by chance, and other times they are due to genetics or to an experiment. From the beginning superheroes generally were the protectors of law and order and lived their respectable middle-class lives in disguise. The more contemporary superheroes, however, are often mutants like the X-Men and have inherited their talents because of some genetic deviation or experiment. Though marginalized and regarded as weird if not dangerous, superheroes tend to use their powers to protect the innocent of the world. However, there are also demonic superheroes who want to rule the world just for the sake of power.

As we tell tales, and as the students create tales, we modify these definitions in discussion, and different legends can be told depending on the demographics of the class. For instance, in Minneapolis there are many Somali, Hmong, Native American, and Mexican children in our classes so it is advisable to introduce a legend or a myth that may come from their culture, especially if the school and the students may be developing units about multiculturalism. For the most part, however, the stories that we choose for our curriculum have a wide appeal, no matter what their origins are, and they are intended to provide students with an understanding of "canonical" texts in Western culture while demonstrating the diversity and richness of stories throughout the world.

For instance, "The Pied Piper" is a German legend that has become internationally known and disseminated. There are hundreds of versions in books, comics, and films, and it raises many significant social questions that are pertinent to our storytelling about mythic gods and superheroes. The piper is a kind of mythic hero, whose behavior is ambivalent. We can ask whether he is a demonic figure who kidnaps the children and leads them away to exploit them or whether he represents divine justice and punishes the mayor and the townspeople for their dishonesty. In addition, the legend could actually be related to a horrible crime committed by the parents, for it may conceal how they abandoned their children or sent them off on a children's crusade. The legend might have been created to cover up the uncanny disappearance of the children from this town. Whatever the case may be, the social contracts between the town leaders and the piper and between the parents and their children are tainted and severed, and the intact community is destroyed by an event so traumatic that it could not be forgotten and thus spreads as a warning to all parts of the world.

Legends

We generally begin the sessions with a retelling of "The Pied Piper," which I discuss in detail in *Creative Storytelling* (pp. 119–21), because it is so effective in introducing legends to students. There are two options to presenting a canonical version of the legend. The first is a retelling of Robert Browning's poem in prose or a reading of the poem, or both; the second is a prose rendition of the legend by the French folklorist Charles Marelle, whose legend was translated and published by Andrew Lang in *The Red Fairy Book*. To show the students how the legend could be made into a more contemporary tale, we often introduce Gianni Rodari's tale "The Pied Piper and the Cars." Tell this story without an ending and then ask the students to supply one. After one student suggests an ending, tell Rodari's endings. This story with its multiple open endings should be used to begin the chair game. The "open-ending game" is important because we shall use it later to animate the students to develop their final play for the Bridges Festival.

Basic Structure of the Session
A retelling of Browning's "The Pied Piper": Tell the students this canonical version.
A retelling of Rodari's "The Pied Piper and the Cars": Tell the students this more contemporary version.

The Pied Piper and the Cars
Once upon a time there was a pied piper. This is an old story. Everyone knows it. A city is invaded by rats, and a young man comes with his magic pipe. He leads the rats to a river where they all drown. Then the mayor doesn't want to pay him. So the pied piper begins to play his pipe again, and he leads away all the children of the city.

Now my story also concerns a pied piper. Perhaps it's the same one. Perhaps not.

Once there was a city that was invaded, but this time it was invaded by cars. They were on the streets, on the sidewalks, on the squares, and under the gates of the city. There were cars everywhere—little ones like tin cans, long ones like ships, with trailers, with campers. There were cars, trucks, vans, and light vans. There were many that moved with great trouble, colliding with other cars, crashing fenders, squashing bumpers, tearing away large mufflers. And finally there were others that did not have any more space in which to move or park. Therefore, the people had to walk. But it was not so easy because the cars occupied all the space available. It was necessary to go around them, to jump over them, or to crawl under them. And from morning to evening all kinds of sounds could be heard.

"Owwww!"

That was a pedestrian who hit his head against the hood of a car.

"Oooh! Owwww!"

Those were two pedestrians who bumped into each other while crawling under a truck. The people became enraged, which is quite understandable.

"It's time that we put an end to this!"

"We've got to do something!"

"Why hasn't the mayor thought of something?"

The mayor heard these protests and muttered, "With regard to thinking about it, I've been thinking about it. I think about it day and night. I thought about it all day Christmas. The fact is that nothing has occurred to me. I don't know what to do, what to say and what measures to take. And my head is not any thicker than anyone else's. Look at how sore my head is!"

One day a strange young man appeared at city hall. He was wearing a sheepskin jacket, sandals, and a cap shaped like a cone. In short, he really looked like a pied piper, however, a piper without a pipe. When he asked to see the mayor, the guard responded dryly, "Why don't you leave quietly. He doesn't have any desire to hear a serenade."

"But I don't have a pipe."

"All the worse. If you don't even have a pipe, why would you want to see the mayor?"

"To tell him that I've come to free the city of cars."

"What? What? Listen, you better move on. Certain jokes don't go over so well here."

"Tell the mayor I'm here. I assure you that you won't regret it."

This was what was said and done so that the guard would accompany him to the mayor's office.

"Good day, mayor."

"Huh, you're a bit quick to say good day. For me it will only be a good day when ..."

"When the city is freed of cars. I know a system to get rid of them."

"You? And who taught you? A goat?"

"It doesn't matter who taught me. Let me try. It won't cost you anything. And if you promise me a certain thing, I guarantee you that, by tomorrow evening, you won't have any more troubles."

"I'm listening. What thing must I promise you?"

"That from tomorrow on the children will always be able to play in the great square, and that there will be a merry-go-round, seesaws, slides, rubber balls, and kites."

"In the great square?"

"In the great square."

"And you don't want anything else but that?"

"Nothing else."

"Well then, let's shake on it. I promise. When will you begin?"

"Right away, Mr. Mayor."

"Go, don't lose a minute."

The strange young man did not even lose a second. He stuck a hand in his pocket and dug out a small pipe carved from the branch of a mulberry tree. And right away, in the office of the mayor, he began to play a bizarre little tune. Once he left the office he continued playing in city hall. Then he crossed the square and headed toward the river.

A moment later ...

"Look! What's that car doing? It's moving by itself?"

"Also the other one!"

"Hey! That one's mine! Who's stealing my car? Thief! Thief!"

"But there is no thief. Don't you see? All the cars are moving."

"They're picking up speed. ... They're running."

"Who knows where they're going?"

"It's my car! Stop, stop! I want my car!"

"Try to put a pinch of salt on the tail."

From all points of the city the cars began moving in an incredible thunderous roar of motors, exhaust fumes, horns, sirens. They moved and moved by themselves.

If one paid careful attention, however, a slight whistle of the pipe could be heard above the uproar, even stronger and more resistant than the uproar; a bizarre tune, a very bizarre tune.

First Ending

The cars moved toward the river. The piper did not stop playing and waited for the cars on the bridge. When the first car arrived—and by chance it was actually the mayor's car—he changed the melody slightly and reached a higher note. As if by signal, the bridge collapsed, and the car sank into the river. Then the current took it far away. And down went the second, then the third, down went all the cars, one after the other, two at a time, in bunches. They sank with a last roar of the motor, a death rattle of the horn. Then the current carried them away.

As the cars were disappearing, the children descended triumphantly into the streets with their balls and their dolls in carriages. They took rides on their bikes and tricycles, and babysitters smiled as they took a stroll.

But the people began to tear the hair out of their heads. They called the fire department and complained to the police.

"And you're letting this madman do this? Stop him, arrest him, tell him to stop playing."

"Dip him into the river a little, that crazy guy with his pipe!"

"The mayor's also become crazy! He's had all our beautiful cars destroyed!"

"He'll pay for it."

"He'll pay for it dearly!"

"Down with the mayor! Resign your post!"

"Down with the piper!"

"I want my car back!"

The people who were the most bold rushed toward the piper, but they stopped before they could touch him. In the air, invisible, there was a wall to protect him, and those bold people beat their fists and kicked with their shoes against this wall in vain. The piper waited until the last car had plunged into the river. Then he also dove into the water and swam to the other side. There he made a bow, turned, and disappeared into the woods.

Second Ending

The cars moved toward the river, one after the other, where they plunged into the water with one final honk of their horns. The last car to plunge was the mayor's car. By this time the great square was already crowded with children who were playing and their joyous cries covered the groans of the city's inhabitants who had seen their cars disappear far away, dragged by the current.

Finally, the piper stopped playing and raised his eyes. Only now did he see the menacing crowd that marched toward him, with the mayor marching in front.

"Are you satisfied, Mr. Mayor?"

"Now I'll show you just how satisfied I am! You think you've done a beautiful thing? Don't you know how much work goes into making a car and how much a car costs? You really chose a beautiful way to free the city ..."

"But I ... but you ..."

"But you, you're a nothing. Now, if you don't want to spend the rest of your days in prison, put your pipe to your lips and make the cars come back from the river. And make sure that they all come back, every single one of them."

"Bravo! Well done! Long live the mayor!" said the crowd.

The piper obeyed. And obeying the sound of his magic instrument, the cars returned to the bank of the river, moved in the streets and the squares to occupy the spaces that they had occupied before, chasing away the children, the balls, the tricycles, and the babysitters. In short, everything returned to the way it was before. The piper walked away slowly, full of sadness, and from then on nobody spoke about him ever again.

Third Ending

The cars moved and moved. ... Toward the river like the rats of Hamelin? Not at all! They moved and moved. ... And at a certain point there was not a single one left in the city, not a single one in the great square. The streets were empty, the alleys were free, the little parks were deserted. Where did the cars disappear to?

Perk your ears and listen. They are now moving beneath the earth. With his magic pipe the bizarre young man dug streets beneath the streets and squares beneath the squares. There the cars were moving. They stopped to take their owners on board, and then they continued on their way. Now there was a place for everyone. Beneath the earth was for the cars. Above was for the inhabitants of the city who wanted to take a stroll while talking about the government, the latest championship match, and the moon. For the children who wanted to play, for the women who ran their errands.

"How stupid I was!" cried the mayor, full of enthusiasm. "How stupid! Why hadn't I thought about this before?"

They made a statue in this city to honor the piper. Actually, two statues. One in the great square, and the other beneath it, placed among the cars that constantly scoot about in their tunnels.

Discussion: How are cars like rats? Why can't the people get rid of the cars? Should we get rid of cars? Do they contribute to pollution? Do we need cars? What other way can we develop transportation? What ways are there to stop pollution? What is the situation like in your city?

Chair game: Make full use of the Rodari story. Try to lead into the game with some sentences such as, "The people were shocked when they saw the piper leading their cars to the river. Some of them managed to jump into their cars. Some on top. It seemed that the cars were going to carry their owners into the river."

Improvisation and theater games led by the teaching artist: Here we generally use the telephone game. Divide the class into their three groups and form circles. Each group is to be given a prompt such as, "Did you hear that Martians invaded New York? The mayor called for security forces." Or "Did you hear that Miami is infested by snakes? The people were fleeing the city." The story continues to be spread until the last member of the group ends it. Once the story is completed, one of the members retells the story to the other two groups.

Writing game: Return to the "What If?" game.

What if the rats were kangaroos?
What if the pied piper were a butcher?
What if the people wanted to tame the rats?
What if rats could talk?
What if rats could be used to help the people?

Legendary Heroes of History

During the past thirty-five years there has been a major tendency to revise U.S. history so that the contradictions in our manifest destiny—our mission of spreading "civilization" to this "savage" continent and creating a kind of promised land of the brave and the free—become more evident. Revisionist history was borne out of the civil rights struggles, the antiwar movement, and the feminist movement of the 1960s and 1970s. The underlying purpose of many different revisionist books was to examine the negative tendencies of U.S. colonialism, slavery, capitalism, and imperialism along with the positive tendencies of democracy, religious toleration, equal rights, inventiveness, class struggle, and solidarity. The revisionists sought and still seek to understand the sources of contemporary social and political problems and to suggest possible solutions to them. For these critics, history is not the dead past. History is not glorification of the United States' rise to power. History makes itself felt in the present to redress wrongs that stem from the past and to chart a new frontier for the United States.

Part of revisionist history means reexamining our heroes and the whole concept of what it means to be heroic. On one hand, this is not innovative because there has always been a predilection in U.S. history and folklore for the nonheroic type, the common man who pulls himself up by the bootstraps, or the pioneer woman, who shows great strength and stamina under difficult conditions. On the other hand, revisionist history is different because it is more critical and it questions whether the common man and pioneer woman who are successful are truly heroic and, more important, truly humane. After all, to be successful in the United States demands ruthless ambition, fortitude, and manliness that has no faults. Heroism, particularly after World War II, demanded devote patriotism and a belief in the United States as a kind of "holy land," whose manifest destiny appeared to include the entire world.

In fact, the United States in the postwar period generated many "new" popular heroes in mass culture, mainly men, like Superman, Batman, Dick Tracy, the Phantom, Captain Marvel, the Lone Ranger, Tarzan, the Shadow, Hopalong Cassidy, Roy Rogers, Gene Autry, the FBI in Peace and War, Popeye, and Little Abner. They were all saviors, and people looked to them for salvation, just as they looked to Roosevelt, MacArthur, and Eisenhower for salvation. And they were encouraged to do so through film and literature. Rugged individualism in the name of liberty, peace, and justice was represented in different ways by these heroes.

The Vietnam War changed all this. Not completely, but certainly the moral authority of U.S. heroism was brought into question. For many young people it became just as manly (and womanly) to resist the war, to refuse to kill for an unworthy cause, and to defend the notion of a gentler, more just United States.

If we look at children's literature from the 1950s to the present, we see that an entire spectrum of heroes was presented in different genres, though the type of the rugged individual as a U.S. hero was generally the predominant one until the early 1970s. If women were heroines, then they were martyr types who sacrificed their dreams and goals for the good of the family and nation. Though many folklorists and left-wing writers tried to change the image of U.S. folk heroes in the 1940s and 1950s—Davy Crockett, Daniel Boone, Buffalo Bill, Johnny Appleseed, General Custer, Abe Lincoln, Paul Bunyan—these individuals were mostly depicted as extraordinary, powerful men who laid the groundwork for democracy and justice in the United States.

Today we know different. Some of these men were Indian killers, racists, and demagogues. Some did not even exist but emanated from the imagination of common people who yearned for certain types of heroes and gladly told tales about these wish-fulfillment heroes. Historians and folklorists have shed a great deal of light on the mythic nature of these heroes, but storytellers and writers of children's literature have been reluctant to critique these heroes in a full-scale way. The direction they have taken has been to find other positive folk heroes representing different cultures and genders in keeping with the ideology of multiculturalism and feminism. Or they have modified the picture of folk heroes to reveal more of their foibles and yet to rerepresent them as basically good men, admirable and exemplary. It is not easy to rewrite or retell U.S. history in the name of truth and to critique the heritage of U.S. heroism, especially when one works with children in schools. So, the depiction of U.S. heroes, especially the folk heroes, becomes the terrain on which we endeavor to project models that we want our children to emulate, notions of U.S. history that we want them to absorb, and directions to take to become citizens of this nation and the world.

Although there may be a spark of truth in U.S. tall tales and legends, we know that they live from exaggeration. Paradoxically, it is because they are not true that they reveal certain true images of what our ancestors wished for and hoped to accomplish in settling our country. In such books as *Cut from the Same Cloth: American Women of Myth, Legend, and Tall Tale*, one of the few books ever published that deals only with female protagonists, edited by Robert San Souci, and *From Sea to Shining Sea*, a collection of multicultural stories, edited by Amy Cohen, we have two poignant examples of how contemporary writers and illustrators take these wishes and dreams seriously and thus revise these tales to revitalize U.S. tradition. Indeed, they call our attention to the fact that we may still be very much in need of the incredible feats of such individuals like Swamp Angel and John Henry, and the legends in these books, or similar ones, can serve as the basis for this session. However, we purposely focus on a female heroine such as Pocahontas and a traditional white male hero such as Johnny Appleseed to compare and contrast legends.

We begin the fantastic binominal by asking for a list of famous people in history, including presidents, generals, religious and political leaders, athletes, and so forth. We stress that the famous person should be from the distant past and should be dead. Each time a student volunteers a name, she or he must explain why the person was famous and tell everything she or he knows about the famous person. The teaching artist writes about five to ten names on the board and then asks for a place or thing to be coupled with a preposition. The students are to choose one of the famous people and link the person with the noun on the board to create an imaginative story based on what the class knows about the individual. After we have completed the fantastic binominal, we tell two tales about a legendary hero and follow our regular structure of discussion, skits, and a writing game.

Myths

In *Creative Storytelling* (pp. 137–150) there are ample suggestions and texts for developing two sessions on myths. Here I want to explain how we incorporate the telling of myths so that they relate to other sessions in our program.

Basic Structure of the Session
The focus is on Greek mythology.
Fantastic binominal: Write a list of the Greek gods on the board. Next to each name explain what the god's function was.

Zeus, king of the heavens and all-powerful god
Hera, queen of the heavens and all-powerful goddess
Poseidon, god of the sea

Hades, god of the lower world
Persephone, goddess of vegetation
Demeter, goddess of agriculture
Hestia, goddess of the hearth
Ares, god of war
Hephaestus, god of fire
Apollo, god of the sun
Artemis, goddess of the wild animals, the hunt and vegetation
Aphrodite, goddess of beauty
Athena, goddess of wisdom
Hermes, god of speech, messenger of the gods
Dionysus, god of drink and spring
Themis, goddess of hospitality

We ask the students to choose a god or goddess, choose a thing or place, and model a mythic story.

Second fantastic binominal: Keep the list on the board, and ask a student to come up front and write a thing or place on the board. Then have the students write their own myths. They can incorporate their own heroes from popular culture.

Retelling of the creation myth: Tell the students the myth of creation.

Creation

There are many stories about how the world was created and why. Well over two thousand years ago, the Greeks believed there were many gods who ruled the universe, and this is the tale they told about the creation of the universe.

From the beginning there was chaos. Stars, planets, comets, meteors all soared through the universe, crashing into one another in darkness. There was no meaning to anything until out of all this chaos came Nyx (night) and Erebus (the unfathomable deep) that produced the first god called Gaea, Mother Earth. To tell you the truth, nobody knows how or why she came into being. But she did, and one time, as she was sleeping, she gave birth to Uranus, Father Sky, and he became her husband, and they had many children together.

The first children to be born were the Hecatonichires and the Cyclopes. You must imagine that they were extraordinary, and extraordinary they were. The Hecatonichires were tremendous and powerful monsters with fifty heads and one hundred hands. The Cyclopes were gargantuan giants with only one eye in the middle of their foreheads. Soon after the Hecatonichires and the Cyclopes came the handsome Titans, enormous and strong but not as destructive as the Hecatonichires, who were wild and played with thunder and lightning and caused many earthquakes. These hundred-handed monsters were hard to tame, and their father, Uranus, was afraid that they might overthrow him one day. So, he eventually locked them into a dungeon deep in the middle of the earth. But his actions did not sit well with Gaea. She was very angry with Uranus, and she called upon her youngest son Cronus (Time) to challenge his father. Well, Cronus sensed that the time had come to end his father's oppression. They had a huge battle, and Cronus was the victor and became lord of the universe.

"My son," Gaea said, "I am pleased that you are lord of the universe, but now it is time to release your brothers from their dungeon."

"No, mother," he replied. "I have no intention of sharing my power with anyone. Let them stay in their prison."

Gaea was once again angry, but there was nothing she could do. In the meantime, Cronus married Rhea, another Titan, and they had five children who became gods: Demeter, the goddess of agriculture; Hestia, goddess of the earth; Hera, goddess of the heavens; Hades, god of the lower world; and Poseidon, god of the sea. However, Cronus was like his own father and felt that his children might take over his throne. Indeed, he had gone to an oracle and learned that history would repeat itself and his own children would rebel against him. Instead of putting them in a prison, he swallowed them as soon as Rhea gave birth. But they did not die because they were immortal. Indeed, they continued to grow inside Cronus's gigantic stomach.

When Rhea was about to give birth to her sixth child, she hid from Cronus and did not tell him about their new son, whom she named Zeus. Secretly she sent him to the island of Crete, where he was raised by nymphs. However, Cronus suspected that Rhea had given birth.

"Do you think you can fool me?" he roared. "I want the baby."

Rhea refused to tell Cronus about Zeus. Instead she wrapped a large stone in a baby blanket and took it to Cronus, who swallowed it immediately without looking inside.

During the next several years, Zeus grew into a strong, powerful god on the island of Crete, and when he became a young man, Rhea felt that he was ready to do combat with Cronus.

"You have five brothers and sisters trapped in your father's belly," she told Zeus. "Your father would have devoured you, too, if I hadn't saved you. The time has come for you to rescue your brothers and sisters!"

Zeus was enraged by his father's actions and began plans to overthrow Cronus. With the help of Rhea and his grandmother, Gaea, the Mother Earth, Zeus was able to force Cronus to throw up his brothers and sisters. Soon thereafter they joined their brother Zeus in the great battle of the gods, for Cronus called upon the Titans, all his brothers and sisters, to come to his aid.

The universe shook. The universe trembled and rumbled and crumbled. It seemed that it might even be devastated. The young gods fought ferociously against the Titans, and at one point, the great Titan Prometheus realized that the gods were going to win the battle, so he switched sides and joined the gods. Moreover, he persuaded Zeus to free the hundred-handed Hecatonichires from their dungeon, and they used thunder, lightning, and earthquakes to defeat Cronus and the Titans. In turn, they were sent to a prison at Tartaus, deep down in the middle of the earth. From then on Zeus took over the lightning and thunder, and whenever he got mad, he threw thunderbolts at anyone who displeased him.

"We shall make Mount Olympus our home," Zeus declared after the war, for it was the highest mountain and it reached into the heavens. Only the gods were invited to live there, with the exception of Prometheus and his brother Epimetheus, the slow thinker. Prometheus always needed to keep an eye on him because Epimetheus often did foolish things and was not particularly wise.

Because Zeus trusted Prometheus so much, he decided to give him and Epimetheus the wonderful task of filling the earth with animals and human creatures. However, Epimetheus foolishly endowed the beasts with many remarkable gifts so that there was nothing left for humans. Indeed, he gave the animals warm fur and feathers to keep themselves warm; sharp teeth and claws to protect themselves; wings to fly; shells for shields; changeable skins to blend in with nature; speed, different sizes, and strength; and fins for swimming underwater.

"What shall we do?" Epimetheus asked. "What's left?"

"Not to worry," Prometheus responded. "I know what we can do."

Prometheus gave humans an upright stance so that they would stand above the animals and look more distinguished. They could look down into the underworld, but most important, they could look up to the heavens and honor the gods. Finally, he gave humans a greater intelligence than the beasts, and he became very fond of them because they were his own creation.

Some say he became much too fond of them because they wasted their intelligence, but that is another story, a story worth telling, for humankind owes a great debt to the Titan Prometheus.

Discussion: What is chaos? Is it possible that Mother Earth could give birth to her own husband? Why was Uranus afraid of his own children? Why was Cronus afraid of his own children? Why do the gods want so much power? Do you think Zeus should have overthrown his own father? Is it possible that there are too many gods? Does this myth remind you of "The Spirit Names the Animal People"? If so, how? Are the animal tales that were told by Native Americans related in some way to the Greek myths?

Retelling of the Prometheus myth: Tell the students the myth of Prometheus.

Prometheus

Though Prometheus the Titan served Zeus, the most powerful of all the gods, he did not trust him, especially because he took little interest in human beings on earth. This irritated Prometheus, especially because it was he who had created the mortals and constantly gave them gifts so they could survive on earth. It was he who taught them woodworking, boat building, number and alphabet recitation, and saddle making. He also showed them how to heal wounds, mine the earth for its precious metals, and design jugs and homes. Nevertheless, Zeus had no sympathy for the humans and would have preferred it if they had simply vanished from the face of earth. This is why he refused to let them know the source of fire.

To be sure, the humans learned to make fires in their huts and caves to keep themselves warm during the winter. They needed fire to cook their meals and to make their weapons. They lit torches to worship the gods and to bring light into dark dwellings. But at the beginning of the world, they did not know where fire came from. It quite often burst from the skies like lightning and set forests and land ablaze. Sometimes it came from the thunderbolts that Zeus threw at the earth when he became mad. Other times it exploded from volcanoes as though it came from the bowels of the earth. People were frightened of the flames, especially when the fire spread and destroyed forests and dwellings. Each time sparks flew through the air and flickering flames appeared, they prayed to Zeus for mercy and help because they did not know how to control fire or use it to create energy and power.

But Zeus only laughed at the humans. He did not trust them. If they learned the source of fire, he felt, they would become arrogant and use it for destructive purposes.

"No!" Prometheus cried out, "You're judging them unfairly. If you trust them, they'll put fire to good use. I promise you they will make the earth into a garden of paradise."

Prometheus had come to Mount Olympus to pray for the mortals, but Zeus only mocked them.

"Look at those puny hopeless creatures!" Zeus roared. "They don't appreciate any of the gifts you've bestowed on them."

"You must give them a chance, sire," Prometheus responded.

"Hah! They'll make a fool of you," Zeus declared.

Hera, Zeus's magnificent wife, tried to help Prometheus, because he was so noble.

"Perhaps he is right," the queen said. "Perhaps the humans will transform earth into a paradise. They will make progress."

"They will only create more and more weapons and destroy the earth if they learn the secret of fire!" Zeus said angrily. "What you call progress is death and destruction!"

"But fire can help cure and heal people. Like the light of your wisdom, fire can illuminate ways toward a better life," Prometheus pleaded.

"You have heard my answer!" Zeus said. "I said no, and I mean no."

But Prometheus was courageous and stubborn, and though Titans are only demigods, they can perform extraordinary feats. Prometheus was particularly clever and tricky. So, when Zeus went to bed for the evening, Prometheus crawled quietly to Zeus's hearth of fire and stole some for the mortals. Then he soared to earth and disclosed the secret of fire to the humans who rejoiced when they learned what fire could do for them. They were so pleased that they worshiped Prometheus as a god.

However, when Zeus discovered the theft, he was enraged, and he summoned Prometheus to Mount Olympus.

"Who do you think you are?" Zeus roared. "What do you think you've done?"

"I've only tried to champion the cause of the humans, and you wouldn't listen," Prometheus replied humbly.

"Well, my champion of humans," Zeus said, "you'll pay mightily for your crime."

"Have mercy," Hera intervened. "Prometheus meant well. Perhaps his crime will turn out to be a good deed."

"I trusted Prometheus," Zeus said.

"And I trust the humans," Prometheus responded.

"You are a fool!" Zeus declared. "They will betray your trust."

"But Prometheus's heart is noble," Hera said. "Remember how he fought for you against Cronus. You must have mercy for his noble heart."

"Yes, I'll have mercy," said Zeus. "He will not die, but he will learn what it means to be a rebel, and he will be reminded each day of what it means to steal fire from Zeus."

"I'm ready," Prometheus declared. "I don't regret my deed. I'm ready for my punishment."

But Prometheus was not really ready for the horrible punishment he was about to receive. In his anger Zeus condemned the hero to be chained alive to a rock in the Caucasus Mountains, and every day a gigantic vulture came and ate his liver. But Prometheus did not die because Zeus had his liver grow anew each night so that the vulture could feast on his liver again the next day.

The noble Prometheus suffered for a long time, and he would have suffered hundreds of years longer if Hera had not taken pity on him. She told Zeus that cruel justice is not justice, and she, too, had a say in this affair. She summoned Heracles, another great Titan, to take his bow and arrow and shoot the vulture, which he did. And when the vulture lay dead, the powerful Heracles carried Prometheus on his shoulders back to Olympus, where Hera honored him and made it known to the humans that Prometheus was the bringer of light.

However, Zeus was angry at Hera and resented that the humans were now enjoying the benefits of fire against his will. So he ordered his son Vulcan to create a beautiful woman out of clay, and he named her Pandora. Then Zeus ordered the goddess Athena to teach her all the domestic skills that women must know until she was perfect. Next Zeus ordered the goddess Aphrodite to teach Pandora how to be graceful and artful until she was the epitome of beauty. Finally, Zeus commanded the god Hermes to train her to use her speech to flatter and charm, to convince and demand, until she was the perfect speaker. When all the gods had put their touch on Pandora, and she was finished, there was no one, man or god, who could resist her charms and beauty.

Zeus was extremely pleased with the final product, and he called upon his trusty Hermes and said, "I want you to take Pandora to Epimetheus, the brother of Prometheus, as a gift. Do this now without fail!"

When Prometheus heard what Zeus was doing, he warned his brother that this gift might be a trick, but Epimetheus thought that Zeus was trying to atone for the cruel manner in which he had punished his brother. Besides, he fell in love with Pandora at first sight, so striking was she, and he married her the next day.

Now, Pandora had a beautiful jeweled box with her that Zeus had given her, and Zeus had told her that it was never to be opened. It was only to be admired. When Epimetheus asked her what was inside the box, she said, "Never, never open it."

"But you must trust me," Epimetheus said.

"Of course I trust you," Pandora replied. "But even I do not know what is inside."

"Don't you want to know?"

"No," she replied. "I'm afraid to disobey the gods."

But the longer the box stood in her room, the more beautiful and attractive and mysterious it seemed, and one day, Epimetheus could not restrain himself. Despite Pandora's warning, he took the box from her and demanded the key, but as soon as he opened it, he was shocked—all the diseases, maladies, troubles, and plagues that were to trouble humankind and animals forever came rushing out of the box. Epimetheus was horrified and ashamed, and he would have killed himself if Pandora had not pointed out to him that Zeus also had put something else into the box that would also stay with humankind. It was Hope, she explained, Hope that humans would eventually triumph over the worst of catastrophes.

And so it was, and so it is.

Discussion: Is Prometheus a hero or a trickster? Was Zeus correct in punishing him? What is justice in this myth? How did Zeus get revenge on Prometheus and humankind? What is the difference between revenge and justice?

Chair game: Mercury, who was the messenger of the gods, was sent to earth to tell the countries that they must stop all wars. Otherwise, Zeus will destroy the earth. But Mercury was kidnapped by Ares, god of war.

Improvisation and theater games led by the teaching artist: Form a large circle with the entire class. Ask a student to enter the circle. Once in the middle, he or she is to demonstrate a super human strength or feature. The other students are to react to the performance and show fear, joy, awe, and so on. Students are to take turns entering the circle and demonstrating their superhuman powers.

Three skits based on Greek myths: Have the students perform three skits.

Writing game: Ask the students if they can think of characters on TV, in films, in comics, and so forth who are similar to the Greek gods and goddesses. Write some of the names on the board. Then write the names of five gods and goddesses on the board. Ask students to choose one Greek god or goddess and one of the popular characters and write a story about them.

Follow-up themes for discussion:

1. What makes for a hero?
2. Why are most of the heroes men?
3. Are there female heroes?
4. Are there heroes today? Who are they?

Heracles and Athena

This session should be devoted to the question of power, and how the gods were constantly using their gifts to satisfy their own particular needs and to compete with one another. We want to explore whether our present-day "gods" behave any better than the Greek gods. The relationship between the Greek gods and the elite leaders and stars of contemporary society can be made clear in discussions. Depending on the age group and knowledge of the students, we should try to draw parallels with current events and the behavior of powerful people. Why did the Greeks create and revere their gods? Do we do the same today? Who are our gods? For the fantastic binominal, write the list of the Greek gods with their powers on the board to refresh the memory of the students. Then ask the students to associate some important persons, including local celebrities, with some of the gods. Then ask for a noun, preferably an object such as a tool, and link them with a preposition. The students are requested to write a tale about one of the contemporary gods on the board.

Superheroes and Popular Culture

We have now reached the stage when we explore the possibility of appropriating and transforming superheroes from contemporary youth culture. Here our emphasis is on challenging sexual and racial stereotypes and questioning the use of violent action to resolve conflict. Are there other heroes that the students should become aware of? How can we introduce them to heroes from history who may serve their interests in a more meaningful way than many of the commodified characters appear to do?

Basic Structure of the Session

Fantastic binominal: Ask students for names of their favorite heroes from TV, film, comics, video games, and so on, and if you are not familiar with them, ask the students who they are and what they do. After you have a list of about eight, ask them for a thing or place to write on the board. Then ask the students to choose a superhero for the story.

The list may consist of some of the following characters:

Wolverine
Harry Potter
Buffy the Vampire Slayer
Spiderman
Jackie Chan
Superman
Batman
Pokémon
Xena

The list will vary depending on what the students are viewing and reading. If most of the characters tend to be male, ask the students whether they also know of strong female characters.

In telling the tale, it is important to focus on the extraordinary power of the superhero as a talent that can be used to bring about peace. If at all possible, try to develop the tale in a way that the students can realize conflict resolution in a nonviolent manner. We want to encourage the notion that superheroes are great because they know how to use constraint and because they struggle for the benefit of all people. They are not interested in displaying their power because they are confident of their power. Only when a situation becomes desperate do they turn to force. More important are such qualities as cleverness, wisdom, patience, and tolerance.

Second fantastic binominal: Using the list on the board, ask the students for another noun (thing or place) and then have them write stories by choosing one of the superheroes and linking it to the noun.

The legend of John Henry: It is important to talk about slavery, the mythic birth of John Henry, and his sacrifice for workers. We always add his wife, Polly Ann, who is also strong and gracious. The tragic ending remains tragic. This tale and the following tale are told as transitional legends that reveal how power can be used for peaceful ends. They are in direct contrast to the superhero tales that the students read and view and will probably write, which is all the more reason to tell these tales to exemplify how power can be channeled for humane purposes.

John Henry

On the very day that President Abraham Lincoln declared there would be no more slavery in the United States, a strange incident happened on a plantation in Alabama. All the slaves had gathered in front of a small shack because a child was about to be born on the day they were freed. All the animals on the plantation and in the nearby woods also came to watch because they had heard this was going to be a special child. And indeed this child was very special. As soon as he popped out of his mother's belly, he could walk and talk.

The father ran out on the porch and announced the birth of his son. "My son, John Henry, can walk and talk," he said.

The crowd was stunned and cried out, "Oooooh, ahhhhh! Oooooh, ahhhhh!"

The father ran back inside and within seconds came back to declare, "John Henry, my son, has just grown to be three feet tall!"

The crowd responded with, "Oooooh, ahhhhh! Oooooh, ahhhhh!"

The father turned once more and reentered the shack. Before long, he returned to the crowd. "My son John Henry's now six feet tall! We need large clothes. We need more food."

"Oooooh, ahhhhh! Oooooh, ahhhhh!" the crowd rejoiced, and people ran and fetched clothes and food for John Henry. Even the animals scattered and searched for food.

Well, John Henry would not stop growing until he was seven feet tall, and that took only seven days.

"My time is up," he cried out. "My time has come to go out into the world!"

His mother sobbed. His father lamented.

"Why must you leave us now?" they asked, and once again all the people and animals gathered in front of the shack.

"I was born a free man, and I'm going to build this land as a free man. You will hear from me," he said as he hugged his mother and father, "and you will hear about me!"

John Henry headed west to the Mississippi River because he had heard that there was a lot of work on the docks and on the boats. No sooner did he arrive than he found a job loading cotton bales onto the boats. He was so strong and powerful that he could carry five-hundred-pound bales by himself and load a boat in half the time it took twelve men to do the work.

John Henry loved the life on the Mississippi, and everywhere he went he found a job because nobody could match him in skill and power. In the evenings he would sit with friends and tell stories and sing songs. One time while he was recalling some adventure in Missouri, he noticed a young woman named Polly Ann glancing at him with her dark brown eyes.

"What are you looking at?" he asked her.

"You," she replied.

"Why me?"

"Because I like you, and you're gonna be my husband," she smiled.

Well, Polly Ann was almost as big and strong as John Henry, and she was certainly more beautiful. Nobody ever dared talk to John Henry the way she did, and he liked her spunk, and before you could say jackrabbit, they were married!

So now the two of them traveled the Mississippi and worked together for several years. Then one day, John Henry said, "I'm getting tired of this sort of life. I've heard they're building a railroad back in West Virginia. Why don't we go there for a change?"

"I'm always ready for a change," Polly Ann responded, and off they went.

Well, when they got to West Virginia, they went to the C & O Railroad, and there was a man named Captain Johnson, who was hiring hundreds of men to lay tracks for the railroad. Trains were new to the country, and the C & O Railroad wanted to cut across the whole of the United States. John Henry was the perfect man, Captain Johnson said, a hammer man who could drive holes through rocks to make the way for the tracks. And Polly Ann, she worked on the tracks until they discovered she was pregnant and had to stop the hard labor. But she continued to work in the kitchens to feed the hungry men who worked hours and hours in the steamy hot weather.

The work was hard and dangerous, and many men died from exhaustion because they had to cut into the wilderness, chop down forests, and burrow through hills.

"We're gonna bring all the people together," John Henry said. "We're gonna connect people all over America with our tracks."

This is what the workers believed, and most of them were blacks who had been freed from slavery and wanted to show the world what they could create. Then there came a time when they came to the Big Bend Mountain in West Virginia, and the railroad men decided to build a tunnel right through this mountain.

"We won't need your work for this mountain," Captain Johnson declared.

"What?" the workers cried out.

"You'll have to find some other jobs," Captain Johnson said. "We're bringing in a special machine that can work better than all you men."

"But what about our families?" they responded. "How are we going to feed them? You can't just lay us off."

"The machine will save us money and time," Captain Johnson said.

"But we're better than any machine!" John Henry shouted.

Just then you could hear *chug-chug-chug, chug-chug-chug,* and a man in a top hat and suit came driving up on a steam machine. It was Chuck Geary, the inventor of a drill machine that he drove up to the mountain and parked in front of all the workers.

"Who said you're better than my machine?" he shouted.

"I did!" John Henry declared.

"You're a fool and don't know what you're talking about."

"I'm a man and smarter and stronger than any machine you can make."

"Hold on, now," Captain Johnson intervened. "I don't want no fights on this here territory. I've got a job to do. A tunnel to build."

"That's what I'm here to do," Chuck Geary declared. "You want a tunnel. Well, I can get through this mountain in one day's time."

"And I can do it faster," John Henry said. "And if all the men worked with me, we could do it in half a day."

"You're a liar!" Chuck Geary yelled.

"Nobody calls me liar and gets away with it!" John Henry was mad.

"We'll see what the truth is," said Captain Johnson. "Let's have a contest. Tomorrow at eight in the morning John Henry will face the machine to see who can dig a tunnel through Big Bend Mountain the fastest. If John Henry wins, you men will keep your jobs. If not, I'll buy the machine from Chuck Geary."

Well, word spread quickly about the contest between John Henry and the machine. The next day at sunrise there were thousands of people gathered before Big Bend Mountain. John Henry stood proud and tall with steel hammers in each one of his hands. Chuck Geary sat on his shiny steam machine with power drivers set to pound the mountain. Captain Johnson had a flag raised high, and as soon as it turned eight o'clock, he cried out, "Ready, set, go!" The flag went down, and *wham!* John Henry whacked the mountain with his hammers, and *wham!* the machine cracked open the mountain.

Bam! Bam! Bam! John Henry's arms were power drills, and he began drilling through the mountain. The crowd cheered as he got a head start on the machine.

Chug, chug, chug! Chug, chug, chug! The machine began to dig a large tunnel, and Chuck Geary kept driving it forward.

Bam, bam, bam! Bam, bam, bam! John Henry kept at it until midday when he came back out of his tunnel to rest for several minutes.

Chug, chug, chug! Chug, chug, chug! Chuck Geary kept going on his machine.

"He's getting ahead of you, John Henry," the people cried.

"Don't worry. I still have the lead!" he responded.

"Not for long," Chuck Geary yelled.

"I better go back into my tunnel," John Henry said.

Chug, chug, chug! Chug, chug, chug! The machine was gaining a lead.

But John Henry kept pounding ahead way into the afternoon. *Bam, bam, bam!*

In the meantime, the thousands of people went around the mountain and gathered at the other end to see who would be the first to emerge. The sounds were terrifying.

Bam, bam, bam! Chug, chug, chug! Slam, whack, bam, chug! Thud, whack, slam, bam!

All of a sudden, the people could see a crack in the mountain. The crack widened, and dirt and rocks began to fall as a hole appeared, and out jumped John Henry. The people roared and danced and sang.

"John Henry! John Henry! He's done it! He's won!"

But then there was silence. Nobody could hear the machine anymore. John Henry looked worried.

"What's going on?" Captain Johnson asked.

"It's Chuck Geary," John Henry replied. "I think he's stuck. I think the machine broke down."

Quickly, John Henry began pounding the mountain where Chuck Geary had been expected to make his entrance. He slammed and whacked the side of the mountain and began making another tunnel. Inside he went and drove onward until he came to poor Chuck Geary who was lying on his machine. He had fainted when the machine broke down. So John Henry picked him up and carried him out of the mountain.

"John Henry! John Henry! He's done it! He's won!" the crowd roared again.

But just as John Henry placed Chuck Geary on the ground, he gasped and held his heart. Then he toppled over, fell to the ground, and lay there dead.

Polly Ann came rushing over to John Henry. Tears filled her eyes. She could not stop sobbing. There was silence. Then Polly Ann stood up and managed a smile.

"It's no time to be sad," she said. "John Henry died for you, and now it's time for you to be glad that you have your jobs and your families. Just do me a favor and never forget my man John Henry. That's all I ask."

And Polly Ann tapped her belly and added, "My baby won't forget either, and the future will be ours."

John Henry was a railroad man,
He worked from six 'till five,
"Raise 'em up bullies and let 'em drop down,
I'll beat you to the bottom or die."

John Henry said to Chuck Geary:
"You are nothing but a common man,
Before that steam drill shall beat me down,
I'll die with my hammer in my hand."

Discussion: Is John Henry a superhero? What happened during the period of slavery in the United States? Who built all the railroads? Why don't workers get credit for all the work they did and do? What has happened to the railroad system in the United States?

Three strong women: See my version of this tale in *Creative Storytelling* (p. 88). This story concerns a mythic wrestler who learns to use power peacefully to end vicious fights.

Chair game: Using one of the superheroes on the board, begin a prompt by placing the hero in danger.

Improvisation and theater games led by the teaching artist: Here we use the machine game. The students are divided into their three groups. One student starts a motion, and another student must attach him- or herself to the first to form a machine. Once the machine is formed, each student takes a turn and steps out of the machine to observe it. In the second part of exercise, the students disassemble and gather together to talk about the machine or activity that they want to represent. Then they form that machine for the other two groups. The others must guess what the machine is. Once the machine is identified, another group performs.

Three "superhero" skits: Have the students perform three skits.

Writing game: Ask the students for more superheroes. Write five names on the board. Then ask for two things and two places. Write these on the board. Have the students write a "salad" story using all the names and nouns on the board.

From Tall Tales to Utopian Tales

In the last weeks of the program, we move toward the production of a play based on the ideas and improvisation of the students and we begin to introduce tales and to animate the students to tell tales based on personal experiences—tall tales, family tales, pourquois tales, and utopian tales. We all have tales to tell, and we tell them in our everyday conversations, phone calls, and e-mails. Yet we often do not realize how our storytelling has deep roots. We do not appreciate the value of our own stories and how they can be artfully shaped to make meaning out of our lives. Sometimes we are afraid to reflect on and examine our own stories for fear that they reveal too much about our inner lives and our relations with other people. Telling a tale involves a certain amount of intimacy: the actual telling can lead to some kind of intimate relations with the listeners; the tale itself might contain intimate elements. Therefore, unless we want to bare our souls—and most of the time we don't—we need to learn to distance ourselves from our own experiences, to make our experiences seem strange, so that we can step back from our encounters and laugh and cry about them with the world around us. Storytelling is a form of artful estrangement. We use stories to come to terms with the strange aspects of our lives and experiences, and learning the art of storytelling can enable us both to conceal and to reveal our innermost needs and desires.

The world is a strange place for young people, and they want to make it familiar so that they can feel at home and more comfortable with it. Paradoxically, the stranger they make the world, the more they will get to know it. This is why art is so powerful and so helpful in their lives. Storytelling, writing, acting, and drawing can enable the students to gain distance from their everyday experiences that are often troubling if not traumatic. So we encourage the students to play with events and occurrences, break them down and apart only to reshape them into forms of expression that have special meaning for them. We want to demonstrate that life can be re-formed if we step back and gain a different perspective on what transpires in each individual's life. We want to bring out the commonality of experiences in families and societies, and at the same time we want to appreciate differences that can be shared.

By moving from tall tales and family stories to utopian narratives, we try to show that change is possible with hope and cooperation. Self-transformation is only possible through social transformation, for if society does not allow for experimentation and innovation, what seems to be reform and change is really fraud and self-deception. A static society or society that does not recognize the value of relativity will permit not a transformation but only a reinforcement of the status quo. In conservative societies there is only role-playing, a switching of roles while power is maintained by elite groups. In progressive societies, all roles are questioned and constantly adapted to the needs of the majority of the people. New roles and identities are sought and pursued so that the rules and limits of society are tested. This testing is different from the arbitrary tests children must undergo to fit into boxes and jobs prepared for them by a socioeconomic system that is basically concerned with its own preservation.

Our storytelling wants to preserve the value of self-transformation and social reform. Therefore, we reserve and guard space to play with those forces that play with us.

Tall Tales Based on U.S. Folklore

It is often thought that tall tales—the boasting of individuals and the exaggeration of actual incidents—are characteristic mainly of U.S. culture. But nothing could be further from the truth. If we recall some of the exploits of the Greek gods, it is easy to realize that most of their stories and tales told about them are fabrications meant to endow them with aura and power. It is therefore important to stress that words can empower both the storyteller and the characters within the story.

We stretch words into narratives that make our lives fascinating and incredible. Wishes are embodied in the stories so that we appear better or more interesting than we are. The plots take twists and turns that incorporate alternatives that we have not experienced. Although tall tales are often likened to lies, they are really daring tests of the credibility of the listeners and the inventiveness of the teller. The limits of truth are constantly being tested through exaggeration and fabrication. The humor of the tall tale explodes the boundaries of arbitrary rules, and this is why the tall tale often engenders a belly laugh from the listener. Such laughter mocks authority and breaks the rules of decorum. In fact, tall tales follow no rules, and any experience or person can be turned into the joke of the narrative, which makes it very dangerous but also delectable.

One of our sessions is therefore devoted to U.S. tall tales, which are closely connected to the legend tradition in the United States. Many of the heroes were common people who had extraordinary talents, were courageous, and were often nonconformists. They may have never existed in reality as depicted in the stories, yet they did exist in the imagination of hundreds and thousands of people who spread these tales for different reasons. Either they needed heroes and heroines as "gods" who might provide hope in their lives or they may have actually met unusual people like the characters in these tales, and thus the characters became real figures to whom they could relate. Not only could they relate to the stories of these figures, but they also embellished them. How many of us have met strange and different people, even in our immediate family, who have prompted us to tell stories about them? How many of us have seen common people do extraordinary things? How many of us have related their adventures time and again, often changing our stories? We are attracted to the unusual and uncanny in our lives because they hint that life can be an adventure and that we, too, can make our lives more adventurous. We preserve U.S. folklore and the tall tales because they remind us that there have always been unique individuals who have exceeded the limits of reality and challenge our imagination. In many ways, the legends and tall tales that have been fabricated reveal more truths about U.S. history than the so-called objective histories.

For some of the better anthologies of U.S. folklore see B. A. Botkin's *A Treasury of American Folklore,* Robert San Souci's *Cut from the Same Cloth: American Women of Myth, Legend, and Tall Tale,* and Catherine Peck's *Treasury of North American Folktales.* They contain marvelous tales about Paul Bunyan, Annie Christmas, Sal Fink, Bess Call, Davy Crockett, Daniel Boone, Kit Carson, Old Sally Cato, Pecos Bill, Mike Fink, Billy Hickok, Johnny Appleseed, and others.

Basic Structure of the Session

Fantastic binominal: Ask students for names of famous people, presidents, actors, or athletes. Ask what makes a person famous or notorious. Can a famous person be notorious? Try to talk about historical characters, local heroes, and current events. Put a list of about eight famous people on the board. Then ask for a thing or a place. Ask them to choose the famous person and then tell a tall tale about the person as a model tale. Repeat the game but have them write stories.

Tell a tale of Annie Christmas: For the first U.S. tall tale I suggest the following one about Annie Christmas because it is closely related to the U.S. legends that we have and it also introduces an African American woman as the major protagonist.

Annie Christmas Stems the Tide

Annie Christmas lit up the streets wherever she went in New Orleans. It wasn't just because she was seven feet tall and always wore a bright red, green, or golden satin dress trimmed with all kinds of bright ornaments. It wasn't just because she always had her twelve children, six sons and six daughters, escort her, six on the right, and six on the left, wherever she went. It was because she was the strongest, feistiest, happiest, and bravest woman that ever paraded along the banks of the Mississippi, which she declared to be her own river. Some say she had no right to lay a claim to that big river. But I say she did, and let me tell you why.

Annie Christmas was born somewhere in the Delta swamps at the base of the Mississippi some time in and around 1850. But no one was certain where and when she was born because Annie Christmas seemed ageless. She just appeared one day along the banks of the Mississippi in New Orleans, and she began loading bales of cotton onto the riverboats faster than any man, animal, or reptile could. Whether a man was black or white, he lived in fear of Annie Christmas, but she had no fear of men, and when she fell in love, she acted like a thunderbolt, and her man felt her passion and power. Well, to tell the truth, some say she loved her six husbands to death, and at one time, she became so fearful of her own strength that she decided to stop marrying after she had her twelfth child and lost her sixth husband.

Annie was tough, and she worked hard. One time, Mike Fink, who was one of the great hunters and roughest frontiersmen in the South, came down to New Orleans from Kentucky. When he was watching the men loading the boats with cotton, he was astonished to see Annie Christmas doing double the work of the men.

"Hey, what you doing that for?" he cried out. "You should be in the kitchen cooking somethin' good for real men."

Now, the trouble with Mike Fink was always his big mouth, because he liked to boast about how great a shooter he was and how he could wrestle grizzlies to the ground, and nobody in New Orleans had ever seen him in action. So he thought he could always get by just on his looks, and he was a goodly built man. But he never counted on meeting Annie Christmas, who stood up and placed her hands on her hips when she heard him call out.

"What did you say, boy?" she asked.

Mike Fink had never seen a woman seven feet tall with bulging muscles, and even though he was a good six feet and strong as an ox himself, he was taken aback when he saw how powerful Annie Christmas was.

"Cat got your tongue?" Annie said. "How'd you like me to fling you on that boat over there?"

"It's a nice day, isn't it?" Mike Fink stuttered and started backing up.

"It's a nice day," Annie responded, "and I think me and the boys here need something to drink and eat. How 'bout you going into the kitchen over there and making us a meal?"

Annie flexed her muscles, and Mike Fink's jaw dropped.

"Glad to, glad to," Mike said, and he backed out of there all the way to Kentucky and never showed his face in New Orleans after that.

Annie Christmas just laughed.

"I'm not going to Kentucky just to get a meal out of Mike Fink!"

No, indeed, she kept working on the docks until she had enough money to buy a keelboat that could carry cotton and other goods up and down the Mississippi. A keelboat is a large flat boat made out of logs, and Annie and her children knew how to navigate that river from New Orleans all the way up to Minnesota. And they had many an adventure that I'd like to tell you about one day, but for now, let me tell you how she saved New Orleans and laid claim to the river.

Now I'm not sure what year it was. Maybe it was 1880. Maybe 1881. Don't matter. What matters is that it was a rainy spring, and Annie Christmas was all alone way up near Minnesota. Her children had all gone and married themselves off, and she was returning to New Orleans on her keelboat with clothes and food for some customers in New Orleans. But she was having a difficult time of it because it was raining cats and dogs up north, and the river was rising and acting up. Everyone up there in Minnesota told her to dock her boat because the rain would not let up and the river would become ferocious.

"In seven days time it will rise up like a tidal wave and rush down south and flood all the towns in Louisiana!"

"It will wipe New Orleans off the face of the map!"

When Annie Christmas heard that her favorite city was threatened, she cried out, "It's my river and my city, and I take responsibility for this here river! I'll ride her down south and stop her shenanigans!"

"You can't do that," the people cried.

"You wait and see," she replied.

So Annie Christmas jumped on top of her keelboat, and she rode that bucking river as though it were a wild horse that needed taming. The Mississippi flung her here and there and everywhere. She almost drowned a hundred times and was knocked off her keelboat five hundred times. But Annie Christmas was a fighter and a survivor, and she finally made it to New Orleans, three days before the floods were going to arrive.

New Orleans was quiet and peaceful, and nobody knew the floods were coming.

"Get up!" she shouted. "If you don't start packing bags of sand along the shores, you won't have a city anymore!"

Scared and frightened, the people of New Orleans jumped out of their beds and began packing the banks of the Mississippi with bags of sand. In the meantime, Annie Christmas called out to her sons and daughters and said to them, "You've been lazy long enough. Now come with me. We're going to build a damn and redirect this wild river toward Texas."

"Why Texas?" one of her sons asked.

"That's just one big desert, son," she answered. "And they could use some water. Besides they got too many gamblers and crooks there, and maybe the water will wipe them away."

Well, you wouldn't have believed your eyes even if you had been there. Annie Christmas took her six huge daughters and six huge sons, and they went a hundred miles north of New Orleans, and within two days they built a gigantic dam covering the Mississippi. Then Annie Christmas showed them how to dig a riverbed heading toward Texas, and they took their shovels and pikes, and within a day there was a sort of canal leading off to Texas.

Just as they finished, they could hear the water rumbling, grumbling, thundering, plundering, roaring, and soaring.

"Here she comes!" Annie Christmas yelled, and just as the first tidal wave hit the dam and bounced off the walls, she jumped on top of it and began wrestling it to the ground. The water ran all over her, but she bounced up and grabbed hold of the tip of the wave and held it in a headlock, forcing the water to enter the riverbed and the canal toward Texas. Up and under she went, but Annie Christmas managed to drag the water away from the walls of the dam toward Texas. She waged a huge battle and almost drowned a thousand times, but she always came back up riding the water until it was clear that the Mississippi would not flood New Orleans.

Annie Christmas disappeared at the end of the day, but her body was never found. Some say she drowned. Some say she became part of the Mississippi, and that's why it's never threatened New Orleans again. Her six daughters and six sons refused to hold a funeral for her.

"She's still alive in our hearts," they declared. And all the people of New Orleans gave their blessing, and to this day they believe that Annie Christmas is still alive.

Discussion: Did Annie Christmas really live? Did Mike Fink really live? Why were stories spread about these characters? Why was the Mississippi River so important? Is it still important? How often are there floods?

Tell a tale of Mike Fink: The second tall tale I recommend is one about Mike Fink, an unusual figure, who may or may not have lived in Kentucky. This version is adapted from Ben Casseday's *The History of Louisville.*

The Adventures of Mike Fink

Now you've heard all about Annie Christmas and how she scared the living daylights out of Mike Fink. Let me tell you, this was no ordinary feat because Mike Fink was no ordinary man. He was one of the most notorious frontiersmen and bargemen in the entire South. He could navigate the Mississippi or any river in the South with the best of the boatsmen. He could shoot and hunt as well as Davy Crockett and Daniel Boone. He could drink and curse and boast with the best of the rugged pioneers. He had a little of the devil in him, and when he grew older, he was always getting into trouble with the law. But, wait, I'm getting ahead of my story.

Mike Fink was actually born in a city, the city of Pittsburgh, Pennsylvania, sometime around 1840 or so. Nobody knows exactly when, but we do know that, as a young boy, he became a scout for the U.S. Calvary and was able to track down enemies of the settlements and any kind of beast that haunted the forests. While he was working as a scout, he came across many a river and soon took up part-time work as a boatsman. Well, he fell in love with the free and wild life of the sailors and bargemen and gave up the life of the scout. His greatest dream was to go to New Orleans down the Mississippi because he heard that the women there were mighty pretty and they all spoke French and that the living was easy. But that's where he met Annie Christmas, who put him in his place, and he stayed away from New Orleans and the Mississippi after his encounter with that strong lady.

But there were other rivers and other states, and Mike soon made Kentucky his home and became known as one of the best riflemen and boatsmen in the state. Big and powerful, Mike loved to drink and tell jokes. He could drink a gallon of whisky in twenty-four hours and tell many a good joke. If his listeners didn't laugh when he told them a funny story, he gave them a beating. They didn't laugh at that, but after they received a drubbing they always remembered to laugh at his stories.

Well, Mike also loved to play practical jokes, and one time he was drifting down the Ohio River on his barge, and he saw a flock of sheep grazing on the shore. He had run out of food, and he thought those sheep would make a tasty meal for him and his men, but he didn't feel like buying the sheep from the farmer. So, in the evening he landed his boat and took a batch of tar that he had been carrying with him and went ashore. After he captured about five or six of the sheep, he smeared their noses and faces with the tar and stuck some down their throats. He then returned to his boat. The next morning he sent one of his men to the farmer.

"Hey, you better get down to the fields to see what's goin' on with your sheep!" the man said. "They look mighty sick to me."

As soon as the farmer got dressed, he rushed to the field, where he saw Mike Fink and some of his men examining the sheep. What's more, he saw that some of his sheep were jumping up and down, bleating, rubbing their noses on the ground, and bumping into each other. The farmer was puzzled and turned to Mike.

"Hey, do you have any idea what the matter is with my sheep?" he asked.

"Don't you know?" Mike replied very gravely.

"Nope," the farmer said. "No idea."

"Did you ever hear of the black murrain?" Mike whispered, as if he didn't want the news to travel.

"Yes," responded the farmer.

"Well, your sheep have got it!" Mike declared. "All the sheep up the river's got it bad. They're dying like rotten dogs—hundreds a day!"

"Terrible! What am I goin' to do?" asked the farmer. "Is there some sort of a cure?"

"Only one as far as I know," said Mike. "The murrain disease can spread quickly, and if you don't shoot the sheep that have got it right away, they'll give the disease to the rest of the flock. Better shoot all those sheep that are infected right away and save the flock. They're gonna die anyway."

"But there's no doctor or man who can tell which sheep are infected and which aren't," the farmer said.

"Hey, my name's Mike Fink!"

And that answer was response enough because Mike Fink was famous throughout Kentucky and Ohio, and people thought he could do just about anything. So the farmer begged Mike to shoot the infected sheep and throw them into the river. That was exactly what Mike wanted, but he pretended to resist.

"It might be a mistake," he said. "The sheep might get well. I don't like to shoot so many sheep. Maybe we better get another opinion here."

"No, no," said the farmer.

Mike continued to resist until the farmer also promised him a couple of gallons of peach brandy if he would do it, and do it fast. Well, Mike finally shot some of the sheep, and he and his men threw them into the water not too far from his flat boat, and the farmer gave him the brandy. Later in the day Mike and his men hauled the sheep aboard the boat and went merrily gliding down the river.

Some say that Mike Fink had no respect for anyone's property or the law. He kept playing so many of his so-called practical jokes and stealing other people's goods that the sheriff of Louisville finally offered a reward for his capture. Mike Fink's jokes were not a laughing matter. But he was not an easy man to arrest.

One day, when his boat was moored at Louisville, an old friend came to him and told him that his family was starving and had no money. Then Mike, who was especially kind to his friends, said, "Don't you worry about that. You go to the sheriff's office and tell the sheriff that you've captured me and want the reward."

"I can't do that," his friend said.

"Don't you worry about me," Mike Fink said. "I'll get free even if they arrest me."

So his friend went to the sheriff and told him where Mike Fink's boat was moored. The sheriff went with some of his men to Mike's boat and placed him under arrest. However, Mike said, "I'll only come with you if you bring me in with my men and barge. That's the only way I'll feel comfortable."

The sheriff agreed, and he fetched a long wagon with oxen attached to it. The boat was set on the wagon, and Mike and his men, with their long poles ready, as if they were still going to float down the river, were put on board, with Mike in the stern. Now the wagon had to climb a hill to the courthouse, and the oxen pulled and pulled and managed to make it up this hill when all of a sudden the booming voice of Mike cried out, "Set poles!" and the end of every long pole was set firmly in the thick mud.

"Back her up!" roared Mike, and down the hill went the wagon, the oxen, the men, and Mike. Once at the bottom of the hill, the sheriff and his men started yelling and complaining. They warned him they would shoot if he dared try anything again. So the oxen pulled and pulled again until they had almost reached the top of the hill when Mike cried out again, "Back her up!" And once more, the wagon rolled backward to the bottom of the hill. A third attempt, however, was successful, and Mike reached the courthouse and was brought before the judge.

"Mike Fink," the judge said. "You're a menace to society. Do you know how many complaints have been filed against you?"

"No, your honor, but I got just as many complaints against the people who filed complaints against me."

Well, the judge didn't laugh at Mike Fink's joke, and that made Mike angry. He grabbed hold of the judge and gave him a good drubbing while his men knocked the rifles out of the hands of the sheriff and his posse. When Mike was done, they ran out of the courthouse, jumped on to their barge, and slid down the hill until they hit water. As they sailed away, Mike waved his red bandanna, which he had fixed on one of his poles, and promised to call again at Louisville whenever the judge had learned to laugh at his jokes.

Discussion: Was Mike Fink a real person? Were there many tales told about characters like Mike Fink in the South and West? Is Mike Fink a

criminal? Did many men act like he did? Should he have been punished? Why does he get away with his jokes? Who told these stories
about Mike Fink? Why?

Chair game: Using one of the names on the board, prompt the students
to tell a tall tale by stretching an ordinary experience in which the person is
involved. If possible, try to make sure that you have some legendary hero
or heroine of your region as one of the possibilities. For instance, in Minnesota it would probably be Paul Bunyan. In Massachusetts, it might be
Paul Revere, and in Illinois, Casey Jones. There are also many legendary
inventors, sports figures, and actors.

Improvisation and theater games led by the teaching artist: Our focus
here is the exaggeration game. Divide the class into three groups and
have the groups sit on the ground, forming circles. The first student is
to begin telling about an ordinary event such as, "I went to school
today." The second student is to take the ordinary event and change it
into something extraordinary: "Along the way I met a giraffe who told
me that school was cancelled." Each student is to add a sentence or two
after the explosion of the extraordinary. The students should continue
the tale until one of the students decides to bring it to an end. One of
the students from the group is to share the story with the other two
groups after they have completed their tales. The idea behind this game
is similar to Kafka's "The Metamorphosis," in which Gregor Samsa
awakes one day to find himself changed into a gigantic insect. What
happens when the extraordinary disturbs our ordinary lives?

Three tall tale skits: Have the students perform three skits.

Writing game: Ask the students to write the names of several legendary heroes or heroines on the board. Then ask them to imagine that
some legendary hero (Davy Crockett, Daniel Boone, Paul Bunyan,
John Henry, etc.) or heroine (Annie Oakley, Annie Christmas, Belle
Star) made his or her way into the twenty-first century and arrived in a
big city like New York, Chicago, Los Angeles, Washington, D.C., or
even Minneapolis. Write the names of the cities on the board and add
names that might be unfamiliar to the students. Provide some background material for the names. What would happen if there were a
catastrophe threatening the city? How would the hero or heroine react?
Encourage the students to use their imagination to tell a tall tale.

Tall Tales Based on Daily Occurrences and Family Stories

We rarely realize how magical our everyday lives are, how they are filled with surprises, strange happenings, tragic episodes, and ludicrous behavior. We are too future oriented to grasp the present. Yet there are ways we can hold time in our hands by paying attention to details that we might otherwise let slip by us. One way to realize the value of small things in life and our daily experiences is through storytelling—noting the past and present in diaries, journals, and notebooks and recalling these events through the spoken word.

Basic Structure of the Session

Fantastic binominal: Bring in newspapers and give each student a sheet or two. Ask several students to read their favorite headlines and choose two nouns from the headlines they read. Model a story based on two nouns that you have written on the board. After you have told your story, two students are to come to the board and write the two nouns from their headline. Students are to write stories based on the nouns. After the students have written their stories based on these nouns, and after three or four have told their stories before the class, the two students who chose the nouns are to read the short newspaper articles from which they took their nouns. If possible, try to encourage a discussion about the differences between the newspaper articles and the stories that the students have created.

Tell your own story: Think of an incident in your own life, and embellish it as best you can in a tall tale. I have told two stories in *Creative Storytelling* that I am fond of retelling. By now you have been leading different parts of the sessions. It is important to share some personal episode with the students, and of course it should be turned into a tall tale of some kind.

Swap tall tales in a circle: Explain the difference between lying and stretching the truth. If the students have difficulty with embroidering their tales, provide them with some examples. For instance, "This morning I got up, went to the bathroom, and began brushing my teeth. When I looked into the mirror, I saw my face, and all of a sudden my reflection began talking to me." Demonstrate how any real daily and ordinary experience can become marvelous. Dreams can come true.

Wishes need to be told and projected as possibilities. Nightmares can be overcome by telling them and acting them out.

Improvisation, theater games, and skits led by the teaching artist: This time each group is to be given a slip of paper that has written on it an ordinary, everyday activity that undergoes a change.

> Taking the bus to school: When you get into the bus, it begins flying.
> Shopping: You enter a store and the toys and articles begin talking and trying to buy you.
> Watching television: When you turn on the set and begin watching your favorite program, the characters invite you into the TV to become part of the show.

Each group is to take this ordinary activity and "stretch" it into a tall tale. The members are to sit in a circle and take turns telling the tale, with each student passing on part of the story to another until someone concludes it. Then the students are to decide how they want to reshape what they have just told into a skit. Once they have all agreed on the plot, they are to rehearse their skit and improvise. The students should be given about fifteen minutes to prepare their skits.

Writing game: Return to the newspapers that were distributed to the students. Ask them to read any headline or story in the newspaper. Then they are to make a tall tale out of the headline or article by stretching the truth. If there is time, they are to share their stories, first by reading the headline or article, and then by reading their stories. Their stories should be kept in their folders along with the headline or article.

The students have an assignment during the week. They are to collect as many family stories as possible, write them down, and bring them to school. Time should be set aside for them to polish their stories, to lengthen them, to revise them, and so forth. They are to keep the stories in their folders. They will be used in the session of week twenty-three.

To facilitate the collecting of family stories at home, the teachers at the Whittier School for the Arts and Marcy Open have developed forms to be used by the students.

Sample 1: Whittier School for the Arts

Directions: Find the oldest member of your family and ask the following questions. If you want more information, feel free to inquire further. Be sure to tell your interviewee the purpose of your lesson and have him or her feel as comfortable as possible. Take some notes and have fun!

1. What is your earliest childhood memory?
2. What is your favorite story from your parents' or your grandparents' life?
3. Who changed your life and what impact did it make on you?
4. What is your favorite family recipe and when is it served?
5. Do you own a favorite object or article of clothing and what is the story behind it?
6. How did your family members come to Minnesota?
7. Are there any fishing or sports stories? Give me the details.
8. Are there any special family remedies or healing techniques that are or were used in your household?
9. Have you ever been given any special recognition? (Awards, plaques, articles, ribbons, etc.)
10. What sad event(s) have you gained wisdom from?
11. What is a quote or saying that you live by?
12. Tell me your favorite joke, riddle, or tall tale.
13. Describe a neighbor that you'll never forget.
14. Do you have a nickname?

Remember to thank your interviewee for sharing his or her time, energy, and experiences.

Sample 2: Marcy Open School

Family stories have a great deal of power. They connect you to your past. Children and adults use stories to shape and reshape their lives. I hope these activities are enjoyed by all.

Do the following:

1. Look through a photo album and find an old picture that looks interesting. Find out information about the picture and write a story. Please bring the picture to class. Maybe your parents will not want to part with it. If so, perhaps you can bring in a photocopy of the picture. Old pictures are special and valuable.

2. Write one other family story. This story should have lots of details. Your story should be almost a page or more. It can be about anyone in your family. Remember the details! The story could be about a lesson your mom or dad learned as a child, family immigrations to this country, a family member's experience at war, or what your parents and grandparents remember about important events in history.

Sample 3: Marcy Open School

Spring Break Homework: Telling Our Stories Family stories have a great deal of power. They connect you to your past. Children and adults use stories to shape and reshape their lives. I hope these activities are enjoyed by all.

1. Interview a family member. First write down ten open-ended questions to ask a family member. Then do your interview.
2. Find out about and write down the origin of your name. When were you born? Who was there? Why were you given the name you have? What do your mother and father remember about the day you were born?
3. Write a story about *you*! It can be from the day your were born up until age five. Something you were told about yourself as an infant or as a toddler.
4. Write three other family stories. These stories should have lots of details. Each story should be almost a page. The stories can be about anyone in your family.

This is the month that we would like you to have a family evening at the school with dinner (pizza, snacks, etc.). The purpose of the evening is to share family stories, to get parents involved, to have them tell stories in a circle.

Family Tales

The family tales are not to be confused with tall tales, although many family tales are the stuff from which tall tales are made. It is important to stress that the tales to be shared are to be as authentic as possible. That is, the tales should come from the participants' experiences within their family and are important to be recalled and remembered. Each family has its own history, and the history is constituted generally by an oral tradition. The repetition of the tales generates a distinctive history that will mark the development of each member of the family.

A family story will be told differently by each member of a family, and it will be different on each occasion that it is told. The sociocultural context will influence the telling of the tale. For instance, the teller may simply want to describe to outsiders how unusual his or her family is, and the description might be altered or heightened depending on the audience. If a tale is told within a family, its purpose might be totally different. The tale might be told to recall a dead member of a family, to bring about reconciliation, or to boast about a certain feat. Within a classroom, the students may learn something about a classmate that will be helpful in their interactions. Too often students have no idea whatsoever of the background of their classmates and what might prompt them to act and behave as they do. A family tale will not solve problems or overcome conflicts within a classroom, but it might provide the basis for greater empathy among the students in a class. This empathy is important at a time when students are shuffled and shuttled about as though they are objects in a massive experiment to improve the human species. The result is that they feel more like guinea pigs than human beings who can learn to cooperate and decide things that are best for themselves.

Sometimes I have initiated the telling of family tales by telling "When Grandfather Becomes a Cat," mentioned by Gianni Rodari in *The Grammar of Fantasy*.[1] It is about a retired old man, a widower, who feels useless at home because everyone, the adults and children, are too busy to spend time with him. Therefore he goes to a small park in Rome that is a sanctuary for stray cats. When the grandfather ducks under an iron bar that separates the sanctuary from the street, he is immediately turned into a handsome gray cat and has the time of his life. After a few hours pass, he returns home, not as the grandfather but as the gray cat, and he is treated like a king. Everyone in the family pets him, and he is given choice pieces of meat and milk. As a grandfather he was a nothing. As a cat he is the center of attention in the home.

Like Rodari, I end the story at this point—the cat, happy at home. Then I ask the students whether grandfathers should be treated in this manner. Is the grandfather really happy as a cat? Should he change himself back into a grandfather? How can he do this? Would the grandfather be better off in a nursing home for the aged? How do we treat the aged in our society? Why don't grandparents live with their families?

Fantastic binominal: Ask the students for the names of members of a family: mother, father, stepmother, stepfather, brother, sister, stepbrother, stepsister, grandmother, grandfather, and so on. Ask the students for an object. For their story, ask them to choose one of the family members and connect him or her with an object, such as grandfather on the car, the car on the grandfather.

Tell a personal tale: Tell a personal tale about a crazy, wonderful person in your family, about a legendary person in your family, or about family incidents. Once again, it is important that the story is not a tall tale. It must be true in some fashion.

Circle is formed, family histories are shared: Students have been asked to collect family stories and histories at home during the week and to write them down at school or at home. The students are asked not to read their stories but to recall what they have written.

Improvisation and theater games led by the teaching artist:

1. The first group of students is to enact the storyteller's family story. The teaching artist is to participate in this play.
2. The second group of students is to enact the teacher's family story. The teacher is to participate in this play.
3. The third group is to choose one member's play by lottery and then dramatize this story.

Writing game: Tell the students to think of a family member about whom they want to write. Place this person in a strange situation or a strange city and country. What would she or he do if confronted by people who are totally different and have unusual customs? For instance, they don't say "hello" when they greet someone. They say "good-bye." They don't say "thank you." Instead, they say, "too bad." Write a story about the confusion experienced by the family member and how he or she manages to survive.

Pourquoi Tales

To a certain extent, the pourquoi tales are related to creation tales because their major purpose is to explain why people and animals developed certain features and characteristics. These tales can be found throughout the world and are generally part of the customary manner that a group, tribe, community, or region has developed to reveal so-called true explanations. Yet pourquoi tales are far from being the truth; they are related to the tall tale insofar as they are humorous and make use of exaggeration and farce. Often they are fables with a moral. Though there may be some plausibility in the story, the pourquoi tales are compelling because they are plausible and ironic. It is not so much the explanation that is important but the inventive and surprising manner in which the narrator pretends to provide evidence. The explanation is generally valid only if one stretches one's imagination. The plots often involve tricks, and many of the animals hark from the trickster tradition. The trick will be played to escape capture and simultaneously to clarify why the world is the way it is or why we are the way we are. The irony is, of course, that pourquoi tales can really never explain anything, even when we want them to do so.

Basic Structure of the Session
Fantastic binominal: Ask students for the names of animals, fish, or birds, such as mouse, shark, duck, beaver, or tiger. After five names are written on the board, ask the students to pose questions about the animals. For instance,

> Why does a mouse love cheese?
> Why does the shark have such big teeth?
> Why does a duck quack?
> Why does a beaver chop wood?
> Why does the tiger have stripes?

Explain to the students that the questions can serve as the basis for a fantastic binominal. Erase the names of the animals and ask the students for five more animals, fish, or birds and write the names on the board. Ask for a thing and then a preposition. The students are to choose one of the animals, fish, or birds and link it with the thing to form a pourquoi tale.

Tell a pourquoi tale: Tell one of the following pourquoi tales taken from *The Complete Fairy Tales of the Brothers Grimm* (3rd edition).

Why Dogs and Cats and Cats and Mice Are Enemies

A dog had loyally served the lion for many years. Therefore, the king of the animal realm thought he would reward his trustworthy servant with honors.

"Listen," he said to the dog one day, "from now on you will be counted among my nobles."

And he gave him a document made out of parchment, elegantly written and glossed with gold, that certified he was an aristocrat. The faithful dog was tremendously happy about all this and went to the cat, with whom he was on most familiar terms, and said to her, "My dear sister, the king has bestowed great honors on me and anointed me an aristocrat. He has given me a document made out of parchment, elegantly written and glossed with gold. Would you please be so kind and keep this document for me and look after it every now and then to make sure that it's not spoiled or stolen until I return to pick it up?"

The cat promised to do this and hid the document in a hole within a tall oak tree where it seemed to be very safe. Moreover, for the sake of her dear brother dog, she diligently checked to see whether the document might be spoiled by rain. Gradually, however, she forgot all about it and let the parchment be. About this time a hungry little mouse found it and nibbled bits of the parchment each day until it was completely torn and tattered.

Soon the dog came back to the cat and asked to have the parchment because he wanted to bring it to a tournament at the king's court. It was then that the cat discovered the catastrophe that the mouse had caused in the tall tree. The cat became so mad at the mouse, and the dog at the cat, that the cat swore she would be the mouse's enemy forever, and the dog swore he would be the cat's eternal enemy. Ever since that time they cannot stand another.

Why Dogs Sniff One Another

The lion had invited most of the animals to a meal, and when they began eating, some animals noticed that the pepper was missing. The lion immediately called upon one of the dogs who was sitting at the large table and told him to run quickly to the next city and fetch some pepper. The dog whined and was very annoyed that he had to leave behind such delicious food that he had already begun devouring with his eyes. However, he went off, otherwise, he would have been beaten. But instead of bringing pepper, he played a trick and ran away with the pepper.

The animals waited an hour and another hour, but the dog did not come. The lion became angry, and he sent the other dogs out to search for the dog with the pepper. As soon as they found him, they were to tear him to pieces. Moreover, they would never receive meat at the king's table any more, only bones, until they found the dog with the pepper and took revenge. Ever since this time dogs sniff each other to try to find the dog with the pepper. But they have yet to find him.

Tell another pourquoi tale: Tell this pourquoi tale adapted from Alcée Fortier's *Louisiana Folk-Tales.*

Why Buzzards Are Bald

Do you know why buzzards are bald? No? Well, I'm going to tell you.

Once upon a time Madam Buzzard was sitting on her nest in an oak tree. Her husband was a good-for-nothing fellow, and she was always starving. At the foot of the tree there was a big hole in which a rabbit was living. Well, Brother Rabbit was large and fat, and every time Madam Buzzard saw him, she wished she could eat him. One day, while Brother Rabbit was sleeping, she took some moss and bricks and closed the hole in the tree. Then Brother Rabbit would not be able to get out and would die of hunger.

When Brother Rabbit woke up and found that he was shut up in the hole, he begged Madam Buzzard to let him out, but she replied each time, "I'm hungry, and I must eat the flesh on your bones."

When Brother Rabbit saw that it was of no use to beg, he stopped speaking, while Madam Buzzard was so glad she had caught Brother Rabbit that she licked her lips when she thought of the good dinner she would make out of the poor rabbit. After a while she did not hear Brother Rabbit move, and she thought he was dead and smothered. So she took away the moss and the bricks that had closed the hole. When she began to go down the opening, however, Brother Rabbit made one jump and got out. After running some distance, he cried out, "You see, you're the one who's caught now. Not me!"

He ran away and went to stay at the home of one of his friends because he was afraid to go back to the oak tree near Madam Buzzard. Some days later, Madam Buzzard, who had forgotten all about the incident with Brother Rabbit, went to take a walk with her children, who had all come out of their shells. They passed near the house of Brother Rabbit's friend. Brother Rabbit was glad, and he thought of how he might take vengeance on Madam Buzzard. He ran into the kitchen and took a large tin pan full of burning embers and hot ashes. When Madam Buzzard and her children passed near the kitchen, he threw all the ashes on them to burn them. Well, you know that buzzards have thick feathers except on the top of their heads. They shook off the embers and ashes, but not quick enough to prevent the feathers on their heads from burning down to the skin.

This is why buzzards are bald and never eat the bones of rabbits.

Discussion: Ask students if they know pourquoi tales. In the discussion the emphasis should be placed on trying to stimulate children's curiosity about why things are the way they are and what might have happened if things had been different. Do we know why birds fly? Do we know why people use forks, knives, and spoons? Do we know why people are so different in their habits and customs?

Chair game: There was once a wonderful child who could never stop asking why. Why? Why? Why? One Christmas eve she hid behind the tree, and at midnight Santa came sliding down the chimney and was greeted with a "why." Why do you always bring presents, Santa? Why? Why?

Improvisation, theater games, and skits led by the teaching artist: Use the following story as a prompt for the students:

There is a group of animals living harmoniously in a jungle. Humans or a corporation run by a sinister man called Ratherford Rumble wants the jungle for its wood and herbs. (Big business interests.) Bulldozers, cranes, and people are going to take over the jungle for the benefit of civilization. The animals try to find out why the humans are doing this and want to know the meaning of civilization and progress, but they do not succeed. The only way the animals can save themselves is if they journey to Mount Paradise and pick a rose from the top of the mountain.

Once they have obtained this rose and return to the jungle, they must circle the jungle, and its scent and aroma will bring about a wall of invisibility and invincibility. The jungle can no longer be seen by the humans. The animals are safe, as is the jungle.

Each group is to take this story, and one group rewrites it in the past, the second present, and the third in the future. Students can invent their own animals and animal masks and costumes. For instance, they can dig into the past and have dinosaurs. They can move to the future and invent strange beasts on another planet. The story can be shifted, and perhaps in the future story, it could be that the animals of a particular planet fear invasion by earthlings.

This tale and its enactment should prep the students for journey plays later in the spring.

Writing game: Each student is to rewrite the jungle story in his or her own words and to change it any way he or she wants.

Utopian Tales: When Wishes Go Awry

Utopian tales are not only about the projections of an ideal society; they are also tales about personal wish fulfillment and hope. A wish is always prompted by the need and desire for change and improvement. To be sure, there are evil wishes, like wishes for revenge or for the defeat of an enemy. These wishes, however, are more like curses than wishes, which generally tend to be more positive and impel us to pursue the object of desire even if there is no magical help or good fortune. Often we place conditions on our selves when we make a wish. For instance, we often say,

"I'll stop eating ice cream for a year, if I can somehow get that gold-trimmed dress."

"I'll get straight A's, if I can somehow find the money to buy a Porsche."

"I won't tease my sister for a year, if my parents will take me to Disneyland."

"I'll give a million dollars to different charities, if I win the lottery."

These are very individualistic wishes, but we also make socially minded wishes, such as,

> "If the war stops, I shall dedicate my life as a doctor to helping people."
> "If all people become vegetarians, I shall look after stray animals."
> "If I were given a million dollars by a stranger, I would set up homes for poor refugees."

We are often sure of what we would wish for, and yet, when presented with the opportunity to have our wishes fulfilled, we betray ourselves or do not know what to do with our good fortune. Sometimes it is best not to have our wishes fulfilled because they keep propelling us to change conditions with our own volition and power.

Basic Structure of the Session

Fantastic binominal: Take out a coin from your pocket and pretend it is a magic coin. Tell the students that the coin can provide three wishes to anyone who is kind for one entire year. In keeping with the tall tale tradition, confide in the students that you are in the third month of being kind to other people, but you are worried about whether you will succeed. Ask the students for names of magic objects, and ask them what the magic of the objects are and what one would have to do to obtain a magic object. Write the magic objects on the board. Then ask the students for a person, animal, or place to begin a fantastic binominal. The students are to link the magic objects with a person, animal, or place.

Retelling of "The Three Wishes": Tell the tale of "The Three Wishes," adapted from Joseph Jacobs's *More English Fairy Tales.*

The Three Wishes

Once upon a time, and to be sure it was a very long time ago, a poor woodcutter was living in a large forest, and every day of his life he went out to cut down trees. Now one day he started out, and his good wife filled his knapsack with food and drink so he could refresh himself during the day. Then he slung the sack over his back and trudged off into the woods. He had marked out a huge oak, which, he thought, would furnish a good deal of timber when he was done chopping it down. As soon as he arrived at the tree, he took his axe in his hand and swung it around his head as though he wanted to cut down the tree with one stroke. However, he had not given one blow when, all of a sudden, he heard some pitiful moans and groans and pleas. Right before his nose he saw a fairy, who begged him and pleaded to spare the tree. As you might imagine, he was dazed with wonderment and fright, and he couldn't open his mouth to utter a word. Finally, he found his tongue and said, "Well, there's no reason for me to harm this tree. No harm to me."

"You've done better for yourself than you know," the fairy replied. "To show I'm not ungrateful, I'm going to grant you your next three wishes whatever they may be."

Upon saying this, the fairy vanished from sight. The woodsman slung his knapsack over his shoulder and started for home. The way was long, and the woodsman kept thinking about the wonderful thing that had happened to him. He could not get it out of his head, which was still whirling by the time he got home so that he wished for nothing than just to sit down and rest. Maybe, too, this was the trick of the fairy. Who can tell? Anyhow he sat down by the blazing fire, and he started to feel hungry even though it was a long time before supper.

"Don't you have anything for supper?" he asked his wife.

"It won't be ready for a couple of hours yet," she responded.

"Ah!" groaned the woodsman. "I wish I had a huge portion of black pudding right before me!"

No sooner had he said these words, when *clatter, clatter, clatter,* what should come down the chimney but a gigantic bowl of the finest black pudding a man's heart could ever wish for. If you think the woodsman was surprised as he stared at the pudding, you should have seen his astonished wife's face!

"What's all this?" she asked.

All at once the woodsman remembered the fairy he had met that morning, and he told his tale from beginning to end, and as he told it, his good wife glowered and glowered, and when he came to the end, she burst out, "You're nothing but a fool, John, nothing but a fool! I wish the pudding was stuck to your nose. I do indeed!"

And before you could say Jack Robinson, there the good man sat, and his nose was longer and covered completely with black pudding.

He tried to pull off the pudding, but it stuck, and they both pulled and pulled until they nearly pulled the nose off. But the pudding stuck.

"What's to be done now?" he said.

"Well, you don't look all that bad," she replied looking hard at him.

But the woodsman took a look in a mirror and almost fainted. He realized that if he was going to make a wish, he had better do it in a hurry. And wish he did that the black pudding might come off his nose. Well, within seconds, the pudding lay in a large bowl on the table. Even though the good man didn't get to ride in a golden coach and the good woman didn't get to wear a dress in silk and satin, they had at least for their supper as fine a black pudding as a man's heart could desire.

Read a different version: Another interesting variant can be found in the collection of *Folktales from Northern India,* collected by William Crooke and Pandit Ram Gharib Chaube.

The Three Wishes There was once a very poor man who made his living by cutting wood in the forest. One day, as he was working hard in utmost misery, the gods Mahadeva and Parvati passed by, and Parvati said to her husband, "You are always blessing someone. Now give a blessing to this poor creature."

"In this life everyone gets his due, and it is useless granting favors to a miserable boor like this," Mahadeva responded.

But Parvati, who had a kind heart, insisted, and at last Mahadeva said to the woodcutter, "Ask for any favor you desire."

"My wife is a witch," the man said, "and I don't dare ask for a favor without consulting her."

"You may consult her," Mahadeva replied, "and when you want to make a wish, spread white plaster on a piece of ground, wash yourself, sit in the middle of the white ground, and make your wish. But you can only ask once, and your wife and son may ask, too."

The woodcutter went home and told his wife what had happened.

"I must have my wish first," she said.

So she did has the god had ordered, and she prayed, "Oh Lord, may my body be turned into gold."

And she got just what she wished. Just then the king of the country, the Raja, was passing by on his elephant, and as he looked into the house of the woodcutter, he saw this woman of gold, and he fell in love with her. So he sent his servants, and they seized her, placed her in a litter, and carried her off to the palace.

When the woodcutter saw that he lost his wife, he too did as the god had ordered and prayed, "Oh Lord, may my wife be turned into a pig."

And so it was.

When the servants opened the litter to take her to the Raja, they found only a dirty pig inside, and when the door to the litter was opened, she ran away and returned to her own house.

As soon her son saw this loathsome animal enter the house, he rushed at her with a club, but his father stopped him and said, "This is your mother, who has been turned into a pig by my wish because I wanted to save her from the Raja. Now you must make your wish."

Then the boy prayed, "Oh Lord, turn my mother into her original shape."

And so it was.

Then Mahadeva said to Parvati, "Now you see why it's useless to try to help miserable creatures like these."

Discussion: Why are the wishes given? Why are the wishes not fulfilled? Whose fault is it?

Chair game: Once there was a poor woman who had three children. She earned her living by sewing, but she could not earn enough to feed them, no matter how hard she worked. One day, on the poor woman's way to work, a very old lady fell in the middle of the street, and the poor woman helped her and brought her to a hospital: "Bless you," said the old lady, "today, and only today, you will have three wishes."

Improvisation and theater games led by the teaching artist: Divide the class into three groups. One member of each group pretends to be a fairy with magic powers and the other members are to decide among themselves what kind of group or family they are. However, they are to be poor or suffering and in need of help. The fairy grants them three wishes, but they do not know how to use them.

Three skits based on the wishing tales and chair game: Have the students perform three skits.

Ask the students for about five wishes: Write the wishes on the board. Ask the students to write a story about how they might be able to have their wishes fulfilled.

Fig. 8.1 Teaching artist Signey Harriday giving advice to a student before a play at Marcy Open School.

8

CREATIVE DRAMA, CROSSING BRIDGES
FESTIVAL, AND EVALUATION

The final weeks of the Neighborhood Bridges program are focused on the preparation for a play, which the students develop on their own with the guidance of the teaching artist, teacher, and set designer. By this time the students have already improvised numerous skits and have been coached in acting and directing. The play that they produce is not intended to be a grand production, nor is it scripted. It is a work in progress that will constantly change up through the day of its performance. Our emphasis is on process, on animating the students to keep changing and improving their works, whether they are stories, skits, illustrations, poems, and so on. They have gradually learned to develop and hone their talents and skills throughout the year, and now we want the three groups in each class to come together as one large group to produce a play prompted by open-ended stories that we present.

During the last month of the program we offer the students a selection of three to four stories, and we ask them to adapt the tales first by setting them in the past, the present, and the future and altering characters and plots. Each group in the class is responsible for each different time period. The stories we tell are often interrupted toward the end so that the students do not necessarily know the ending and have to supply their own endings. Sometimes we tell the complete story because it is sufficient to ask them to adapt the story in another time period. The students are given total freedom in reshaping and transforming the characters, plot, background, and ending of the story. The changes are made through discussions and rehearsals.

Once the three different versions are performed by the three different groups, we bring all the students together and brainstorm how all three groups can use the ideas from the three different plays to form a new play in which all the students will act. As soon as we decide more or less on how the plot will be developed and what characters will be needed, we write the characters and scenes on the board and begin to test out the ideas of the students by improvising the different scenes. The roles are not assigned at the beginning. After a week or two of improvisation with the students switching roles, we ask them to decide on how they want the roles to be chosen.

As soon as we have decided on the roles, the basic plotline of the play, and the setting, we invite a set designer from the Children's Theatre Company into the class to help us design the sets and costumes that will be made from found materials brought in from homes, streets, and vacant lots.

"How Six Made Their Way in the World" and "Seven Brooms"

We generally have a folder of several tales that the teaching artist can select as possibilities for the play. Both of the suggested tales presented here are ones that demand collective and individual action against exploitation. It is important that the students be encouraged to play with the roles and motifs. For instance, because "How Six Made Their Way in the World" involves mainly male protagonists, we encourage the students to choose women as protagonists as well. Instead of a male soldier, they may experiment with a female soldier. Instead of a sharpshooter, we might have a thrower who can hit any target in the world. In "Seven Brooms" the theme of sexism is already pronounced, and it may be interesting to stop the story at the point where Fortuna is given three tasks to fulfill to see what ideas the students conceive and how they will work through problems. Both stories can also be told in their entirety because there are many characters and motifs that lend themselves to experimentation just by changing the time and setting. The students vote on which one of the tales they want to adapt.

Fantastic binominal: This may be a good time to ask students to think of all the monsters or evil characters they know. Write the names of about ten monsters (giants, ogres, witches, Dracula, Voldemort, Hitler, Darth Vader) on the board. Then ask the students for a place or object. Suggest that the tale they write should be about the overcoming of the monster. Why is he or she evil? What is evil? What does the monster represent? How can evil be overcome?

First story: Tell "How Six Made Their Way in the World" adapted from *The Complete Fairy Tales of the Brothers Grimm.* This tale either should be told in its entirety or should be stopped just as the princess is about to win the race, as indicated below.

How Six Made Their Way in the World

Once upon a time there was a man who had mastered all kinds of skills and worked hard. One day the king drafted him to serve in his army, for he needed all the hardworking men he could find. Well, this man fought in the war for three long years, and he fought bravely and was wounded many times. But when the war was over, he was discharged and received just three pennies for traveling expenses.

"Just you wait!" he cried out to the king's officers. "I won't put up with this. If I find the right people, I'll force the king to turn over all the treasures of his kingdom to me."

Full of rage he went into the forest, and there he saw a man tearing up six trees as if they were blades of wheat. "Will you come and travel with me?" he asked. "I could use a man like you and I'll pay you well."

"Yes," the man answered. "But first I want to bring this little bundle of firewood home to my mother." He took one of the trees and wrapped it around the others, lifted the bundle onto his shoulders and carried it away. Then he returned and went off with his new friend, who said, "We two shall certainly make our way anywhere in the world."

After they had walked for a while, they found a huntsman who was kneeling down and taking aim with his gun at something.

"Huntsman, what are you going to shoot?" the master asked him.

"There's a fly sitting on the branch of an oak tree two miles from here. I want to shoot out its left eye," he answered.

"Oh, come with me," said the man. "If we three stick together, we'll certainly make our way anywhere in the world."

The huntsman was willing and went with him. As they approached seven windmills, they saw the sails rotating swiftly, even though no wind was coming from any direction and no leaves were stirring.

"What in the world can be driving those windmills? There's not a breeze around," the man said. He continued on with his companions for about two miles, and then they saw a man sitting on a tree. He was holding one nostril closed while blowing through the other.

"My goodness! What are you doing up there?" the man asked.

"Two miles from here are seven windmills," he said. "I'm blowing them so that they'll turn."

"Oh, come with me," said the man. "If we four stick together, we'll certainly make our way anywhere in the world."

So the blower got down from the tree and went along with them. After some time they saw a man standing on one leg, while the other leg was lying unbuckled on the ground next to him.

"You've made things comfortable for yourself," said the man. "Time for a rest, I suppose?"

"I'm a runner," he answered, "and I've unbuckled my leg so that I don't run too fast. When I run with two legs, I go faster than any bird can fly."

"Oh, come with me. If we five stick together, we shall certainly make our way anywhere in the world."

Now the six came to a city where the king had proclaimed that whoever ran a race against his daughter and won would become her husband. But whoever lost would have to pay for it with his head. Then the man appeared before the king and said, "I want to race but under he condition that one of my servants runs for me."

The king answered, "Then his life must also be placed at stake, and you and he will forfeit your lives if you lose."

When they agreed on the terms and everything was set the master buckled on the runner's other leg and said to him, "Now show us how quick you are and help us win."

The runner and the king's daughter were both given jugs and set off running at the same time. Yet within seconds after the king's daughter had run but a short stretch, the spectators could no longer see the runner, for he soared by them like the wind. In a short time he arrived at the spring, filled the jug with water, and turned around. Halfway back, however, he was overcome by fatigue, put the jug on the ground, lay down, and fell asleep. For his pillow he had taken a dead horse's skull that had been lying on the ground so that he would not be too comfortable and would wake up in time to continue the race. In the meantime, the king's daughter, who was much better at running than ordinary people, had reached the spring and was hurrying back with her jug of water. When she saw the runner lying asleep on the ground, she was delighted and said, "Now the enemy's been delivered into my hands." She emptied his jug and continued running.

Everything would have been lost for the runner if the huntsman had not by chance been standing on top of the castle and if he had not seen everything with his sharp eyes.

"I'll make sure that the king's daughter does not defeat us!" he said, and he loaded his gun and aimed so carefully that he shot the horse's skull right out from under the runner's head without hurting him. The runner awoke, jumped up, and saw that his jug was empty and that the king's daughter was way ahead of him. However, he did not lose heart, but ran back to the spring with the jug, filled it with water, and managed to beat the king's daughter home, with ten minutes to spare.

"You see," he said, "it was about time that I really started using my legs. I wouldn't exactly call that *running*, what I was doing before."

However, the king was vexed—and his daughter even more so—that a common discharged soldier should win the race. Therefore, they consulted with each other, seeking a way to get rid of him and all his companions as well. Finally, the king said to her, "I've got an idea. Don't fret. They'll never show their faces around here again." Then he went to the six and said, "I want you to eat, drink, and be merry," and he led them to a room that had an iron floor. The doors were also made of iron, and the windows were lined with iron bars. In the room there was a table covered with delicious food, and the king said to them, "Go inside and enjoy yourselves."

When they were inside, the king had the door locked and bolted. Then he summoned the cook and commanded him to make a fire and keep it going under the room until the room became burning hot. The cook did that, and it began to get hot in the room. The six, who were sitting at the table, felt very warm, but they thought this was due to the food. However, when the heat became greater and greater and they wanted to leave the room, they found the doors and windows locked. Now they realized that the king had devised an evil plan to suffocate them.

"He won't succeed!" said the man with the cap. "I'm going to let a frost come that will put the fire to shame and send it crawling away."

So he put his cap on straight, and immediately there was a frost, causing all the heat to disappear and the food on the table to freeze. After two hours had passed and the king thought the men had all perished in the heat, he had the door opened and he looked in to see how they were. Yet when the door was opened, all six of them were well and vigorous. Indeed, they declared that it would be nice to get outside and warm themselves, for the food had frozen to the dishes because of the cold conditions in the room. The king stormed furiously down the stairs, scolded the cook, and asked him why he had not done what he had ordered. But the cook answered, "There's more than enough heat. Just look for yourself."

The king saw a tremendous fire blazing under the iron room and realized that he could not get the better of the six men by doing something like that. So he tried to think of something new to get rid of the unwelcome guests. He summoned the ex-soldier and said, "If you will accept gold and give up your claim to my daughter, you can take away as much gold as you like."

"That's fine with me, Your Majesty," he answered. "If you give me as much as my servant can carry, I won't claim your daughter."

The king was satisfied with that, and the ex-soldier added, "In two weeks I shall return to fetch the gold." Then he summoned all the tailors in the entire kingdom, and for two weeks they had to sit and sew a sack. When it was finished, the strong man, who could tear up trees, swung the sack over his shoulder and went to the king, who said, "Who's that powerful fellow carrying such a bundle of canvas on his shoulder? Why, it's as big as a house!" Suddenly the king became horrified and thought, "What a lot of gold he'll carry away!" So the king ordered that a ton of gold be brought, and all of that took sixteen of his most powerful men to carry, but the strong man grabbed it with one hand, put it into the sack and said, "Why don't you bring more right away? This will barely cover the bottom."

Gradually, the king had his whole treasure brought, and the strong man tossed it all into the sack, but it only became half full.

"Bring some more!" the strong man cried. "These few crumbs aren't enough to fill it."

So seventeen thousand wagons of gold from all over the kingdom had to be driven to the spot, and the strong man stuffed it all into the sack, along with the oxen that were harnessed to the wagons.

"Since I don't have the time to inspect everything," he said, "I'll just take what comes until the sack's completely full."

When everything was in the sack, there was still room for a lot more, but the strong man said, "I think it's time to put an end to this. Sometimes one has to tie up a sack even if it's not quite full." Then he hoisted it onto his back and went away with his companions.

When the king saw one single man carrying away all the treasures of his kingdom, he was furious and ordered his cavalry to pursue the six men and take the sack away from the strong man. Members of the king's regiment soon caught up with the men and called to them, "You're our prisoners! Put down the sack with the gold, or else you'll be cut to pieces!"

"What did you say?" asked the blower. "We're your prisoners? Before that ever happens, all of you will soon be dancing around in the air." With that he held one nostril and blew through the other at the two regiments, sending them flying in every which direction, up into the blue and over hill and dale. Some were scattered this way, others that way, while a sergeant begged for mercy. Because he was a brave fellow, who had nine wounds and did not deserve to be humiliated, the blower let up a bit, and the sergeant came out of it without being harmed. Then the blower said to him, "Now go home to the king and tell him, all he has to do is send a few more men, and I'll blow them all sky high!"

When the king received the message, he said, "Let those fellows go. There's something extraordinary about them."

So the six men brought their wealth back home, divided it among themselves and their friends, and lived happily until their death.

Second story: "Seven Brooms" is an adaptation of an Italian folktale. This tale either should be told in its entirety or should be stopped just as Fortuna is sent off to carry out the three tasks as indicated below.

Seven Brooms

Many years ago in my mother's town called Casino, not far from Naples, there was a merchant by the name of Domenico, somewhat chubby and pompous, who, on the birth of his seventh daughter, flung open the windows of his house and yelled,

"Seven brooms! Seven brooms!"

But just as he was about to close the windows with an air of satisfaction, he heard from across the street,

"Seven swords! Seven swords!"

It was his neighbor, Guiseppe, whose wife had just given birth to their seventh son. Well, this merchant was just as stout and full of himself as was Domenico, and he laughed loudly and shouted at Domenico,

"Seven brooms! What good are they? They'll sweep you clean!"

"Oh yeah," responded Domenico, "seven swords will stick you where it hurts!"

"And your lousy brooms," Guiseppe raged, "will get stuck in the stinking garbage of your miserable house!"

"Well, then your swords will have their tips cut off by the piles of dirt and dung hanging from the rafters of your house!"

"You blabbermouth. Bimbo! You were born in a madhouse!"

"You slobbermouth. Decrepit weenie! They should lock you up and throw the keys away!"

"Pork chop!"

"Weasel!"

Now, it may be difficult for you to imagine, but this ranting and raving continued for many years. Every day Domenico and Guiseppe flung open their windows and began with "Seven brooms!" and "Seven swords!" And every day the people of my town laughed at their antics and wondered whether they would ever make peace. But their yelling went on until Domenico's youngest daughter turned sixteen. Her name was Fortuna, and she was Domenico's favorite. It was she who always asked why her father hung his head in shame each time he turned and closed the window. And he would answer,

"He's right, you know. Though I love you and your sisters dearly, what good are seven brooms compared to seven swords?"

And Fortuna would smile at him and brighten his day by saying, "Wait and see, Papa. We'll sweep him off his feet. Don't you worry. We'll sweep him off his feet!"

It seemed, however, that nothing would ever happen in our little town to change things, until a messenger from the king arrived and announced that the king's wife had been kidnapped by a strange sorcerer living on top of a glass mountain. The king sent his knights to rescue her, but very few of the king's men managed to scale the walls of the mountain, and those who succeeded had been turned to stone by this mysterious sorcerer, who had stolen the queen just so he could listen to her play the harp. He prided himself on being a connoisseur of heavenly harp music.

"The king's not worthy of such music!" the sorcerer declared. "He's a boor, and the music is wasted on him."

Believe me, these remarks enraged the king. Though it was true that he preferred to hunt with his hounds and duel with his knights in tournaments, he loved his wife, and most of all he loved the fact that her pasta dishes were just as delicious as her music. So, he promised a huge treasure to any able-bodied man who could rescue his wife from the sorcerer.

"All the money you can carry from the king's treasury!" proclaimed the messenger, who left the town as soon as he had alerted everyone in the vicinity.

Well, when Guiseppe heard this news, he called his youngest son, Settimo, who loved to take on challenges that involved brute force, but I must also tell you he was not especially bright. Nevertheless, his father gave Settimo a sturdy horse and armor and then sent him on his way to rescue the king's wife. Then Guiseppe flung open the window of his house and yelled and gloated,

"Hail to the seven swords! We'll soon be rich! Very rich!"

Domenico kept his window shut, but Fortuna ran to her father and said, "Papa, give me a horse and armor, and I shall rescue the king's wife."

At first, Domenico refused and said, "What can a girl like you do? What good is a little broom like you?"

But Fortuna pleaded until he relented and gave her a horse and armor. Nobody would recognize her dressed as a knight, he thought. Then he secretly sent her off on her journey, for he was fearful she would fail, and he did not want to be shamed in public.

In the meantime, Settimo charged recklessly through the forest without caring for anything in his path. His horse trampled over a large anthill, killing many of the poor little insects. Then he stormed through a stream, tossing many small fish onto the bank where they flapped and floundered. Soon after he tore through the bushes and trees, knocking down nests of little sparrows onto the ground. When he reached the glass mountain, his horse kept sliding down the slope, but Settimo kicked it mercilessly and whipped it until the powerful steed made it to the top, where the sorcerer courteously greeted Settimo with a smile. "Good day, young man," he said, "I assume you've made your way here to rescue the queen."

"How'd you know?" responded Settimo. "Well, anyway, you're right, and I'm going to kill you right now."

"Not so hasty," said the sorcerer. "You know you have to perform three tasks before you're allowed to kill me."

"I do?" Settimo was not so sure of himself.

"Of course you do," the sorcerer said. "Haven't you ever read a fairy tale?"

"Well … I'm not much of a reader," Settimo confessed.

"Now, here's what you have to do," the sorcerer told him. "First you must travel to the dark blue sea and dive deep down into the water where you'll find a humongous whale. Then you must pry open its gigantic mouth and take the pure white pearl. After you do that you must enter the deep dark forest and go to the dreary dragon's cave. You must avoid his spitting fire and then grab the sparkling diamond that lies at its clawed feet. Finally, you must climb the golden mountain up to the dazzling peak where you will find the thorny eagle's nest. Then you must steal the glittering golden egg. Once you do all three tasks, you may try to slay me."

"You mean I've got to do all that?" Settimo asked. "That's asking a lot."

The sorcerer looked carefully at Settimo, and out of frustration, he said, "You're right, you pitiful blockhead. You're going to need all the assistance you can get. So, sit down and wait. Help is on its way."

"But I'm hungry!" Settimo complained.

"Not if you're made of stone," said the sorcerer, who clicked his fingers. Settimo was suddenly changed into stone.

"Now I can go back and listen to the queen's divine music," the sorcerer said to himself. "I've never heard anyone play the harp the way she does."

In the meantime, Fortuna came upon the poor ants who were desperately trying to rebuild their anthill. So she got off her horse and helped them restore their homes. When she was done, the ants cried out, "Kind Fortuna, what a wonderful deed! You can count on us in your time of need."

As Fortuna continued on her way, she came across the poor fish still flapping on the bank of the stream. Quickly she dismounted her horse and gathered all the fish and placed them back into the water. Then the fish cried out, "Kind Fortuna, what a wonderful deed! You can count on us in your time of need."

Then Fortuna got back on her horse and entered the dark forest. As she rode along, she noticed the crushed nests and little sparrows on the ground. Again she dismounted and gathered the nests, fixed them, and placed them back on the trees with the little sparrows in them.

"Kind Fortuna," they cried, "what a wonderful deed! You can count on us in your time of need."

Finally Fortuna arrived at the foot of the glass mountain, and when she realized that it was impossible for her horse to carry her to the top, she got off and began climbing the mountain by knocking little holes in the glass for her feet. She was so graceful and skillful that she managed to climb the mountain in a few hours. When the sorcerer saw her coming, he pretended that he hadn't been expecting her.

"Well now," he said, "what brings you here, young lady? No need to pretend you're a knight. Surely you don't want to rescue the king's wife?"

"And why not?" Fortuna asked.

"Well, despite your armor, my dear," responded the sorcerer, "you have nobody to protect you, and you certainly don't have the strength to perform the tasks that I have in mind for you."

"Try me," Fortuna said. "There may be more to me than you can see."

"I'm sorry, my dear," the sorcerer said politely, "but I'm afraid that I shall have to give you a partner, for I fear a young woman like yourself may not be up to the tasks that I have in store for you."

So the sorcerer clicked his fingers, and suddenly the stony Settimo came to life again.

"Why did you have to turn me into stone? I'm still hungry!" Settimo began whimpering.

"Stop your babbling," the sorcerer ordered. "Here is your partner, and together you must complete the tasks that I gave you before."

And he repeated the exact same tasks to Fortuna that he had given Settimo, but this time he said, "You must work together, and bring back the pearl, the diamond, and the golden egg. If one of you fails to help the other, you'll both be turned to stone. Now off you go!"

Fortuna could not believe her ears. She felt that Settimo was too dumb to help her, while Settimo was enraged because he felt that Fortuna was too soft and would get in his way. They looked at each other dumbfounded and then headed down the mountain. The sorcerer smiled. He knew they would never get along, and now he could listen to the lovely harp music without being disturbed.

When Fortuna and Settimo got to the bottom of the mountain, she told him to follow her through the forest, and she began running.

"Wait," he cried. "The armor's weighing me down!"

"Take the darn thing off!" Fortuna answered and kept racing through the bushes and bramble. Settimo managed to toss off the armor, but he kept his sword and hacked his way through the woods.

When Fortuna reached the stream, she called out to the fish. "Oh little ones, my need is great, it's you who will decide my fate."

Well, I know you won't believe this, but the fish swam to the surface and quickly taught her how to dive deeply and hold her breath for hours. But Settimo almost drowned when he tried to dive, and he had to rest on shore. So Fortuna swam to the deep blue sea and dove deep down into the water. When the whale saw her coming toward him, he was so astounded that he gasped and opened his mouth. Out flew the pure white pearl, and Fortuna grabbed it and carried it to the shore.

"Great!" yelled Settimo, and his eyes grew wide when he saw the beautiful pearl. "Let's bring it back to the village and sell it."

"Don't be foolish, Settimo," Fortuna said. "The king has promised a fortune if we rescue his wife."

"Right," he replied. "Right."

"You wait here," she said. "I'll be back in a jiffy."

Fortuna quickly brought the pearl to the sorcerer, who was somewhat flabbergasted.

"And your partner?" he asked. "Where is he?"

"He's waiting for me," Fortuna said.

"Well, be off, be off," he responded and was now worried that Fortuna might ruin his plans. He was getting so used to listening to the queen's music that he did not want to give her up.

When Fortuna returned to the forest, she found Settimo sleeping under a tree. She gave him a gentle kick in his rear.

"Get up, Settimo, we don't have time to lose!"

"What's going on?" Settimo asked drowsily.

"Follow me," and off went Fortuna, running like a deer and winding gracefully in and out of the trees. Settimo bumped his head several times in his desperate attempt to keep up with her, and he was glad when she finally stopped in front of the anthill. Then she knelt down and whispered softly to the ants, "Oh little ones, my need is great, it's you who will decide my fate."

Within minutes the ants came out of their hill and taught Fortuna how to bore through the ground and into the sides of mountains. Settimo laughed. He tried to show them that his sword was much better and knocked down a few trees to prove it. But Fortuna ignored him, as did the ants. She crept carefully to the back of the dragon's cave, and Settimo called her a coward.

"Watch!" he said, and he went around front and challenged the dragon to a fight.

"Owww!" Settimo screamed when the dragon's flames began to scorch him, and while the dragon was spitting fire out of the front of the cave, Fortuna bore a hole in the back and entered the cave. The dragon was tossing flames at Settimo and showing off so much that it did not notice when Fortuna stole the sparkling diamond right from under its pot-sized belly. Off she went and took it to the sorcerer, while Settimo climbed an oak tree and had to spend the night listening to the owls and bats who offered to share the insects they caught so that he wouldn't go to bed on an empty stomach.

When daylight came, Fortuna returned and helped Settimo climb down from the tree. Then she whistled and cried out to the sparrows, who were chirping on nests in a nearby tree. "Oh little ones, my need is great, it's you who will decide my fate."

Within seconds the sparrows came out of their nests, and I know this seems impossible, but they taught Fortuna how to fly. And because she was so graceful and skillful, she learned in a jiffy, and she soared to the golden mountain, where she waited patiently until the eagle left its nest. Then she dashed through the air, seized the golden egg, and returned to the spot where she had left Settimo. Exhausted, she lay down to rest.

"Let me take a short nap," Fortuna said, "and then we'll go to the sorcerer and take the queen back to her husband."

"Of course," Settimo agreed. "I'll keep guard over the golden egg."

But no sooner did Fortuna fall asleep than Settimo grabbed the egg and headed toward the glass mountain. Once he managed to climb to the top, he approached the sorcerer and said, "Here it is, the golden egg! Now, give me the queen in return."

"Hmmm," said the sorcerer. "Did you get this all by yourself?"

"Of course I did."

"Where's Fortuna?"

"She got stuck in some bushes. Besides, she wasn't much of a help. I had to learn how to fly to the top of a mountain to get this egg," Settimo remarked, "and believe me, that's something a girl could never do."

"Oh," said the sorcerer, "if you can fly, then I suppose you can fly to the top of the tower over there where I keep the queen."

"I could," said Settimo, "but I'm a bit exhausted right now."

"Oh, do give it a try," the sorcerer urged him. "If you can't do it, you'll be spending the rest of your life as a stone."

When he heard this, Settimo became frightened, and his face turned red. He began flapping his arms and rushed toward the tower. As he approached, he jumped into the air and collided with the stone wall.

After he bounced off the wall, the sorcerer clicked his fingers, and poor Settimo was changed once again into a stone statue.

About an hour later, Fortuna arrived at the top of the mountain, and she, too, approached the sorcerer.

"Well, what do you have for me, my dear?" the sorcerer asked.

"To tell you the truth, I've failed you and myself," Fortuna reported. "I lost the golden egg, and I've lost Settimo."

"Well, that's a shame, Fortuna," the sorcerer responded, "but I shall give you one last chance to redeem yourself. If you can fly to the top of the tower and fetch the queen's harp, you will have your way."

The sorcerer did not have to repeat himself, for Fortuna was in the air before he could finish the sentence. She flew to the top of the tower, entered the room, curtsied before the queen, grabbed the harp, and returned to the sorcerer before anyone knew what was happening.

The sorcerer was impressed. "My dear, you've exceeded my expectations and my wishes as well. Not only shall I give you the king's wife, but you may have as much of my treasure as you desire."

"Thank you, kind sir," she said. "I don't want your treasure. But I would like that stone statue over there." And she pointed to Settimo. "And my only request is that you tell me the magic words that will make him human again."

The sorcerer was puzzled, but he granted her wish and put Settimo in a cart that was drawn by a horse. So Fortuna drove the cart with Settimo and the queen and her harp in the back, bobbing up and down over the rocky road. When she arrived at the king's palace, the king ran to meet his wife. Though he was most grateful and rejoiced, he was also very perplexed.

"How did you do this?" he asked Fortuna. "You're just a girl. But what am I saying? It doesn't matter. What matters is that my wife has returned. What can I do for you? How much money do you want?"

But Fortuna just smiled and said, "I already have my reward." She pointed to the stone statue and drove off, seated on her cart with Settimo in the rear. After she had journeyed several hours, she approached the little town of Casino. As soon as the people saw her coming, they rushed out of their homes onto the streets and began cheering. Then, when they finally noticed Settimo standing as a stone statue in the back of the cart, they burst out laughing and chased the cart until Fortuna arrived in front of her father's house and called out, "Papa, Papa, look at what I've brought you!"

Domenico came rushing out of the house with his wife and six daughters, and he beamed with pride when he saw Fortuna, who waved her hand over Settimo and cried out, "Seven brooms! Seven brooms!"

Suddenly Settimo became human again. His face turned red, and it became even redder when his father Guiseppe came out of his house and hung his head in shame.

Now some say that soon after this event, Fortuna and her six sisters married Settimo and his six brothers, who wanted to change their shame into fame. But to be frank, all this is gossip. The truth is that Fortuna had swept the sorcerer off his feet, and soon after she returned to Casino, he came riding into town with his six brothers. Anyone who's grown up in Casino knows what happened after that. They all know my mother's story and how I came to be. And, if you don't believe me, just come and listen to what they have to say.

Improvisation and theater games: Depending on which tale the students decide to adapt for their play, the improvisation will focus on skits that shift the time period of the story. The students are divided into their three groups. Group one will be asked to set the story in a specific time in the distant past. Group two will be asked to set the story in the present. Group three will be asked to set it in the future. The following is a list of story ideas if the students choose "How Six Made Their Way in the World":

Past: Keep story basically as it is but set it at the time of the French Revolution or American Revolution.
Present: The soldier may be sent to serve his country in South America or Africa, and when he returns home, he is not treated well.
Future: The soldier is sent to Mars to fight for his country.

The following are story ideas if the students choose "Seven Brooms":

Past: Keep the story as is with the merchants living in a small village in Italy.

Present: Have the story take place in a small town in northern Minnesota.

Future: Have the story take place on another planet.

Writing game: Return to the "What If" game and ask the students questions that pertain to "How Six Made Their Way in the World" and "Seven Brooms." For instance, what if the king treated the soldier more fairly? What if the soldier lost the race to the princess? What if Fortuna fell in love with Settimo? What if Settimo overcame the sorcerer?

The School Production and Crossing Bridges Festival

In the past, when there were only three or four schools involved in the Neighborhood Bridges program, we brought all the classes to the Children's Theatre Company, where they performed their plays on the main stage in front of parents, relatives, friends, and other guests. It was generally a day in which pen pals would meet, and the children would tour the theater. However, because we have close to ten schools and eighteen classes in the program, there are now two festivals, and we try to bring together classes from different schools that have been corresponding with one another.

Before the performance at the Children's Theatre, each class does a dress rehearsal in the its own classroom. Once the dress rehearsal is completed, the teaching artist leads a discussion about the work on plays, sets, costumes, movement, and music. If there is time, the students are asked to design a program for the play that is then produced and handed out at the Children's Theatre. There is generally one or two performances of the play within the school before the students travel to the Children's Theatre Company.

Every student in the class is involved in the final production. We want to share and show off what the students have learned and to involve the community at large in the final production. Everyone is aware that the plays are works in progress, just as the children themselves are in a process of developing their talents and social awareness. Plans are already under way to develop a second stage in the Neighborhood Bridges program that will enable the students to use what they have learned in a second year of the program that is focused on creating a play in the fall that the students will perform in other schools of the district during March, April, and May. The methods and principles of the Neighborhood Bridges program will serve as the basis for adapting a story, and more time will be spent with training the children in the fundamentals of producing a play, including building sets, making costumes, directing, writing scripts, and learning dramaturgy. On the basis of a pilot program that we have developed at the Children's Theatre Company, the students will not only perform their own plays at other schools in Minneapolis and St. Paul but also lead discussions about their work and conduct workshops with students from the other schools.

Students' speaking out and acting out are fundamental to their education. The fundamentals they learn help them cultivate their imagination and critical literacy. Storytelling and creative drama celebrate their individual talents.

The Importance of Children's Theater

Fig. 9.1 Students from the Children's Theatre Company rehearsing "The Giant" in Berlin.

9

POLITICAL CHILDREN'S THEATER IN THE AGE OF GLOBALIZATION

Thirty years ago I went to Germany to write about the famous director Peter Stein's Schaubühne am Halleschen Ufer and other experimental political groups sprouting in the aftermath of the student movement of the 1960s. While I was in Berlin, a friend told me that the most significant political theater was not really the Schaubühne, or any other theater for adults, but a children's theater called Grips, founded by the writer Volker Ludwig. Its members, who used to perform in a political cabaret for adults, had recently turned their attention to developing unusual political plays for children that incorporated rock music and Brechtian dramaturgical methods such as the estrangement effect and didactic lessons. At first I was not going to follow up on this tip, but I was glad I did, for the production I saw by Grips, which means something like common sense and implies using your intelligence politically to understand the world, overwhelmed me. And unlike the spectacular Schaubühne and many other so-called political theaters of that time, Grips continues to do what it has been doing for thirty years: to challenge and provoke children and adults to change their lives, if not society as a whole.

Ludwig, who has remained the director and major writer of Grips, sought from the very beginning to link theater to emancipatory education. He has often remarked that Grips's plays are designed to show our condition as changeable and to reveal the possibilities for social transformation and critical thinking. As he stated, "Primarily this means that we want to encourage children to ask questions, to understand that criticism is their undeniable right, to enjoy creative thinking, and to gain pleasure from seeing alternatives."[1] How does the Grips ensemble, which has constantly responded to changing political conditions, bring this about? Almost all of their plays are Brechtian *Lehrstücke* (learning plays) and are performed in a cabaret style that enhances the estrangement effect and allows for pleasure in learning. The adult actors do not try to mimic children or act naturalistically. On the contrary, social conditions and events are explained and demonstrated from children's point of views based on political principles of solidarity that the actors are encouraged to display. The plays do not present solutions but show possible alternatives to conditions that are oppressive or self-defeating. The plays are not ends in themselves; they do not preach the right answers, nor should they be performed this way. They want to teach how enjoyable it can be to master and use critical thinking.

Each scene of a Grips play tends to be a social experiment, a testing of the social conditions to see if perhaps some other form of organization might make more sense and allow for more freedom of movement and development. Characters represent antagonistic principles, and as they are unmasked, the social relations underlying the principles become more visible, as in the case of *Mannomann!* (1973), an early play about male chauvinism; *Bella, Boss und Bulli* (1995), a drama about bullying; and *Melodys Ring* (2000), a musical about racism and the prejudicial treatment of political émigrés. The characters step out of their roles to show what the conditions are and how they act on people in all social classes in given circumstances. The songs of the plays further illustrate the importance of using a critical approach to a problem, rather than searching for easy solutions. Cabaret performance has been the dominant influence on the actors and the playwrights because it is illusion smashing, frank, quick, jovial, and, yet, serious. Many of the Grips's productions and techniques can be repetitive, but they have worked effectively and artistically to engage audiences to think about

political commitment. Ludwig has a remarkable gift for writing provocative plays and maintaining the organization of his theater so that
Grips constantly intervenes in daily politics. Over the years he has hired
many cohorts, who have made the aesthetic and social mission of the
theater stronger, and, more than any children's theater I know, Grips
has resisted forces of compromise and continues to demonstrate how
children's theater can address ordinary children's daily struggles with
the authorities and institutions that govern their lives and ours.

But this chapter is not about Grips, which even in Berlin is special
and unique.[2] Rather, it is an attempt to grasp why we need an alternative, not just to the lily-white, run-of-the-mill, middle-class children's
theater but also to the youth entertainment industry whose spectacles
make the productions of the middle-class children's theater seem even
radical at times. First I want to hark back to Walter Benjamin's essays
on children's literature and culture,[3] in particular to his seemingly anti-
quated essay "Program of a Proletarian Children's Theater," to explain
in more depth what I mean by "children's political theater." Then I
want to say a few blunt words about the state of children's culture in the
United States and how it is organized—that is, homogenized—for
them. Finally, I want to discuss different kinds of unspectacular children's theater that thrive in the nooks and crannies of public realms.

The Timeless Walter Benjamin

By 1928 Walter Benjamin, a thinker before his time and perhaps
beyond our times, who as a collector of children's books had already
expressed an interest in children's literature, began to do some work for
the radio as a commentator on children's culture. The same year he
wrote a curious piece titled "Program of a Proletarian Children's
Theater"—curious because Benjamin knew very little about children's
theater, which nobody took notice of—that forty years later, in the late
1960s and 1970s, shaped the way West German activists approached
children's culture. Benjamin wrote the "Program" for the Latvian director Asja Lacis whose work he admired and with whom he was very
much in love.[4] Benjamin met Lacis on the Isle of Capri in 1923. A dedicated communist, Lacis was startlingly intelligent and beautiful and
played a short but important role in developing a unique children's theater in the Soviet Union during the agitprop years of the revolution. In

1928 she was sent to Berlin as a Communist cultural worker to do experimental drama with young people at the Liebknecht House. Benjamin sought to assist her by writing a theoretical framework for a new political children's theater. The result, based on their conversations, was a provocative and analytical statement designed to further a type of theater work that stressed spontaneity and collective and autonomous work by young people. Accordingly, the new political theater for children was to focus on process rather than on results, to integrate children's intuition, and to raise the participants' awareness of social and economic differences.

In the 1920s, a period of cultural war in Weimar Germany, theater became a battlefield, a hotly contested space, and an open realm for experimentation that ranged from the agitprop work of Erwin Piscator to the opulent productions of Max Reinhardt. All the major parties—the Social Democrats, the Communists, and the Nazis—formed youth groups that made theater experiments part of their political work and propaganda. Theater was considered a weapon that could be used to win the minds and bodies of the young. Because this political aspect of theater was less obvious in the mainstream middle-class *Luxustheater*, which catered to the elite and generally produced charming fairytale plays for children of the educated classes at appropriate times such as Christmas, Benjamin declared,

> The theater of the present-day bourgeoisie is economically determined by profit. Sociologically it is, above all, an instrument of sensation in front of and behind the curtains. It is different with the proletarian children's theater. Just as the first firm grip of the Bolshevists was used to raise the red flag, so their first instinct was to organize the children. In this organization the proletarian children's theater has developed as its core, as the basic motif of the bolshevist education. This fact is borne out by a countercheck. It works out this way: from the viewpoint of the bourgeoisie, nothing is more dangerous for children than theater.[5]

Benjamin's use of terms such as "bourgeois," "bolshevist," and "proletarian" and his strident tone should not put us off. After all, he was writing for his comrades at that time and for Lacis. He was trying to make a crucial class and experiential distinction that holds true even today: a political children's theater that addresses the concerns of the majority of children—who, then, as now, are poor and disadvantaged—fuses play and reality, and allows children to become more conscious of how they can explore and experiment with forces that act on them. This indeed makes theater dangerous, but not just for today's corporate and professional elite groups. Political theater that prompts children and animates them to take charge of their acts and actions means taking a risk. It is risky for all social classes. Such theater will upset authorities and institutions and make itself suspect because of its carnivalesque nature. When free to explore, children will cross all sorts of lines, and they will often do so in politically incorrect ways, something even Benjamin did not grasp.

Or did he? Benjamin went on to say,

> The productions of this theater [proletarian children's theater] are not the real goal of the strenuous collective work accomplished in the children's clubs, something that is the case with the great bourgeois theater. In the children's proletarian theater, productions are incidental. One could say: they come about out by mistake, almost as a whim of the children, who interrupt their studies in this way and basically never bring them to a close. The leader [the adult in charge of group work] places less value on completion. More important are the tensions which are resolved in such productions. The tensions of the collective work are the educators.[6]

Such tensions between individuals and social conditions are explosive, demanding patience and comprehension on the part of the theater's adult leaders and the young people. Emphasizing the status of children as independent agents, Benjamin conceived of young people, especially between the ages of six and sixteen, as supremely qualified directors: they were *erdenfern* and *unverfroren*—that is, they were not yet fixed and bound to earth but were fluid and malleable. They could take ordinary situations and turn them around so as to reflect their own tastes and needs.

Key ideas of Benjamin's "Program" and his essays on children's culture were in direct opposition to the reigning pedagogical principles and discipline of his period when formal German idealism and middle-class notions of what was appropriate for children regulated youthful enthusiasm and naive susceptibility.

> The proletarian pedagogics demonstrates its superiority by guaranteeing children the fulfillment of their childhood. The place [theater, school, or youth center] in which this happens, does not have to be isolated from the area of class struggles. Their issues and symbols can be played out—may even have to be—in that place. But, in playing them out, the forms need not dominate the child. They will not demand this. ... New forces, and new inspirations will appear which the [adult] leader may not have gleaned at all from the work. Only through the wild release of the children's imagination will the leader become acquainted with these forces and inspirations. Children, who have played theater in this way, have become free in such productions. Through play they have fulfilled their childhood. They do not take any remnants with them that might later inhibit an unsentimental activity due to tearful childhood memories.[7]

If I summarize some of the more important ideas of Benjamin's "Program," their subversiveness will become apparent.

- All books, toys, clothes, plays, films, and other products for children are created within a socialization process and are the products of the prevailing means of production and reception. In this regard they form important parts of the bourgeois public sphere. They were and still are used as prescriptions for the "good" of children who are to be raised and disciplined in pedagogically approved ways. They are also class specific even when they do not appear to be so. Their inescapable prescriptiveness can be suspended only by children who appropriate them on their own terms and use them to create their own world, one that functions according to relatively new rules.
- From the bourgeois perspective, the carefully designed and censored production of children's objects—and nowadays this would include film, TV programs, video games, clothes—greatly determines their reception. Children are to be protected from reality and are to see, read, and buy only what adults believe is good for them. In other words, in the enlightened bourgeois tradition,

children are to be raised as passive and obedient spectators and readers.

- It has always been illusory to believe in predictable, positivist social conditioning. Children are not automatons. To develop their own identities, they read and play with what has been printed, produced, manufactured, and organized not only for them but for an adult world—and they especially like to play with garbage and junk.
- Only through play can children create an environment that will enable them to pursue their own interests, which they intuit and need to articulate in a free space.
- A true childhood, in which the child functions as player, collector, and producer of his or her identity, is impossible in the traditional public sphere, for there a child's life is narrowly prescribed and reflects the interests of hierarchical classes.
- By developing a proletarian public sphere—that is, a proletarian children's theater, a children's theater from below—one creates the conditions for producing new plays, new books, and new insights that inspire continual reformation. At the heart of children's play is the reformation of the world.

Benjamin realized that new children's books, new toys, and new children's plays had to be specific to one's social class. That is, they had to come out of the realm of experience of children of the lower classes, and that the role of adults was to cultivate the artistic abilities of the children so that they could autonomously and clearly articulate their wishes, dreams, and needs. Given the fact that social class structure has greatly changed since Benjamin's time and is much different in the United States, it is important to elaborate Benjamin's notion of social class, which was readily understood during the Weimar period. Today in the United States the old divisions between the proletariat, petit bourgeoisie, agrarian class, middle class, and upper class no longer function as cleanly as they did in Benjamin's Germany. The ideology of consumerism tends to erase or conceal differences so that, in the United States, everyone appears to belong to the affluent middle class as soon as one has sufficient money to buy a particular item that may denote membership in the middle class. Class boundaries are thus easy to cross and transgress. Because the international conglomerates that produce books, toys, clothes, plays, music, and so on seek the lowest common denominator, any boy and girl can subscribe momentarily to a social class or group and feel wealthy, important, strong, or cool. The purpose of production in our age of consumerism is to conceal class and make it appear as if we can all belong to one class called "American."

Multiculturalism actually contributes to the concealment of class differences because it emphasizes cultural differences without exploring or showing how class operates within ethnic groups and it argues for inclusion in the "grand" middle class of the United States. But, whatever is produced by the United States' underclasses and nonmainstream groups eventually becomes appropriated by the professional and corporate classes in keeping with their interests and marketed for everyone. Cultural homogenization makes it extremely difficult to demarcate a class-specific game, toy, film, or play. The discourse of the professional and corporate classes in the public sphere and in the cultural industry tends to foster a notion of one nation or one family under God which can enjoy the fruits of our American life if we all do our respective jobs and keep the economy working and flourishing. Such occlusion of social class difference makes it all the more important to find the differences and to grasp why and how they exist.

For children in the United States to have a true childhood, in Benjamin's sense of the term, they must live and interact within both public and private spheres and be allowed to use their imaginations freely, to notice class differences, to grasp the ideology of consumerism,[8] and to deal with imposed religions, ideologies, and pressures. Consumerism is not only an ideology; it is the major practice of most adults in the Western world, and children are cultivated according to their class to learn to buy items and sell themselves to earn their place in society. Accordingly, in work and play with children, adult leaders should not function in Benjamin's ideal "proletarian sphere" merely as observers who receive new impulses from the creative efforts and productions of the children. Rather, they should encourage and guide children, fostering awareness of class, gender, and ethnic distinctions, how consumerism works, and how the spectacles of society blind them.

Within this learning process the adults cannot be afraid to voice their own ideological opinions and must be honest with the children. Moreover, they must also learn how to learn from the children who will appropriate everything that comes their way as consumers with very particular needs.

The theses that Benjamin put forward in "Program of a Proletarian Theater" served many years later to stimulate the German critics Oskar Negt and Alexander Kluge to formulate the important notion of the "children's public sphere":

> When children want to recognize and realize their own sensuality, that is, to catch hold of themselves, they need a more emphatic spatial realm than adults. They need much more room for freedom of movement, places which allow for a much more flexible field of action in which things are not fixed once and for all, defined, tagged with names, with signs forbidding what to do. ... As with each proletarian public sphere, the children's public sphere has the tendency to include the totality of the society; it does not let itself be organized in small groups. It cannot be the intention of the children, when they organize themselves for themselves and try to bring about self-regulation, to pay for this free space with a massive withdrawal from reality and withdrawal from the adult world because all objects are connected to another and to the children and belong to this world. Therefore, the children's public sphere cannot be brought about without a material public sphere that involves parents, and without public children's realms in all social classes, which can make connections with one another.[9]

I'll have more to say about the possibilities for a children's public realm in the present-day world of globalization in a moment, but for now it is important to stress that Negt and Kluge's theoretical formulations are based on Benjamin's observations that included all forms of children's culture. In this respect, one cannot write about one form of children's culture without taking into consideration other forms and their production and reception. For instance, Benjamin believed that there could not be a new children's literature or theater unless the social and political conditions were radically changed. As he remarked in *Einbahnstraße:*

It is foolish to grumble pedantically about the production of objects appropriate for children—illustrative materials, toys, or books. Ever since the Enlightenment this concern has involved the most grumpy speculations of educators. Their absorption in psychology prevents them from recognizing that the earth is full of the most incomparable objects that capture the attention of children who use them. Full of the most distinct objects. Indeed, children are disposed in a special way to seek out any work place where they can see how things are concretely made. They feel irresistibly attracted to garbage and junk left over from building, gardening, housework, sewing, or carpentry. In these objects of junk they recognize the face, the face of the world of things that turns right to them, to them alone. In this world of things they do not imitate the works of the adults. Rather they bring stuff of very different kinds together in a new volatile way through what they produce in play. As they do this, children form their world of things by themselves, a small world in the large one. One would have to have an eye for the norms of this small world of things if one wants to create deliberately for children and not to give priority to one's own activity with all that it requires regarding instruments, but to let oneself find the way to the children.[10]

Though some of Benjamin's ideas tend to be idealistic and anachronistic, much of his critique is still valid today and can enable us to grasp the conditions and contradictions that limit the formation of a children's public sphere conceived in the 1970s by Negt and Kluge. More than ever before children's lives are segmented and constrained by tightly knit institutional and cultural forces that limit autonomous movement and decrease the potential for playing with alternatives. Instead of the expansion of a children's public sphere in the spirit of Negt and Kluge, we have restricted zones that determine whether a child merits an entrance ticket to discover his or her talents.

Children and Children's Culture in the Age of Globalization

Children in the United States have become insatiable consumers of manufactured identities that falsely promise excitement and happiness. This creates a major dilemma for children's theater: how to attract an audience while at the same time avoiding absorption into the culture industry where it would be subjected to the forces of globalization, which turn everything into spectacle. Because the transformation of theater into spectacle diminishes the threat of theater to the dominant forces of power within our present-day institutionalized public spheres, it is important to understand the distinction between the two. In his provocative book *The Society of the Spectacle*, written in the heyday of the student revolution in France, Guy Debord declared,

> By means of the spectacle the ruling order discourses endlessly upon itself in an uninterrupted monologue of self-praise. The spectacle is the self-portrait of power in the age of power's totalitarian rule over conditions of existence. The fetishistic appearance of pure objectivity in spectacular relationships conceals their true character as relationships between human beings and between classes. A second Nature thus seems to impose inescapable laws upon our environment. But the spectacle is by no means the inevitable outcome of a technical development perceived as *natural;* on the contrary, the society of the spectacle is a form that chooses its own technical content. If the spectacle—understood in the limited sense of those "mass media" that are its most stultifying superficial manifestation—seems at times to be invading society in the shape of a mere *apparatus,* it should be remembered that this apparatus has nothing neutral about it, and that it answers precisely to the needs of the spectacle's internal dynamics.[11]

There are many problems with Debord's overall analysis such as his attribution of monolithic power to the state and his conviction that we are living in a totally administered society, a viewpoint that he shared with other eminent postwar critics, including Theodor Adorno, Max Horkheimer, Herbert Marcuse, and Louis Althusser. They were not entirely wrong, but they did not give enough credit to the resilience and sheer inventiveness of human beings: even in the most oppressive and totalizing circumstances we create spaces for alternative lifestyles and find ways to undermine the abuses of power and unveil the spectacles that tend to prevent us from seeing alternatives.

Still, what I find immensely useful in Debord's work is his category of the "spectacle" because it enables us to grasp that what is shown through the mass media conceals power relations. The spectacle is artificial, a social construct, as academicians are fond of saying today, that reveals little about society but produces and reproduces power relations that maintain and reinforce the status quo. As such, the spectacle dominates everyday life by adjusting our vision and reducing us to mere spectators and thus engendering alienation. Debord argued that the more the spectator watches, "the less he lives; the more readily he recognizes his own needs in the images of need proposed by the dominant system, the less he understands his own existence and his own desires. The spectacle's externality with respect to the acting subject is demonstrated by the fact that the individual's own gestures are no longer his own, but rather those of someone else who represents them to him. The spectator feels at home nowhere, for the spectacle is everywhere."[12]

We need only think of the staging of "authentic" emotions on the TV talk shows and reality programs, the pathetic interviews, the courtroom trials, and so on to realize how people perform emotions and end up looking like replicas of themselves. However, it is not just this deep alienation of emotions that the spectacle fosters. Numerous critics, who have written on popular culture, have repeatedly pointed out how the spectacle dumbs down or seeks to dumb down the audience, especially children. But the spectacle does more than dumb down the public; it engenders commensurate modes of behavior that make the projected image valid. The only hope, so it seems for children, is that their lives may be validated according to the expectations of the mass media and the institutions that are connected to them. Or put another way, there is no way that children can avoid the insistent spectacles of popular culture. Whether they will become what the culture industry presents as ideal is an open-ended question. In fact, the culture industry does not care in the least what happens to children just as long as they are configured and compatible with the operational system of the industry and agree to consume and just as long as they are disposed to be turned into professionals to maintain the system in some capacity and into actors for commercials, TV programs, videos, and whatever engenders profit for the industry. Benjamin was right when he talked about the profit motive of bourgeois theater, but he underestimated the power of the culture industry.

Theater as spectacle is everywhere. It is invasive—it invades our minds and bodies through the technological means of the mass media. For example, when President Bush came to visit a special school in

St. Paul, Minnesota, in 2001 to push his education program based primarily on rote testing, his entire visit was scripted from the moment he left Washington, D.C., to the moment he arrived in St. Paul, met with teachers and children, was photographed by the press, and was filmed for television. Though he did ad-lib at times, he did not make a fool of himself because he stuck to his script as much as possible and knew how to smile and look concerned about the children. Mission accomplished, he returned home to view his performance. Everyone had joined in—the authorities, the Republican mayor, who was already planning to run for senator to replace the liberal Paul Wellstone, the children, the parents, the press. No dissenters were visible or asked to question the spectacle. The audience was a captive one. Though Bush spoke about how his educational plans would benefit children, there was only one person—or should I say groups of people—who was going to profit from this spectacle and who had a political agenda to push as the spectacle.

Children's theater as spectacle furthers the pauperization, if not prostitution, of children: material pauperization, pauperization of the mind, prostitution of the body, and prostitution of talent. Much of children's theater today prevents critical thinking by children even as it presents itself as moral, serious, patriotic, and God fearing. Public spectacles are rampant, and children cannot escape their vamped-up ideologies. To be sure, they are not passive victims and recipients of the shows and objects they consume. They continue to play with garbage, but even the garbage won't help them form new meanings if globalization persists, and they may become just like shrubs—dried-up bushes.

But shrubs are also wooden Howdy Doodies—funny, cute, adorable puppets who trip over their own strings and delude themselves and believe that they do not have strings attached to them. Yet they are jerked constantly by the same corporate forces they represent. They are devoid of identity. Globalization contributes to the devastation of identities of all people, especially children, but it does this in a very class-specific manner. In perhaps the most astute and concise analysis of globalization I have read, Zygmunt Bauman remarked,

> To put it in a nutshell: *rather than homogenizing the human condition, the technological annulment of temporal/spatial distances tends*

to polarize it. It [globalization] emancipates certain humans from
territorial constraints and renders certain community-generating
meanings extraterritorial—while denuding the territory, to
which other people go on being confined, of its meaning and its
identity-endowing capacity. For some people it augurs an
unprecedented freedom from physical obstacles and unheard-of
ability to move and act from a distance. For others, it portends
the impossibility of appropriating and domesticating the locality
from which they have little chance of cutting themselves free in
order to move elsewhere. With "distances no longer meaning
anything," localities, separated by distances, also lose their
meanings. This, however, augurs freedom of meaning-creation
for some, but portends ascription to meaninglessness for others.
Some can now move out of the locality—any locality—at will.
Others watch helplessly the sole locality they inhabit moving
away from under their feet.[13]

With the dissolution of public places, or public spheres, communities break down. One of the ironies of polarization is that it leaves these
loose bunches of people, who are no longer bound by community, open
to homogenization and uniformity. Desperate for meaning, people
want to belong to some sort of meaning-producing group, be it a
church, sports team, cult, choir, or fan club, and they seek a way to
belong, to fit in, and to protect themselves from homogenization that
makes their local community meaningless.

This is the paradox, I think, that evades Bauman. As he correctly
remarked, globalization brings about polarization and fractures communities. Yet it also seeks to replace religious and social forms of community with a consumer ideology and organized forms of play and
work that tend to homogenize behavior and to limit the development
of class and political consciousness.[14] Seemingly diverse and enclosed
groups that seek to form distinct identities are actually more uniform
and similar than they realize, and they mimic each other; all forms of
interaction revolve around the same customary practices, which make
activities into commercial undertakings and children into consumers.

Here are two brief examples that pertain to children: organized sports
and school. Instead of forming part of what Negt and Kluge called a
"children's public sphere," organized sports and schools prevent the creation of such a sphere. Indeed, all youth culture—that is, manufactured

popular culture—works against the autonomy of the young, and their space for movement and self-development is becoming more and more narrow as commerce encroaches on their alternative spaces and as globalization seeks to expand its grasp.

The pressure to conform and celebrate uniformity begins, in U.S. sports, before children turn five years old, when they learn to train their bodies and minds and to perform according to adult expectations—how to move, to behave, to feel; what uniforms to purchase; what logos are best to wear; how to invest one's energy; what can be gained by playing the game in certain ways. Whereas only forty years ago children would organize themselves for the most part on streets, backyards, driveways, sandlots, fields, ponds, and playgrounds and develop their own games and rules of the games, almost all these areas have been expropriated and consumed by adults and reorganized according to imposed conditions of the authorities and private owners. This is not to say that children no longer invent and play their own games on their own terms. But the dominant forms of sports are associated with the professionalization of the sport so that the young child is raised, educated, and groomed to think of selling his or her body for profit at a certain point in time. If those expectations cannot be fulfilled, there are others, such as perfecting one's body so that it looks like a machine. Even young girls cannot avoid the homogenization of sports. The so-called revolution in women's sports is a joke: more and more girls seek to resemble the boys in the manner in which they violently play games of every kind to achieve number one status. Competition, profitability, self-promotion, and mimicry are the guidelines that blind spectator and participant alike. Corporate needs and rules have altered and dictated the way many sports are played today. What might have been an important feature of schooling at the end of the nineteenth century and the beginning of the twentieth century—physical education—has become an exercise in self-denial instead of self-expression.

The purpose of the school and schooling, which was in part to foster self-expression within the limits of ruling-class norms, has, of course, changed and will continue to change in the coming years. The most startling transformations are connected to the encroachment of business corporations into public and private schools and the privatization of public schools.[15] Whereas the focus used to be on children and how they might be assisted in defining their identity, it has shifted conclusively toward adult expectations of preparing their children for careers or economic disposability, toward the expectations of the state to maintain a certain level of functional literacy needed by the business world and government to reproduce themselves, and toward the religious and educational leaders and experts who have conflicting views about effective teaching methods and standards. Whatever the focus may be, the child is merely the object of experimentation. There are, of course, numerous schools that prove to be the exception, such as the ones run according to the Montessori, Reggio Emilia, and Waldorf (Rudolf Steiner) philosophies. However, even these schools are endangered species in a world where spectacle invades classrooms and halls to minimize alternative viewpoints and to institute pledges of allegiance to fake gods and countries.

Children's Theater as the Unspectacular

Theater cannot avoid spectacle, and in fact, most of theater and children's theater is spectacle. By spectacle I mean a theater that produces shows for the show's sake, not for the sake of children. It panders to the entertainment industry's expectations and basically conceals power relationships in the way Debord demonstrated. Shows that show off are the traditional fairy-tale plays or plays based on classical or soon to be classical children's literature. They show off talent while concealing the connections to the daily struggles of children trying to grasp how art can play a role in their immediate lives. Children's theater as spectacle is imitative of Broadway and Hollywood musicals, and although numerous performances are captivating and deal with social issues, they divert attention as divertissement from the mediations and connections that bind children into the corporate interests of the public sphere that will exploit and make good use of the children's talents. A good example of the perniciousness of children's theater as spectacle is *A Christmas Carol*. Generally speaking, the larger adult theaters throughout the United States, as well as some of the more privileged wealthy children's theaters, will produce plays during the holidays to bring joy and happiness to children. For instance, the famous Guthrie Theatre in Minneapolis reproduces ad nauseam a version of Dickens's *Christmas Carol* every December—not to prompt children to think about capitalism, misers, poverty, and exploitation but to exhibit the grandiose stage effects and fine acting. The focus on the spectacle is a focus on celebrity, a glorification of the famous theater and its famous actors that detracts from the relevance of Dickens's story to contemporary conditions. After all, if the play were to be performed to convey his social message, it might ruin the afternoon or evening of pleasure for children and their families. Therefore, *A Christmas Carol* is always produced to ease the conscience of the rich and to celebrate philanthropy without questioning it. The spectacle is part of a dumbing-down process and imagines that children cannot think for themselves. Children's theater as spectacle meets the social class expectations of its providers and glorifies their interests.

But fortunately not all theater is spectacle, and work in the theater can also endanger the spectacle itself, just as Benjamin said it can become dangerous for the bourgeoisie. There were and still are many forms of theater that are subversive and invert the spectacle to make it unspectacular. Theater demands space for constant experimentation with the world of objects and for self-experimentation with one's body and mind. Therefore, we can and must question all children's spectacular theater that calls on the young to perform the prepared scripts of their lives. Whether it is a Broadway play, a classical drama, or an adaptation of a famous novel, these plays have a minimal value for the lives of children unless they can appropriate them. For them to appropriate these scripts means that they must have the freedom of space and time to investigate the nature of the texts; how they were produced, received, and distributed in their time; and whether there may be meaning leftover for their lives. If so, it is this leftover signification that will form the basis of the children's play and production, if they even want to produce anything.

I do not mean to dismiss and judge a priori the production of traditional plays such as *A Christmas Carol, Cinderella, The Three Musketeers, Little Orphan Annie, The Wizard of Oz, Pippi Longstocking, Peter Pan,* and so on in the professional children's theater or in schools. I have often been struck by the excitement and pleasure children exude when they watch a live performance of a play. They see and imbibe so many things that escape me. They are not passive as spectators, and yet they are introduced to certain prescribed ways of performance with which they cannot actively play or question. Even question-and-answer sessions after a play or exploring the stage after a performance is not conducive to the creation of a children's public sphere. These activities do not lead to self-exploration and critical examination of the production of their environment.

Benjamin was very insistent that plays not be performed for children. Rather, children should develop their own plays with the guidance of adults, who are also part of the learning process. All other theatrical forms he disregarded as bourgeois and discounted as spectacle, although he did not use that term. This position, I think, is too narrow. No matter what children watch as spectators in a spectacle, they will take over some tiny aspect and cherish and cultivate it in original ways. There is, however, no doubt in my mind that the most effective political theater for children demands physical and intellectual immersion in a project of the children's conception and undertaking.

That being said, there are numerous theatrical groups in the Western world formed by adults only, or with a mixture of adults and children, and they are doing unusual unspectacular work that can be considered politically subversive or threatening, and thus enlightening and empowering. Grips is that kind of a theater, which produces plays written and performed by adults that are intended to provoke children and adults to question the political relations of their personal lives. Within the walls of its own theater, a Grips performance provides a brief glimpse of how play can challenge the spectacle and offer a children's public sphere as an alternative that comprehends the adult world.

Children's theater conceived, practiced, and performed by adults to animate children to consider the alternatives to the power relations of the spectacle opens up fissures in the totalizing tendencies of global capitalism. There is no one model of such political children's theater, and, perhaps, even the term *political* may not be the just term to describe some of the important experiments I have seen in the past ten years. Nevertheless, I shall use the term *political children's theater* to refer to the unspectacular as I discuss some of the performances I was fortunate to have experienced in Minneapolis and St. Paul at the International Children's Theater Festival sponsored by the Ordway Theater as well as individual productions at the Children's Theatre

Company of Minneapolis and visits by different international groups. The political nature of the aesthetics of some of these small companies is not always immediately visible, and yet it is what sustains the intentionality of the plays developed to focus the attention of young spectators so that they can glimpse the power relations that prevent them from seeing how the world is actually made and affects their personal lives.

Reviewing the Unspectacular

When we talk about children's theater, it is never clear what we mean. Do we mean theater for the very young, ages three to ten years, or for teenagers? Are there plays and performances that are age specific? Should plays be censored and made appropriate for the sensitivities of certain age groups? Why even make distinctions? Aren't the best plays and performances for children productions that appeal to people of all ages?

It would take another book to answer these questions, but certainly discrete distinctions can be made with regard to the reception of plays by children. Although the best work is universal, many theater groups create modes of production expressly designed for the comprehensibility of a certain age group.

For instance, Dockteatern Tittut (The Peek-a-Boo Puppet Theatre, Sweden), Mimika Theatre (England), Theater Terra (the Netherlands), and the Catherine Wheels Theatre Company (Scotland) all have created plays that address very young audiences and use space and sound in unusual and careful ways to address issues of alienation, loneliness, and loss. The actors, directors, and designers invest care and thought in all their productions. This adult investment in animating children to ponder complex existential problems is, I think, what is of value to political children's theater.

I saw two plays, *Langel and the Horse Named Blue* and *Wanna Be Wolf,* performed by the Dockteatern Tittut in Minneapolis, and what struck me about its work was the manner in which it openly used puppets, dolls, and the scenery to tell simple narratives with great poetry, humor, and poignancy. *Langel and the Horse Named Blue* concerned a boy who has a best friend named Gudmar, but a blue horse comes between them, and jealousy almost ends their friendship. *Wanna Be Wolf,* based on a book by Ulf Stark, was a delightful shadow-puppet play about a wolf, with whom nobody wants to play, because she is so zany and wild, and a rabbit, who is so shy that he is scared of his own shadow and nobody wants to play with him. They meet and exchange identities, and through this exchange, they play with one another and "come out of themselves" to become good friends.

All the plays created and produced by Dockteatern are intended for children between the ages of two and six years, and the audience is generally limited to thirty or forty spectators. The atmosphere of intimacy and the music of the plays are soothing, and the brevity of the plays (approximately thirty minutes) enables the children to relax and concentrate. The dialogue, sounds, rhymes, and songs are intended to demonstrate how language and relations can be played with and transformed, recalling how children interact with one another in their own imaginary play in homes, on the street, in parks, and in playgrounds. The puppets are used almost like found objects that children pick up on the street or in the house and play with in an imaginary game. There is nothing overtly political about the plots of the plays or the dramatic style of Dockteatern, and yet the unpretentious acting that makes everything visible to the children is exactly the opposite of spectacle theater. The actors talk to the children before and after the performance and invite them to touch and look at the sets and puppets. These interactions show respect for the children's intelligence. There is nothing sweet about Dockteatern. The language is idiomatic, and though the characters and colors are marvelous, the problems depicted are real ones that the very young confront in their everyday lives.

The struggles of daily life also shaped Mimika Theatre's production of *Landscapes*, which I saw at the 2002 International Children's Theater Festival at the Ordway Center for the Performing Arts in St. Paul. Like the Dockteatern actors, Mimika's two puppeteers limit the audience to twenty children, taking them two at a time into a dimly lit canvas tent filled with music based on sounds from nature. Mimika does a great deal of work with special education children and takes its play into schools. Perhaps, *play* is the wrong word for *Landscapes. Panorama* might be a better term. The audience was taken on a journey through a desert, a tropical rainforest, the sea, and Antarctica. The scenery kept changing, and the animals and birds that populated these regions also underwent change. As the children watched, they were clearly being taught something about the climate, the environment, and the beasts. Each region, however, was not a peaceful domain, for the animals preyed on one another and played with one another. There was a sense of survival of the fittest, but with the twinkle of an eye, for the smaller creatures managed to escape the predators. Here, too, the puppeteers were visible for much of the time, and after the play came to a close, they sat and talked with the children and showed them how they worked the puppets and scenery. Although the magic of the performance was thereby dispelled, the art was passed on, and the children may later experiment in much the same way that the actors did.

Although it is clear that Dockteatern, which has been in existence for twenty-five years in Stockholm, is well-funded, neither Dockteatern nor Mimika makes a great deal of money, and it is the unselfish dedication of the actors to educating children through their experimental art that comes through in the best of the small groups I have seen in the past ten years. There is an insistent pursuit to link the personal to the social and political. Dramatic conflict demands theatrical cooperation through narratives that touch on core existential problems. For instance, at the 2001 Ordway International Children's Theater Festival, the Dutch troupe Teater Terra performed the touching play *Swan's Down* about a child's confrontation with death. Simon, a small boy, played by a large puppet, lives near the sea with his father. Though we are unaware of this fact at the beginning of the play, they are mourning the death of the boy's mother, who recently drowned. Thanks to a friendship that the boy develops with a mother swan, he begins to take joy in life again. However, a nasty neighbor recklessly kills one of the swans, and this tragedy, although upsetting, enables the boy to empathize with the mother swan and come to terms with the loss of his own mother. At one point, Simon has an argument with his father, who is overly anxious that his son may drown like his wife, and the boy runs away from home. However, the swan repays his kindness by bringing him back to his father and bringing about a reconciliation. Performed by three actors on a proscenium stage with no change of scenery, this play moved slowly and yet had a poetic flow: the actors did not waste a gesture or word, nor did they seek to create a melodrama. Rather, the reserved and somewhat blunt acting style and the spare scenery captured a mood of loss that was gradually overcome by the boy who shared his feelings with the young spectators without trying to over-whelm them.

The Catherine Wheels Theatre Company (Scotland) also performed a touching drama titled *Martha* at the 2002 Ordway Festival that con-cerned overcoming loneliness. A grumpy woman named Martha lives in a shack by the sea. She has tacked a sign on her shack that says "Don't knock. Just go away!" Most people are scared of her, and even the mailman, who tries to befriend her, is driven away. Martha appears to be satisfied looking at the world through a telescope. Then, all of a sudden, a stray white goose shows up at her shack and begins to pester and play with her. The glum Martha trys to chase him away, but the goose keeps returning until he gets sick and cannot be found. Worried, Martha searches for the bird and brings him into her home, where she nurses him back to health. They form a friendship and play together, and Martha's temperament changes and she becomes an agreeable and joyful person. When the goose disappears overnight to join his flock, Martha becomes somewhat despondent but realizes why the goose had to leave. Soon after she joins the mailman on an outing and she appears to have overcome her loneliness.

Performed by two actors, Gill Robesons and Annie Wood, founders of this group, the play had no young characters, unless one considers the goose a kind of wild, uncontrollable, loveable child. The goose was a rod puppet and was manipulated by Robesons, who also played the mailman and who was forgotten about by the spectators because of the deft way he became part of the goose. Once again, the setting was spare, and the actors took a simple situation—the outcast condition of a disgruntled older woman, which is often incomprehensible to young people—and turned it into a poignant drama about the possibility for change and friendship.

The didactic elements of these unspectacular dramas for the young-est spectators were not overly emphasized by any of the groups I have discussed thus far. Metaphors and puppets were all used to give the children distance as the adult actors concentrated on telling a simple fantastic story as realistically as possible. This style was in stark contrast to that in two productions for teenagers that I witnessed at the Interna-tional Children's Theater Festivals of 2001 and 2002. Both were highly realistic, involved violence, and were intended to raise discussions about particular incidents after the performance.

The Stones, written and performed by Tom Lycos and Stefon Natsou of the Zeal Theatre (Australia), is based on an actual event that took place in Melbourne. Two boys kicked rocks from a freeway overpass for fun, and they accidentally caused the death of a driver. The boys, who were thirteen and fifteen years old, were charged with manslaughter and brought to trial. The verdict was "not guilty" at the end. But here, ultimately, the audience is called on to deliver the verdict, for the play ends with one of the boys realizing how reckless he had been and the other just relieved that he was "getting off." Lycos and Natsou consulted the officer in charge of the Australian case while writing the play several years ago, and they added aspects from other similar incidents that have taken place throughout the world. They play all the roles in the play—the boys, officers, attorneys—in a small space with minimum change of costume in front of the spectators. They never identify with their characters, but in good Brechtian fashion they use the play to demonstrate how small acts of vandalism can lead to tragedy. Neither one of the boys is particularly sympathetic, and this feature of the play and the way it is performed without stereotypes adds to its powerful effect. The play is similar to a documentary but it is more effective because it calls on the spectators to reveal what they have learned in the end and to make judgments.

The work of the Teatergruppen Mariehønen is also based on the Brechtian *Lehrstück* methodology. Here the set, which can easily be transported to schools or open spaces, acts as a metaphor of life. An equilateral triangle surrounds a box that contains large boxing gloves; a lighting rig at each point of the triangle is used as the designated space of each of the characters, who usher the spectators into the area as if they were going to witness a boxing match. The characters, all in their early teens, are Poul, who is sensitive and modest and has a good home life; Stevens, a bully, who takes pleasure in making life hell for Poul; Norman, who is imaginative and nervous and whose father is an alcoholic and beats him and his mother; and Henrietta, nicknamed Henry, who has just moved to the city because her parents are going through a divorce. She has a tough veneer and does not want anyone to know that she is suffering. The play begins at the end of the school year. Stevens beats up Poul and makes him promise that on the first day of school in the fall he will wear girl's clothing to indicate that he is a sissy. Poul spends the summer with his friends Norman and Henrietta and he tries to learn how to box so he can defend himself in the fall. However, Stevens frequently interferes with them, as do their conflicts at home. All their personal problems emerge as they engage in the boxing ring of life. In the end they find a way to put an end to the turmoil and violence of bullying, which they confront inside and outside their homes.

The actors of Teatergruppen do not mimic teenagers. Instead, they illustrate the dramatic situations in which teenagers may find themselves at any given moment. Making full use of the boxing metaphor, they reveal the shifting sides of the different combats that the characters are obliged to enter, whether they want to or not. Though the bully is defeated in the end, it is not a final defeat, nor are all the problems of the teenagers put to rest. What becomes clear, however, is that there are many ways to defend oneself and that friendship and solidarity are essential when one is confronted by tyranny.

There are hundreds of tiny groups like Teatergruppen Mariehønen and Zeal Theatre in the Western world, formed by adults who have a message they want to deliver to children to change or affect their lives. Their work varies according to their grasp of the power relations of the social world in which they interact. As adults, they are generous with their time and commitment to children or a political cause and are poorly paid. Characteristically their best work is unspectacular, enabling their audiences to unravel some of the blinding forces that control their lives. The unspectacular is the crucial element of the children's public realm. When children and adults play not to show off the social and political forces that prescribe and dictate their lives but to show how to play with these same forces in cooperation with one another, they form the unspectacular that is dangerous to theater of spectacle.

A Nonconclusive Conclusion

I hesitate to conclude this chapter with an assessment of children's theater today or with some pronouncement of what children's theater should become for it to be authentic or proletarian. But I do want to make a few remarks about educational children's theater or theater through education that generally takes place unseen in thousands of schools in the Western world in many different forms. In the United States, my focus of attention, it is this type of theater work, closest to what Benjamin envisioned as proletarian children's theater, that is the first to be cut in schools when there are budget problems and crunches. In the age of shrubs and globalization, theater and arts programs are especially "dangerous" and are being visibly crunched, whether they have a political purpose or not.

Nevertheless, these programs and the tiny, if not minuscule, groups of adults who work with children in these programs are crucial to support and maintain if the unspectacular is going to thrive as a subversive force—and I think that is our only hope for it—and to survive as a subversive force. Fortunately (or some might say, unfortunately) the theater of the spectacle and the society of the spectacle feed off the unspectacular as parasites and need the life force of the unspectacular to expand their interests and make themselves appear to be interesting and interested in their spectators. So, it will always be possible to do educational theater in the nooks and crannies of public spheres and institutions.

In Minneapolis there are several small groups that seek to enter the fissures of institutionalized schooling, some that simply seek to impart artistic skills to children and entertain them, some with a social and political agenda. I want to close with a summary of a project developed at the Children's Theatre Company of Minneapolis because this large and wealthy theater is an example of how such traditional middle-class theaters, while creating spectacles, can transcend themselves through subversive unspectacular work and perhaps can eventually transform their main stage into a public theater of the people.

Taking a Giant Step and Building Bridges in the Junior Conservatory
For many years the Children's Theatre Company has run an actor training program (the Junior Conservatory) for students in the late afternoon on Monday, Tuesday, and Wednesday and on weekends. Traditionally the students are divided into two classes: eight- to twelve-year-olds and thirteen- to sixteen-year-olds. They are trained in acting, music, and dance, and some of the youngsters are granted scholarships. A few of the students are recruited or audition for plays performed on

the main stage of the Children's Theatre Company, but the majority are enrolled in these courses for their own benefit and they generally produce a small skit at the end of each semester.

In the winter of 2002, Maria Asp, who directs the acting session of the Junior Conservatory and is the assistant director of the Neighborhood Bridges program, came to me and asked for some material for her class of eight- to twelve-year-olds. I gave her the story "The Giant and His Suit of Armor," which I had translated from German, by Edwin Hoernle, who had written political fairy tales during the Weimar period. The tale concerns a young giant, who is kidnaped by dwarfs from another country and transformed into their slave, even though he is more powerful than they are. While in captivity, he builds a suit of armor to protect himself from the punishment of the dwarfs, and he even realizes that he is stronger than the dwarfs. Yet, the years of humiliation and degradation have made him so anxious and afraid that he never rebels against his masters and remains in chains for the rest of his life. Hoernle wrote this tale to critique the unwillingness of workers to take charge of their own lives and to change the miserable conditions under which they worked.

Asp joined with two other Junior Conservatory teachers, Marya Hart (music) and Matt Jensen (dance), to adapt the story and make it into a play. Working very much in the Benjaminian mode, they sought to prompt, coach, and guide the young actors to develop their own play based on the story. In this multidisciplinary project the students explored the vocabulary of modernism through the music of Hanns Eisler and Kurt Weill and created modern dance pieces, including a contemporary "ballet mechanique." They were also introduced to Brecht's theories and techniques of epic theater and tradition of the *Lehrstück* (learning play). By the late spring of 2002, the students under the guidance of Asp, Hart, and Jensen performed their play "The Giant" for a general public consisting of parents, relatives, friends, and members of the Children's Theatre Company staff.

The actors used old costumes from the Children's Theatre Company and found objects in a small studio theater to demonstrate the helplessness and foolishness of giants. (Instead of one giant, they had three.) They formed a chorus to comment on the actions of the dwarfs and the giants. Their gestures and words brought out their own thinking about the situation of the giants as representative of workers and common people. Though there was some confusion between the giants and the dwarfs at times, and the songs were not always clear or appropriate for the action, the half-hour skit was a remarkable work in progress that revealed how much the students had learned and how well they could work together to develop their own play.

This play was not, however, finished. Shortly after the production, Hart came up with the idea of reworking the skit for the 2003 International Brecht Conference that was to take place in Berlin. At the same time I was already holding discussions with Peter Brosius about the possibility of developing a small theater group with Neighborhood Bridges students to perform their improvised skits at other schools. It occurred to me that the work in the Junior Conservatory, which was already connected to Neighborhood Bridges through Maria Asp, might serve as the testing ground for the Gorilla Theater of Neighborhood Bridges.

It did not take much time for me to make arrangements with the International Brecht Society and Grips Theater to schedule a performance during the Brecht Conference at the end of June 2003. Following the performance, there was to be a panel discussion with Volker Ludwig, Albrecht Dümling, and other educators attending the conference. Asp, Hart, and Jensen spent the fall of 2002 applying for grants and raising money for all fourteen students, who were to fly to Berlin in June 2003. Because I was going to spend the 2002–2003 academic year in Europe, I had discussions with Asp, Hart, and Jensen about the development of the play and strategies for collaboration with a class at the John F. Kennedy School in Berlin. The Minneapolis students would have pen pals and perform their play not only at the Brecht conference but also at the JFK School. The preparations were to begin in January at the Junior Conservatory, and any student who applied to participate in this special class was accepted. Students from the Neighborhood Bridges program were recruited. Scholarships were given to all students who needed support.

Asp, Hart, and Jensen worked intensely with a group of fourteen students (ages nine to fourteen) from January until June, when they set out for Berlin. Here is the report that Asp filed with a German cultural agency that cosponsored the event:

On Monday, June 23, the Children's Theatre Company manager Deb Pearson joined the teachers, students, and four parent-chaperones and set off for Germany. After an exciting plane change in Reykjavik [Icelandic Airlines gave a special reduction for the group] we landed safely in Frankfurt am Main. Our next adventure was taking two trains to the beautiful town of Lutherstadt Wittenberg. After a delicious German meal, the sleepy travelers collapsed in their beds at the charming medieval youth hostel.

The next day we spent exploring the town. The students loved the historic buildings and relaxed on the shores of the Elba River. They were most impressed, however, by a school designed by the famous painter Michael Hundertwasser. We spent a great deal of time walking around this fabulous building, spending hours letting our eyes be pulled along the winding paths and visiting with the students inside.

The next day we boarded a train for Berlin. After settling in at our new hostel near the Technical University of Berlin, we grabbed a quick bite to eat and began rehearsing our show at the Schiller Theater-Werkstatt, a small studio theater, where Grips performs some of its plays. A local musician, Toby Schiller, joined us and enriched our live musical accompaniment with his clarinet and saxophone playing. He was a great addition to our group.

Our next days were full of wonderful activities, including sightseeing, rehearsing, meeting pen pals, making new friends with other students at our hostel, enjoying German food, and shopping. Some of the highlights included seeing the Berlin Ensemble, the Church of Memories, the Berlin Tower, the Tiergarten, the Brandenburg Gate, the Reichstag, the amazing architecture of Potsdammer Platz, Alexander Platz, and the musical performance by Peter Sicher and pianist Claus Schäfer. The students especially enjoyed seeing two plays, *Linie 1* and *Melodys Ring,* performed at the Grips Theater. Many of them bought copies of the *Melodys Ring* sound track, got autographs from the actors, and sang the songs throughout their time in performance. The Grips plays were an inspiration for our students.

The culminating event was the students' performance of "The Giant" on Sunday, June 29. They were sensational. It was as though they had truly been inspired by their new surroundings. The Schiller Theater-Werkstatt was filled to capacity with scholars of theater from around the world and a general public. After the performance, there was a brief break followed by a captivating panel discussion led by Jack Zipes, Volker Ludwig, and Albrecht Dümling. The reflection by both scholars and student performers was profound. No one left the theater. In particular, our students amazed the audience by their insights into their own work and responses to questions.

We had only one day in Frankfurt am Main on our way back to Minneapolis, but the students loved walking around the town and exploring the old churches and fountains. We were quick to realize that there were more extraordinary places and things to do and see so that we all needed to return to Germany again some day.

We met and exceeded our goals. The students created a theatrical piece where their voices were heard examining contemporary and historical issues. Moreover, their exploration of German history and culture will continue, and they demonstrated an uncanny ability to draw parallels with developments in our present-day world. Many of the students picked up the language at an incredible rate. Several continue to write to their pen pals and plans for reunions are under way. The students became an ensemble and felt welcomed by the German people. We all made many new friends and contacts. Already we have received interest from organizations and colleges to continue this kind of work with young people in other communities.

Indeed, their willingness to cross bridges and spread what they have learned in their sphere of activity, that is, to apply their learning to the world, brings us back to one of the key notions in Benjamin's "Program of a Proletarian Children's Theater": "Children, who have played theater in this way, have become free in such productions. Through play they have fulfilled their childhood." Certainly, it is impossible to speak about his "Program" today without revising and expanding it. History has changed childhood. History has changed the proletariat. But history has not changed the conditions under which children play and labor to define themselves to struggle against oppression in the family, schools, and community and to articulate their needs. Benjamin saw a specific proletarian theater as a means that would enable children (the most oppressed) to come to terms with conditions that were not of their own making. He demanded, perhaps too rigidly, a theater in which the children could voice their wants and develop projects that spoke to their needs. This type of theater work is still possible, but it is a theater work that must cut across all social classes in schools and community centers, and it must also include the unspectacular theater productions of adults, whose care and concern for children are expressed in their unusual performances that touch the minds and emotions of the young. Whether such unspectacular work will become more visible and have an impact on society does not depend entirely on children's theaters, but political children's theater must continue to question the purpose of such theaters and confront the society of the spectacle if it wants to keep the vital, "dangerous" impulse of theater alive.

Bibliography

I have divided the bibliography into three parts: Anthologies of Folk and Fairy Tales, Fables, Legends, and Myths; Tales by Individual Authors; and Reference Works. It is based on the bibliography in *Creative Storytelling: Building Community, Changing Lives,* but it has been extensively revised. By no means are these lists complete or intended to designate some type of definitive catalog of the best tales, fables, legends, and myths for storytelling. Most of the tales and reference works that I have listed are texts with which I have worked and which have been useful to me. In particular, I recommend that storytellers, teachers, and other interested readers adapt the tales to suit their interests. Because it is often difficult to find a good bibliography of tales and references for storytelling, I have tried to provide the most recent books on the topic and to include books that also contain additional references that supplement my work.

Anthologies of Folk and Fairy Tales, Fables, Legends, and Myths

Abrahams, Roger D., ed. 1985. *Afro-American Folktales.* New York: Pantheon.

Achebe, Chinua. 1996. *Things Fall Apart.* Expanded ed. with notes. London: Heinemann.

Aesop. 1954. *Fables of Aesop.* Translated by S. A. Handford. Harmondsworth: Penguin.

Afanas'ev, Aleksandr Nikolaevich. 1945. *Russian Fairy Tales: 1855–1864.* Translated by Norbert Guterman. New York: Pantheon.

Andersen, Hans Christian. 1974. *The Complete Fairy Tales and Stories.* Translated by Erik Christian Haugaard. New York: Doubleday.

Arbuthnot, May H., ed. 1952. *Time for Fairy Tales.* Chicago: Scott, Foresman.

Asbjørnsen, Peter Christen, and Jørgen Moe. 1960. *Norwegian Folk Tales.* New York: Viking.

Auerbach, Nina, and U. C. Knoepflmacher, eds. 1992. *Forbidden Journeys: Fairy Tales and Fantasies by Victorian Women Writers.* Chicago: University of Chicago Press.

Badoe, Adwoa. 2001. *The Pot of Wisdom: Ananse Stories*. Illustrated by Wague Diakite. Toronto, ON: Groundwood/Douglas & McIntyre.

Barbeau, Marius. 1958. *The Golden Phoenix and Other French Canadian Fairy Tales*. Retold by Michael Hornyansky. New York: Walck.

Barchers, Suzanne I., ed. 1990. *Wise Women: Folk and Fairy Tales from around the World*. Littleton, Colo.: Libraries Unlimited.

Basile, Giambattista. 1932. *The Pentamerone of Giambattista Basile*. Translated and edited by N. M. Penzer. 2 vols. London: John Lane the Bodley Head.

Berry, Jack, trans. 1991. *West African Folk Tales*. Edited by Richard Spears. Evanston, Ill.: Northwestern University Press.

Bierhorst, John, ed. 1976. *The Red Swan: Myths and Tales of the American Indians*. New York: Farrar, Straus & Giroux.

Botkin, B. A., ed. 1944. *A Treasury of American Folklore*. New York: Crown.

Botkin, B. A., ed. 1947. *A Treasury of New England Folklore: Stories, Ballads and Traditions of the Yankee People*. New York: Crown.

Botkin, B. A., ed. 1949. *A Treasury of Southern Folklore*. New York: Crown.

Briggs, Katharine M., and Ruth L. Tongue, eds. 1965. *Folktales of England*. Chicago: University of Chicago Press.

Briggs, Katharine M., ed. 1980. *Nine Lives: The Folklore of Cats*. New York: Pantheon.

Brody, Ed, Jay Goldspinner, Katie Green, Rona Leventhal, and John Porcino, eds. 2002. *Spinning Tales, Weaving Hope: Stories of Peace, Justice and the Environment*. 2nd ed. Philadelphia: New Society Publishers.

Bruchac, Joseph. 1991. *Native American Stories*. Golden, Colo.: Fulcrum.

Burg, Marie. 1965. *Tales from Czechoslovakia*. London: University of London Press.

Bushnaq, Inea, ed. 1986. *Arab Folktales*. New York: Pantheon Books.

Calvino, Italo, ed. 1980. *Italian Folktales*. Translated by George Martin. New York: Harcourt Brace Jovanovich.

Caro, Frank de, ed. 1992. *The Folktale Cat*. Illustrated by Kitty Harvill. Little Rock, Ark.: August House.

Carter, Angela, ed. 1990. *Old Wives' Fairy Tale Book*. New York: Pantheon.

Carter, Angela, ed. 1990. *The Virago Book of Fairy Tales*. Illustrated by Corinna Sargood. London: Virago.

Carter, Angela, ed. 1993. *Strange Things Sometimes Still Happen: Fairy Tales from around the World*. Illustrated by Corinna Sargood. London: Faber and Faber.

Chase, Richard, ed. 1943. *The Jack Tales*. Boston: Houghton Mifflin.

Chase, Richard, ed. 1948. *Grandfather Tales*. Boston: Houghton Mifflin.

Chase, Richard, ed. 1956. *American Folk Tales and Songs*. New York: New American Library.

Christianesen, Reidar T., ed. 1964. *Folktales of Norway*. Chicago: University of Chicago Press.

Clarkson, Attelia, and Gilbert B. Cross, eds. 1980. *World Folktales: A Scribner Resource Collection*. New York: Scribner.

Clouston, W. A. 2002. *Popular Tales and Fictions*. Edited by Christine Goldberg. Santa Barbara, Calif.: ABC-CLIO.

Coffin, Tristram Potter, and Hennig Cohen, eds. 1974. *Folklore from the Working Folk of America*. New York: Anchor/Doubleday.

Cohen, Amy, ed. 1994. *From Sea to Shining Sea*. New York: Scholastic.

Colum, Padraic. 1964. *The Children of Odin: The Book of Northern Myths*. New York: Macmillan.

Colum, Padraic, ed. 1937. *Legends of Hawaii*. New Haven, Conn.: Yale University Press.

Courlander, Harold. 1996. *A Treasury of African Folklore*. New York: Marlowe.

Crane, Thomas Frederick. 1889. *Italian Popular Tales*. Boston: Houghton Mifflin.

Crane, Thomas Frederick. 2001. *Italian Popular Tales*. Edited by Jack Zipes. Santa Barbara, Calif.: ABC-CLIO.

Creeden, Sharon. 1994. *Fair is Fair: World Folktales of Justice*. Little Rock, Ark.: August House.

Creeden, Sharon. 1999. *In Full Bloom: Women in Their Prime*. Little Rock, Ark.: August House.

Crooke, William, and Pandit Ram Gharib Chaube. 2002. *Folktales from Northern India*. Edited by Sadhana Naithani. Santa Barbara, Calif.: ABC-CLIO.

Crossley-Holland, Kevin, ed. 1980. *The Norse Myths*. New York: Pantheon.

Crossley-Holland, Kevin, ed. 1987. *British Folktales*. London: Orchard Books.

Curtin, Jerome. 2002. *Creation Myths of Primitive America*. Edited by Karl Kroeber. Santa Barbara, Calif.: ABC-CLIO.

Datlow, Ellen, and Terri Windling, eds. 1993. *Black Thorn, White Rose*. New York: William Morrow.

Datlow, Ellen, and Terri Windling, eds. 1994. *Snow White, Blood Red*. New York: William Morrow.

Datlow, Ellen, and Terri Windling, eds. 1995. *Ruby Slippers, Golden Tears*. New York: William Morrow.

Davis, Donald. 1993. *Jack's First Job*. Little Rock, Ark.: August House.

Dégh, Linda, ed. 1965. *Folktales of Hungary*. Chicago: University of Chicago Press.

Dorje, Rinjing. *Tales of Uncle Tompa: The Legendary Rascal of Tibet*. San Rafael, CA: Dorje Ling, 1975.

Eberhard, Wolfram, ed. 1965. *Folktales of China*. Chicago: University of Chicago Press.

El-Shamy, Hasan M., ed. 1979. *Folktales of Egypt*. Chicago: University of Chicago Press.

Erdoes, Richard, and Alfonso Ortiz, eds. 1984. *American Indian Myths and Legends*. New York: Pantheon.

Field, Rachel, ed. 1929. *American Folk and Fairy Tales*. New York: Scribner.

Fitzgerald, Burdette S. 1962. *World Tales for Creative Dramatics and Storytelling*. Englewood Cliffs, N.J.: Prentice Hall.

Fontaine, Jean de la. 1988. *The Complete Fables of Jean de la Fontaine*. Translated by Norman B. Spector. Evanston, Ill.: Northwestern.

Fortier, Alcée, ed. 1895. *Louisiana Folk-Tales*. Boston: Stechert.

Frere, Mary. 2002. *Old Deccan Days or Hindoo Fairy Legends*. Edited by Kirin Narayan. Santa Barbara, Calif.: ABC-CLIO.

Glassie, Henry, ed. 1985. *Irish Folk Tales*. New York: Pantheon.

Grimm, Jacob, and Wilhelm Grimm. 1981. *The German Legends of the Brothers Grimm*. Translated and edited by Donald Ward. 2 vols. Philadelphia: Institute for the Study of Human Issues.

Grimm, Jacob, and Wilhelm Grimm. 2003. *The Complete Fairy Tales of the Brothers Grimm*. 3rd expanded ed. Translated and edited by Jack Zipes. New York: Bantam.

Grundtvig, Svend. 1914. *Danish Fairy Tales*. Translated and edited by Gustav Hein. New York: Crowell.

Hadley, Eric, and Tessa Hadley. 1985. *Legends of Earth, Air, Fire, and Water*. Illustrated by Bryna Waldman. New York: Cambridge University Press.

Haley, Gail. 1970. *A Story a Story: An African Tale*. New York: Atheneum.

Harris, Joel Chandler. 1955. *The Complete Uncle Remus*. Edited by Richard Chase. Boston: Houghton Mifflin.

Hart, Carole, Letty Cottin Pogrebin, Mary Rodgers, and Marlo Thomas, eds. 1974. *Free to Be ... You and Me*. New York: McGraw-Hill.

Hearn, Michael Patrick, ed. 1988. *The Victorian Fairy Tale Book*. New York: Pantheon.

Hearne, Betsy, ed. 1993. *Beauties and Beasts*. Illustrated by Joanne Caroselli. Phoenix, Ariz.: Oryx Press.

Hickox, Rebecca. 1997. *Zorro and Quwi: Tales of a Trickster Guinea Pig*. New York: Doubleday.

Jacobs, Joseph, ed. 1892. *Celtic Fairy Tales*. London: David Nutt.

Jacobs, Joseph, ed. 1890. *English Fairy Tales*. London: David Nutt.

Jacobs, Joseph, ed. 1892. *Indian Fairy Tales*. London: David Nutt.

Jacobs, Joseph, ed. 1894. *More English Folk and Fairy Tales*. London: G. P. Putnam.

Jacobs, Joseph, ed. 2002. *English Fairy Tales and More English Fairy Tales*. Edited by Donald Haase. Santa Barbara, Calif.: ABC-CLIO.

Jaffe, Nina. 1994. *Patakín: World Tales of Drums and Drummers*. New York: Henry Holt.

Jagendorf, Moritz, ed. 1948. *New England Bean-Pot: American Folk Stories to Read and to Tell*. New York: Vanguard Press.

Jagendorf, Moritz, ed. 1949. *Upstate Downstate: Folk Stories of the Middle Atlantic States*. New York: Vanguard Press.

Jones, Gwyn. 1956. *Scandinavian Legends and Folk-Tales*. Illustrated by Joan Kiddell-Monroe. Oxford: Oxford University Press.

Judd, Mary Catherine. 1901. *Classic Myths*. Chicago: Rand McNally.

Keding, Dan. 1998. *Beyond the Hero*. Little Rock, Ark.: August House.

Kennerly, Karen, ed. 1973. *Hesitant Wolf and Scrupulous Fox: Fables Selected from World Literature*. New York: Random House.

Komroff, Manuel, ed. 1928. *The Great Fables of All Nations*. Illustrated by Louise Thoron. New York: Dial.

Leland, Charles G. 1884. *The Algonquin Legends of New England: Myths and Folklore of the Micmac, Passamaquoddy, and Penobscot Tribes*. Boston: Houghton Mifflin.

Livo, Norma, and Dia Cha. 1991. *The Folk Stories of the Hmong*. Englewood, Colo.: Libraries Unlimited.

Livo, Norma, and George Livo. 1999. *The Enchanted Wood and Other Tales from Finland*. Englewood, Colo.: Libraries Unlimited.

Lofaro, Michael A., ed. 2001. *Davy Crockett's Riproarious Shemales and Sentimental Sisters: Women's Tall Tales from the Crockett Almanacs (1835–1856)*. Mechanicsburg, Pa.: Stackpole.

Louis, Liliane Nérette. 1999. *When Night Falls, Kric! Krac!: Haitian Folktales*. Englewood, Colo.: Libraries Unlimited.

Lurie, Alison, ed. 1980. *Clever Gretchen and Other Forgotten Folktales*. New York: Crowell.

Lurie, Alison, ed. 1993. *The Oxford Book of Modern Fairy Tales*. Oxford: Oxford University Press.

MacDonald, Margaret Read, ed. 1992. *Peace Tales: World Folktales to Talk About*. Hamden, Conn.: Linnet Books.

MacDonald, Margaret Read, ed. 1993. *Tom Thumb*. Illustrated by Joanne Caroselli. Phoenix, Ariz.: Oryx Press.

MacKaye, Percy. 1926. *Tall Tales of the Kentucky Mountains*. New York: Doran.

Malpezzi, Frances, and William Clements. 1992. *Italian-American Folklore*. Little Rock, Ark.: August House.

Marshall, Bonnie. 2002. *Tales from the Heart of the Balkans*. Englewood, Colo.: Libraries Unlimited.

Maspero, Gaston. 2002. *Popular Stories of Ancient Egypt*. Edited by Hasan El-Shamy. Santa Barbara, Calif.: ABC-CLIO.

Massignon, Genevieve, ed. 1968. *Folktales of France*. Chicago: University of Chicago Press.

McKinley, Robin, ed. 1986. *Imaginary Lands*. New York: Greenwillow.

McNeil, Heather. 2002. *The Celtic Breeze: Stories of the Otherworld from Scotland, Ireland, and Wales*. Englewood, Colo.: Libraries Unlimited.

Megas, Georgios A., ed. 1970. *Folktales of Greece*. Chicago: University of Chicago Press.

Mieder, Wolfgang, ed. 1979. *Grimms Märchen—Modern*. Stuttgart: Reclam.

Mieder, Wolfgang, ed. 1985. *Disenchantments: An Anthology of Modern Fairy Tale Poetry*. Hanover: University Press of New England.

Minard, Rosemary, ed. 1975. *Womenfolk and Fairy Tales*. Boston: Houghton Mifflin.

Noy, Dov, ed. 1963. *Folktales of Israel*. Chicago: University of Chicago Press.

O'Faolain, Eileen. 1954. *Irish Sagas and Folk-Tales*. Illustrated by Joan Kiddell-Monroe. New York: Henry Z. Walck.

O'Sullivan, Sean, ed. 1966. *Folktales of Ireland*. Chicago: University of Chicago Press.

Paredes, Americo, ed. 1970. *Folktales of Mexico*. Chicago: University of Chicago Press.

Peck, Catherine, ed. 1998. *Treasury of North American Folktales*. New York: Quality Paperback Book Club.

Pellowski, Anne. 1984. *The Story Vine: A Sourcebook of Unusual and Easy-to-Tell Stories from around the World*. New York: Macmillan.

Phaedrus. 1992. *The Fables of Phaedrus*. Austin: University of Texas.

Phelps, Ethel Johnston, ed. 1978. *Tatterhood and Other Tales*. Old Westbury, N.Y.: Feminist Press.

Phelps, Ethel Johnston, ed. 1981. *The Maid of the North: Feminist Folk Tales from around the World*. New York: Holt, Rinehart & Winston.

Philip, Neil, ed. 1988. *The Cinderella Story*. London: Penguin.

Pino-Saavedra, Yolanda, ed. 1968. *Folktales of Chile*. Chicago: University of Chicago Press.

Pogrebin, Letty Cottin, ed. 1982. *Stories for Free Children*. New York: McGraw-Hill.

Ragan, Kathleen, ed. 1998. *Fearless Girls, Wise Women and Beloved Sisters: Heroines in Folktales from Around the World*. New York: Norton.

Ramanujan, A. K., ed. 1991. *Folktales from India*. New York: Pantheon.

Randolf, Vance, ed. 1955. *The Devil's Pretty Daughter and Other Ozark Folk Tales*. New York: Columbia University Press.

Ranke, Kurt, ed. 1966. *Folktales of Germany*. Chicago: University of Chicago Press.

Rattray, R. S., ed. 1930. *Akan-Ashanti folk-Tales*. Oxford: Oxford University Press.

Reneaux, J. J. 1990. *Cajun Folktales*. Little Rock, Ark.: August House.

Roberts, Moss, ed. 1979. *Chinese Fairy Tales and Fantasies*. New York: Pantheon.

San Souci, Robert, ed. 1993. *Cut from the Same Cloth: American Women of Myth, Legend, and Tall Tale*. Illustrated by Brian Pinkney. New York: Putnam.

Saxon, Lyle, Edward Dryer, and Robert Tallant, eds. 1987. *Gumbo Ya-Ya: A Collection of Louisiana Folk Tales*. Gretna, La.: Pelican.

Schimmel, Nancy, ed. 1992. *Just Enough to Make a Story*. Berkeley, Calif.: Sisters' Choice Press.

Schreiber, Morris. 1960. *Stories of Gods and Heroes: Famous Myths and Legends of the World*. New York: Grosset and Dunlap.

Seki, Keigo, ed. 1963. *Folktales of Japan*. Chicago: University of Chicago Press.

Sierra, Judy, ed. 1992. *Cinderella*. Phoenix, Ariz.: Oryx Press.

Spagnoli, Cathy. 1998. *Asian Tales and Tellers*. Little Rock, Ark.: August House.

Spagnoli, Cathy, and Paramasivam Samana. 1999. *Jasmine and Coconuts: South Indian Tales*. Englewood, Colo.: Libraries Unlimited.

Stephens, John Richard, ed. 1993. *The King of the Cats and Other Feline Fairy Tales*. London: Faber and Faber.

Straparola, Giovan Francesco. *The Facetious Nights of Straparola*. Translated by William G. Waters. Illustrated by E. R. Hughes. London: Lawrence and Bullen.

Taube, Karl. 1993. *Aztec and Maya Myths*. Austin: University of Texas Press.

Thompson, Stith, ed. 1966. *Tales of the North American Indians*. Bloomington: Indiana University Press.

Thompson, Stith, ed. 1968. *One Hundred Favorite Folktales*. Illustrated by Franz Altschuler. Bloomington: Indiana University Press.

Tong, Diane, ed. 1989. *Gypsy Folktales*. New York: Harcourt Brace Jovanovich.

Torrence, Jackie. 1994. *The Importance of Pot Liquor*. Little Rock, Ark.: August House.

Tyler, Royall, ed. 1987. *Japanese Fairy Tales*. New York: Pantheon.

Uchida, Yoshiko. 1949. *The Dancing Kettle and Other Japanese Folk Tales*. Illustrated by Richard C. Jones. New York: Harcourt, Brace, and World.

Ugorji, Okechukwu. 1991. *The Adventures of Torti: Tales from West Africa*. Trenton, N.J.: African World Press.

Van Etten, Teresa Pijoan de. 1990. *Spanish-American Folktales*. Little Rock, Ark.: August House.

Vigil, Angel. 1994. *The Corn Woman: Stories and Legends of the Hispanic Southwest*. Englewood, Colo.: Libraries Unlimited.

Vigil, Angel. 2000. *The Eagle on the Cactus: Traditional Stories from Mexico*. Englewood, Colo.: Libraries Unlimited.

Walker, Deward E., and Daniel Matthews. 1994. *Nez Perce Coyote Tales: The Myth Cycle*. Norman: University of Oklahoma Press.

Weinreich, Beatrice, ed. 1989. *Yiddish Folk Tales*. Translated by Leonard Wolf. New York: Pantheon.

Williams-Ellis, Amabel. 1960. *More British Fairy Tales*. London: Blackie.

Williamson, Duncan. 1983. *Fireside Tales of the Traveller Children*. Edinburgh: Canongate.

Williamson, Duncan. 1985. *The Broonie, Silkies and Fairies*. Edinburgh: Canongate.

Wolkstein, Diane. 1980. *The Magic Orange Tree and Other Haitian Folktales*. New York: Schocken.

Wyatt, Isabel. 1962. *The Golden Stag and Other Folk Tales from India*. Illustrated by Anne Marie Jauss. New York: David McKay.

Yolen, Jane, ed. 1986. *Favorite Folktales from around the World*. New York: Pantheon.

Young, Richard Alan, and Judy Dockrey, eds. 1993. *African-American Folktales for Young Readers*. Little Rock, Ark.: August House.

Zeitlin, Steven J., Amy J. Kotkin, and Holly Cutting Baker, eds. 1982. *A Celebration of American Family Folklore: Tales and Traditions from the Smithsonian Collection*. New York: Pantheon.

Zipes, Jack, ed. 1986. *Don't Bet on the Prince: Contemporary Feminist Fairy Tales in North America and England*. New York: Methuen.

Zipes, Jack, ed. 1989. *Beauties, Beasts, and Enchantment: French Classical Fairy Tales*. New York: New American Library.

Zipes, Jack, ed. and trans. 1989. *Fairy Tales and Fables from Weimar Days*. Hanover: University Press of New England.

Zipes, Jack, ed. 1991. *Spells of Enchantment: The Wondrous Fairy Tales of Western Culture*. New York: Viking.

Zipes, Jack, ed. 1993. *The Trials and Tribulations of Little Red Riding Hood*. 2nd ed. New York: Routledge.

Zipes, Jack, ed. 1994. *The Outspoken Princess and the Gentle Knight*. New York: Bantam.

Zipes, Jack, ed. 2001. *The Great Fairy Tale Tradition: From Straparola and Basile to the Brothers Grimm*. New York: Norton.

Zipes, Jack, ed. 2003. *The Great Treasury of Sicilian Folk and Fairy Tales Collected by Laura Gonzenbach*. New York: Routledge.

Tales by Individual Authors

Ade, George. 1914. *Ade's Fables*. New York: Doubleday.

Ade, George. 1960. *Fables in Slang and More Fables in Slang*. New York: Dover.

Alexander, Lloyd. 1973. *The Foundling and Other Tales*. New York: Dutton.

Alexander, Lloyd. 1977. *The Town Cats and Other Tales*. New York: Dutton.

Appiah, Peggy. 1967. *Tales of an Ashanti Father*. Illustrated by Mora Dickson. Boston: Beacon.

Babbitt, Natalie. 1974. *The Devil's Storybook*. New York: Farrar, Strauss.

Barber, Antonia. 1987. *The Enchanter's Daughter*. London: Jonathan Cape.

Browning, Robert. 1926. *The Pied Piper of Hamelin*. Illustrated by Frances Brundage. New York: Saalfield.

Calmenson, Stephanie. 1989. *The Principal's New Clothes*. Illustrated by Denise Brunkus. New York: Scholastic.

Coolidge, Olivia E. 1949. *Greek Myths*. Illustrated by Edouard Sandoz. New York: Houghton Mifflin.

Carrick, Donald. 1982. *Harald and the Giant Knight*. New York: Clarion Books.

Carter, Angela. 1970. *The Donkey Prince*. New York: Simon & Schuster.

Carter, Angela. 1979. *The Bloody Chamber*. New York: Harper & Row.

Cole, Babette. 1986. *Princess Smarty Pants*. New York: G. P. Putnam.

Cole, Babette. 1987. *Prince Cinders*. New York: G. P. Putnam.

Coombs, Patricia. 1975. *Molly Mullett*. New York: Lothrop, Lee & Shepard.

Corbalis, Judy. 1986. *The Wrestling Princess and Other Stories*. London: André Deutsch.

Corrin, Sara, and Stephen Corrin. 1989. *The Pied Piper of Hamelin*. San Diego, Calif.: Harcourt Brace Jovanovich.

Coville, Bruce. 1984. *Sarah and the Dragon*. New York: Lippincott.

Curtin, Jeremiah. 1931. *Fairy Tales of Eastern Europe*. New York: Robert McBride.

Curtin, Jeremiah. 1975. *Myths and Folk Tales of Ireland*. New York: Dover. Original edition, *Myths and Folk-Lore of Ireland*. Boston: Little Brown, 1890.

Dahl, Roald. 1982. *Revolting Rhymes*. London: Jonathan Cape.

Diamond, Donna. 1981. *The Pied Piper of Hamelin*. New York: Holiday House.

Dove, Mourning. 1933. *Coyote Tales*. Edited by Heister Dean Guie. Caldwell, Idaho: Caxton.

Dunstan, Mike. 1992. *Of Fisherman, Felons, Farmers, Fools ... and Resourceful Sisters*. Torquay, England: Audley Park Secondary School.

Gardner, John. 1975. *Dragon, Dragon and Other Timeless Tales*. New York: Knopf.

Gardner, John. 1976. *Gudgkin the Thistle Girl and Other Tales*. New York: Knopf.

Godden, Rumer. 1970. *The Old Woman Who Lived in a Vinegar Bottle*. Illustrated by Mairi Hedderwick. New York: Viking.

Hazeltine, Alice I. 1961. *Hero Tales from Many Lands*. Illustrated by Gordon Laite. New York: Abingdon.

Hughes, Ted. 1985. *How the Whale Became and Other Stories*. London: Faber.

Kennedy, Richard. 1987. *Collected Stories*. New York: Harper & Row.

Kipling, Rudyard. 1884. *The Jungle Book*. London: Macmillan.

Kramer, Rita. 1987. Rumpelstiltskin: His Story. *South Dakota Review* 25 (summer 1987): 78–81.

Lee, Tanith. 1972. *Princess Hynchatti and Some Other Surprises*. London: Macmillan.

Lee, Tanith. 1983. *Red as Blood or Tales from the Sisters Grimmer*. New York: Daw.

Lobel, Anita. 1983. *The Straw Maid*. New York: Greenwillow Books.

Macmillan, Cyrus. 1920. *Canadian Wonder Tales*. London: John Lane.

Mahy, Margaret. 1974. *The Changeover*. New York: Scholastic.

Martin, Rafe. 1990. *The Hungry Tigress: Buddhist Legends and Jataka Tales*. Berkeley, Calif.: Parallax Press.

Martin, Rafe. 1993. *The Rough-Face Girl*. New York: Scholastic.

Mayer, Mercer. 1980. *Herbert the Timid Dragon*. New York: Golden Press.

McKinley, Robin. 1981. *The Door in the Hedge*. New York: William Morrow.

Munsch, Robert. 1980. *The Paper Bag Princess*. Illustrated by M. Marchenko. Toronto: Annick Press.

Myers, Bernice. 1985. *Sideny Rella and the Glass Sneaker*. New York: Macmillan.
Paterson, Katherine. 1981. *The Crane Wife*. Illustrated by Suekichi Akaba. New York: Morrow.
Raddall, Thomas Head. 1943. *The Pied Piper of Dipper Creek and Other Tales*. Toronto: McClelland & Stewart.
Redgrove, Peter. 1979. *The One Who Set Out to Study Fear*. London: Bloomsbury.
Rockwell, Anne. 1994. *The Robber Baby: Stories from the Greek Myths*. New York: Greenwillow.
Rosen, Michael. 1985. *Quick, Let's Get Out of Here*. Harmondsworth: Puffin.
Rushdie, Salman. 1990. *Haroun and the Sea of Stories*. New York: Viking.
Schickel, Richard. 1964. *The Gentle Knight*. New York: Abelard-Schuman.
Scieszka, Jon, and Steve Johnson. 1991. *The Frog Prince Continued*. New York: Viking.
Sendak, Jack. 1966. *The King of the Hermits and Other Stories*. New York: Farrar, Straus & Giroux.
Shannon, Monica. 1926. *California Fairy Tales*. Illustrated by E. C. Millard. New York: Stephen Daye.
Shapiro, Irwin. 1965. *Heroes in American Folklore*. Illustrated by Donald McKay and James Daugherty. New York: Julian Messner.
Shorto, Russell. 1990. *Cinderella and Cinderella's Stepsister*. Illustrated by T. Lewis. Secaucus, N.J.: Carol Publishing Group.
Skurzynski, Gloria. 1979. *What Happened in Hamelin*. New York: Four Winds Press.
Storr, Catherine. 1955. *Clever Polly and the Stupid Wolf*. London: Faber and Faber.
Stoutenberg, Adrien. 1966. *American Tall Tales*. Illustrated by Richard M. Powers. New York: Viking.
Tolstoy, Leo. 1962. *Fables and Fairy Tales*. Translated by A. Dunn. New York: New American Library.
Turin, Adela, Francesca Cantarelli, and Wella Bosnia. 1977. *The Five Wives of Silverbeard*. London: Writers & Readers Publishing Cooperative.
Turin, Adela, and Sylvie Selig. 1977. *Of Cannons and Caterpillars*. London: Writers and Readers Publishing Cooperative.
Viorst, Judith. 1982. *If I Were in Charge of the World*. New York: Athenaeum.
Waddell, Martin. 1986. *The Tough Princess*. Illustrated by Patrick Benson. New York: Philomel Books.
Walker, Wendy. 1988. *The Sea-Rabbit or, the Artist of Life*. Los Angeles: Sun & Moon Press.
Williams, Jay. 1978. *The Practical Princess and Other Liberating Tales*. New York: Parents Magazine Press.
Yep, Laurence. 1989. *The Rainbow People*. New York: HarperCollins.
Yep, Laurence. 1991. *Tongues of Jade*. New York: HarperCollins.
Yolen, Jane. 1983. *Tales of Wonder*. New York: Schocken.
Yolen, Jane. 1985. *Dragonfield and Other Stories*. New York: Ace Books.
Young, Maud. 1910. *Celtic Wonder Tales*. Dublin: Maunsel.
Zaum, Marjorie. 1985. *Catlore*. New York: Atheneum.

Reference Works

Abernethy, Rose L. 1964. A Study of Existing Practices and Principles of Storytelling for Children in the United States. Ph.D. diss., Northwestern University.
Ackermann, Elfriede Marie. 1944. *Das Schlaraffenland in German Literature and Folksong*. Chicago: University of Chicago Press.
Altmann, Anna E., and Gail de Vos. 2001. *Tales, Then and Now: More Folktales as Literary Fictions for Young Adults*. Westport, Conn.: Libraries Unlimited.

Alvey, Richard G. 1974. The Historical Development of Organized Storytelling for Children in the United States. Ph.D. diss., University of Pennsylvania.

Anderson, Graham. 2000. *Fairytale in the Ancient World*. London: Routledge.

Apple, Michael W. 1990. *Ideology and Curriculum*. 2nd ed. New York: Routledge.

Apple, Michael W. 1995. *Education and Power*. New York: Routledge.

Apple, Michael W. 1996. *Cultural Politics and Education*. New York: Teachers College.

Apple, Michael W. 2000. *Official Knowledge: Democratic Education in a Conservative Age*. 2nd ed. New York: Routledge.

Apple, Michael W. 2001. *Educating the "Right" Way: Markets, Standards, God, and Inequality*. New York: RoutledgeFalmer.

Applebee, Arthur. 1978. *The Child's Concept of Story: Ages Two to Seventeen*. Chicago: University of Chicago Press.

Appleby, Joyce, Lynn Hunt, and Margaret Jacob. 1994. *Telling the Truth about History*. New York: Norton.

Aronowitz, Stanley. 2000. *The Knowledge Factory: Dismantling the Corporate University and Creating True Higher Learning*. Boston: Beacon.

Baker, Augusta, and Ellin Greene. 1977. *Storytelling: Art and Technique*. New York: R. R. Bowker.

Barbour, Philip. 1970. *Pocahontas and Her World*. Boston: Houghton Mifflin.

Barchers, Suzanne. 1988. Beyond Disney: Reading and Writing Traditional and Alternative Fairy Tales. *The Lion and the Unicorn* 12 (December): 135–50.

Barton, Bob, and David Booth. 1976. *Writers, Critics and Children*. New York: Agathon Press.

Barton, Bob, and David Booth. 1990. *Stories in the Classroom: Storytelling, Reading Aloud and Roleplaying with Children*. Portsmouth, N.H.: Heinemann.

Bauman, Richard. 1986. *Story, Performance, and Event: Contextual Studies of Oral Narrative*. Cambridge: Cambridge University Press.

Bauman, Zygmunt, 1998. *Globalization: The Human Consequences*. New York: Columbia University Press.

Bauman, Zygmunt. 2001. *Community: Seeking Safety in an Insecure World*. London: Polity.

Beckett, Sandra. 2002. *Recycling Red Riding Hood*. New York: Routledge.

Bellamy, John G. 1984. *Robin Hood: An Historical Inquiry*. Bloomington: Indiana University Press.

Benjamin, Walter. 1968. *Illuminations*. Translated by Harry Zohn. New York: Harcourt, Brace and World.

Benjamin, Walter. 1970. *Über Kinder, Jugend und Erziehung*. Frankfurt am Main: Suhrkamp.

Berger, John. 1972. *Ways of Seeing*. Harmondsworth: Penguin.

Bettelheim, Bruno. 1976. *The Uses of Enchantment: The Meaning and Importance of Fairy Tales*. New York: Knopf.

Bierlein, J. F. 1994. *Parallel Myths*. New York: Ballantine.

Blatt, Glora T., ed. 1990. *Once upon a Folktale: Capturing the Folktale Process with Children*. Portsmouth, N.H.: Heinemann.

Bloch, Ernst. 1959. *Das Prinzip Hoffnung*. 3 vols. Frankfurt am Main: Suhrkamp.

Bloch, Ernst. 1986. *The Principal of Hope*. Trans. Neville Plaice, Stephen Plaice, and Paul Knight. 3 vols. Cambridge, MA: MIT Press.

Bok, Derek. 2003. *Universities in the Marketplace: The Commercialization of Higher Education*. Princeton, N.J.: Princeton University Press.

Breen, Robert. 1978. *Chamber Theatre*. Englewood Cliffs, N.J.: Prentice Hall.

Breneman, Lucille N., and Bren Breneman. 1983. *Once upon a Time: A Storytelling Handbook*. Chicago: Nelson-Hall.

Brodie, Richard. 1996. *Virus of the Mind: The New Science of the Meme*. Seattle, Wash.: Integral Press.

Brown, Norman O. 1947. *Hermes the Thief: The Evolution of a Thief*. Madison, WI.: University of Wisconsin Press.

Bruchac, Joseph. 1997. *Tell Me a Tale: A Book about Storytelling*. New York: Harcourt.

Bruner, Jerome. 1986. *The Culture of Education*. Cambridge, Mass.: Harvard University Press.

Bruner, Jerome. 1990. *Acts of Meaning*. Cambridge, Mass.: Harvard University Press.

Bruner, Jerome. 2002. *Making Stories: Law, Literature, Life*. New York: Farrar, Straus and Giroux.

Brunvand, Jan Harold. 1968. *The Study of American Folklore: An Introduction*. New York: W.W. Norton.

Brunvand, Jan Harold. 1981. *The Vanishing Hitchhiker: American Urban Legends and Their Meanings*. New York: W. W. Norton.

Calame-Griaule, Geneviève. 1991. *Le Renouveau du Conte/The Revival of Storytelling*. Paris: Centre National de la Recherche Scientifique.

Camporesi, Pietro. 1976. Capitolo qual narra l'essere di un mondo novo trovato nel Mar Oceano. In *La maschera di Bertoldo: G.C. Croce e la letteratura carnevalesca*. Turin: Einaudi, pp. 309–11.

Casseday, Ben. 1852. *The History of Louisville*. Louisville, Ky.: Hull & Brother.

Chambers, Adrian. 1991. *The Reading Environment: How Adults Help Children Enjoy Books*. South Woodchester: Thimble Press.

Chittenden, Patricia, and Malcolm Kiniry, eds. 1986. *Making Connections across the Curriculum: Readings for Analysis*. New York: St. Martin's.

Christensen, L. 1994. Building Community from Chaos. In *Rethinking Our Classrooms*. Milwaukee: Rethinking Schools, pp. 50–55.

Clodd, Edward. 1898. *Tim-Tit-Tot: An Essay of Savage Philosophy*. London: Duckworth.

Coles, Robert. 1989. *The Call of Stories*. Boston: Houghton Mifflin.

Collins, Rives, and Pamela Cooper. 1997. *The Power of Story: Teaching through Storytelling*. Scottsdale, Ariz.: Scarisbrick.

Cooper, Pamela J., and Rives Collins. 1992. *Look What Happened to Frog: Storytelling in Education*. Scottsdale, Ariz.: Gorsuch Scarisbrick.

Cooper, Patsy. 1993. *When Stories Come to School: Telling, Writing and Performing Stories in the Early Education Classroom*. New York: Teachers and Writers Collaborative.

Cross, Gary. 2000. *An All-Consuming Century: Why Consumerism Won in Modern America*. New York: Columbia University Press.

Davies, Bronwyn. 1989. *Frogs and Snails and Feminist Tales: Preschool and Gender*. Sydney: Allen and Unwin.

De Bono, Edward. 1972. *Children Solve Problems*. London: Allen Lane.

Debord, Guy. 1995. *The Society of the Spectacle*. Translated by Donald Nicholson-Smith. New York: Zone Books.

Dégh, Linda. 1994. *American Folklore and the Mass Media*. Bloomington: Indiana University Press.

Dégh, Linda. 2001. *Legend and Belief: Dialectics of a Folklore Genre*. Bloomington: Indiana University Press.

Denning, Stephen. 2000. *The Springboard: How Storytelling Ignites Action in Knowledge-Era Organizations*. Boston: Butterworth-Heinemann.

Dorson, Richard, ed. 1973. *America in Legend: Folklore from the Colonial Period to the Present*. New York: Pantheon.

Dundes, Alan, ed. 1982. *Cinderella: A Casebook*. New York: Garland, 1982.

Dundes, Alan, ed. 1989. *Little Red Riding Hood: A Casebook*. Madison: University of Wisconsin Press.

Durrell, Ann, and Marylin Sachs, ed. 1990. *The Big Book of Peace*. New York: Dutton.

Dyson, Ann Haas. 1997. *Writing Superheroes: Contemporary Childhood, Popular Culture, and Classroom Literacy*. New York: Teachers College Press.

Egan, Kieran. 1986. *Teaching as Storytelling: An Alternative Approach to Teaching and Curriculum in the Elementary School*. Chicago: University of Chicago Press.

Eliade, Mircea. 1963. *Myth and Reality*. Translated by Willard R. Task. New York: Harper & Row.

Ellis, Brian "Fox." 1997. *Learning from the Land: Teaching Ecology through Stories and Activities*. Englewood, Colo.: Teacher Ideas Press.

Estés, Clarissa Pinkola. 1993. *Women Who Run with the Wolves: Myths and Stories of the Wild Woman Archetype*. New York: Ballantine.

Fischer, Gerhard. 2002. *Grips: Geschichte Eines Populären Theaters (1966–2000)*. Munich: Iudicium.

FitzGerald, Frances. 1979. *America Revised: History Schoolbooks in the Twentieth Century*. Boston: Little, Brown.

Flack, Jerry. 1997. *From the Land of Enchantment: Creative Teaching with Fairy Tales*. Englewood, Colo.: Libraries Unlimited.

Foley, John. 1986. *Oral Tradition in Literature*. Columbia: University of Missouri Press.

Fox, Carol. 1993. *At the Very Edge of the Forest: The Influence of Literature on Storytelling by Children*. London: Cassel.

Fox, Geoff, and Michael Benton. 1985. *Teaching Literature from Nine to Fourteen*. Oxford: Oxford University Press.

Freire, Paulo. 1971. *Pedagogy of the Oppressed*. Translated by Myra Bergman Ramos. New York: Herder and Herder.

Freire, Paulo. 1997. *Pedagogy of Hope*. Translated by Robert R. Barr. New York: Continuum.

Fritz, Jean. 1983. *The Double Life of Pocahontas*. Illustrated by Ed Young. New York: G. P. Putnam.

Garvie, Edie. 1990. *Story as Vehicle: Teaching English to Young People*. Clevedon U.K.: Multilingual Matters.

Gillard, Marni. 1995. *Storyteller Storyteacher: Discovering the Power of Storytelling for Teaching and Living*. York, ME.: Stenhouse.

Giroux, Henry A. 1989. *Popular Culture: Schooling and Everyday Life*. New York: Begin & Garvey.

Goforth, Frances, and Carolyn Spillman. 1994. *Using Folk Literature in the Classroom*. Phoenix, Ariz.: Oryx Press.

Hearne, Betsy. 1989. *Beauty and the Beast: Visions and Revisions of an Old Tale*. Chicago: University of Chicago Press.

Heath, Shirley Brice. 1983. *Ways with Words: Language, Life and Work in Communities and Classrooms*. Cambridge: Cambridge University Press.

Heinig, Ruth Beall. 1992. *Improvisation with Favorite Tales into the Reading/Writing Classroom*. Portsmouth, N.H.: Heinemann.

Heinig, Ruth Beall. 1993. *Creative Drama for the Classroom Teacher*. 4th ed. Englewood Cliffs, N.J.: Prentice Hall.

Holt, David, and Bill Mooney. 1997. *The Storyteller's Guide*. Little Rock, Ark.: August House.

Hyde, Lewis. 1998. *Trickster Makes This World: Mischief, Myth and Art*. New York: Farrar, Straus and Giroux.

Hynes, William J., and William G. Doty, eds. 1993. *Mythological Trickster Figures: Contours, Contexts, and Criticism*. Tuscaloosa, AL.: University of Alabama Press.

Jaffe, Nina. 1995. Storytelling at the Crossroads. *Forkroads: A Journal of Ethnic-American Literature* I: 73–76.

Jaffe, Nina. 2000. Bringing Storytelling and Folk Narrative into Classroom Life. In *Revisiting a Progressive Pedagogy: The Developmental Interaction Approach*, edited by Nancy Nager and Edna K. Shapiro. Albany: State University of New York Press, pp. 161–78.

Kennery, Karen, and Herbert Kohl. 1968. *Fables: A Curriculum*. New York: Teachers and Writers Collaborative.

Kinder, Marsha. 1991. *Playing with Power in Movies, Television, and Video Games: From Muppet Babies to Teenage Mutant Ninja Turtles*. Berkeley: University of California Press.

Kohl, Herbert. 1973. *Reading, How To*. New York: Dutton.

Kohl, Herbert. 1988. *Making Theater: Developing Plays with Young People*. New York: Teachers and Writers Collaborative.

Kohl, Herbert. 1994. *"I Won't Learn from You" and Other Thoughts on Creative Maladjustment*. New York: New Press.

Kohn, Alfie. 1999. *The Schools Our Children Deserve: Moving beyond Traditional Classrooms and "Tougher Standards."* Boston: Houghton Mifflin.

Kozol, Jonathan. 1991. *Savage Inequalities*. New York: HarperCollins.

Kraus, Anne Marie. 1998–99. *Folk Tale Themes and Activities for Children*. Vol. 1, *Pourquoi Tales;* Vol. 2, *Trickster and Transformation Tales*. Englewood, Colo.: Libraries Unlimited.

Kroeber, Karl. 1990. *Retelling/Rereading: The Fate of Storytelling in Modern Times*. New Brunswick, N.J.: Rutgers University Press.

Landay, Lori. 1998. *Madcaps, Screwballs & Con Women: The Female Trickster in American Culture*. Philadelphia: University of Pennsylvania Press.

Lanshear, Colin, and Peter L. McLaren, eds. 1993. *Critical Literacy: Policy, Praxis and the Postmodern*. Albany: State University of New York Press.

Lawrence, John, and Robert Jewett. 2002. *The Myth of the American Superhero*. Grand Rapids, Mich.: Eerdmans.

Leach, Penelope. 1994. *Children First*. New York: Knopf.

Leith, Dick. 2002. *Storyteller's Keywords*. Papyrus Series No. 3. Combe Martin, England: Daylight Press.

Levorato, Alessandra. 2003. *Language and Gender in the Fairy Tale Tradition: A Linguistic Analysis of Old and New Story Telling*. London: Palgrave.

Lewinsohn, Richard. 1954. *Animals, Men, and Myths*. New York: Harper & Brothers.

Lipman, Doug. 1995. *The Storytelling Coach: How to Listen, Praise, and Bring Out People's Best*. Little Rock, Ark.: August House.

Livo, Norma J. 2003. *Bringing Out Their Best: Values, Education, and Character Development through Traditional Tales*. Westport, Conn.: Libraries Unlimited.

Livo, Norma J., and Sandra A. Rietz. 1986. *Storytelling: Process and Practice*. Littleton, Colo.: Libraries Unlimited.

MacDonald, Margaret Read. 1993. *The Storyteller's Start-Up Book: Finding, Learning, Performing and Using Folktales*. Little Rock, Ark.: August House.

Maguire, Jack. 1998. *The Power of Personal Storytelling: Spinning Tales to Connect with Others*. New York: Putnam.

Marx, Anthony W. 2003. Review of Derek Bok's *Universities in the Marketplace*. *International Herald Tribune*, 22 May, p. 18.

Mason, Harriet, and Larry Watson. 1991. *Every One a Storyteller: Integrating Storytelling into the Curriculum*. Portland, Ore.: Lariat Productions.

McChesney, Robert W. 1999. *Rich Media, Poor Democracy*. Urbana: University of Illinois Press.

McDrury, Janice and Maxine Alterio. 2003. *Learning Through Storytelling in Higher Education: Using Reflection and Experience to Improve Learning*. London: Kogan Page.

McGovern, Charles, Susan Strasser, and Mattias Judt, eds. 1998. *Getting and Spending: European and American Consumer Societies in the Twentieth Century.* Cambridge: Cambridge University Press.

McGovern, Charles. 2002. *Sold American; Inventing the Consumer, 1890–1945.* Chapel Hill, N.C.: University of North Carolina Press, 2002.

McNeely, Deldon Anne. 1996. *Mercury Rising: Women, Evil, and the Trickster Gods.* Woodstock, Conn.: Spring.

McRae, John. 1985. *Using Drama in the Classroom.* Oxford: Pergamon.

Mieder, Wolfgang. 1987. *Tradition and Innovation in Folk Literature.* Hanover: University Press of New England.

Mieder, Wolfgang. 1993. *Proverbs Are Never out of Season: Popular Wisdom in the Modern Age.* Oxford: Oxford University Press.

Molnar, Alex. 1996. *Giving Kids the Business: The Commercialization of America's Schools.* Boulder, Colo.: Westview Press.

Morgan, Norah, and Juliana Saxton. 1987. *Teaching Drama: A Mind of Many Wonders.* Portsmouth, N.H.: Heinemann.

Morgan, Norah, and Juliana Saxton. 1991. *Teaching, Questioning and Learning.* London: Routledge.

Nager, Nancy, and Edna K. Shapiro, eds. 2000. *Revisiting a Progressive Pedagogy: The Dvelopmental Interaction Approach.* Albany: State University of New York Press.

Neelands, Jonothan, and Tony Goode. 1990. *Structuring Drama Work: A Handbook of Available Forms in Theatre and Drama.* Cambridge: Cambridge University Press.

Negt, Oskar and Alexander Kluge. 1974. *Öffentlichkeit und Erfahrung.* Frankfurt an Main: Suhrkamp.

Niemi, Loren, and Elizabeth Ellis. 2001. *Inviting the Wolf In: Thinking About Difficult Stories.* Little Rock, Ark.: August House.

O'Neill, Cecily, and Alan Lambert. 1982. *Drama Structures: A Practical Handbook for Teachers.* Portsmouth, N.H.: Heinemann.

Ong, Walter. 1982. *Orality and Literacy: The Technologizing of the World.* London: Routledge.

Orenstein, Catherine. 2002. *Little Red Riding Hood Uncloaked: Sex, Morality, and the Evolution of a Fairy Tale.* New York: Basic Books.

Paley, Vivian Gussin. 1997. *The Girl with the Brown Crayon: How Children Use Stories to Shape Their Lives.* Cambridge, Mass.: Harvard University Press.

Peck, M. S. 1987. *The Different Drum: Community and Making Peace.* New York: Simon & Schuster.

Peck, M. S. 1993. *A World Waiting to Be Born.* New York: Bantam.

Pellowski, Anne. 1990. *The World of Storytelling: A Practical Guide to the Origins, Development and Applications of Storytelling.* New York: Wilson.

Piaget, Jean. 1976. *Judgment and Reasoning in the Child.* Translated by Marjorie Warden. Towata, N.J.: Littlefield, Adams.

Piaget, Jean. 1977. *The Development of Thought: Equilibration of Cognitive Structures.* Translated by Arnold Rosin. New York: Viking.

Piaget, Jean. 1981. *The Psychology of Intelligence (1947).* Translated by Malcolm Piercy and D. E. Berlyne. Towata, N.J.: Littlefield, Adams.

Pleij, Herman. 2001. *Dreaming of Cockaigne: Medieval Fantasies of the Perfect Life.* Translated by Diane Webb. New York: Columbia University Press.

Propp, Vladimir. 1968. *The Morphology of the Folktale.* Edited by Louis Wagner and Alan Dundes. Translated by Laurence Scott. 2nd rev. ed. Austin: University of Texas Press.

Propp, Vladimir. 1984. *Theory and History of Folklore.* Edited by Anatoly Liberman. Translated by Adriadna Y. Martin and Richard P. Martin. Minneapolis: University of Minnesota Press.

Radin, Paul. 1956. *The Trickster: A Study in American Indian Mythology*. New York: Schocken.

Ranch, Jonathan. 1993. *Kindly Inquisitors: The New Attacks on Free Thought*. Chicago: University of Chicago Press.

Ravitch, Diane. 2003. *The Language Police: How Pressure Groups Restrict What Students Learn*. New York: Knopf.

Readings, Bill. 1996. *The University in Ruins*. Cambridge, Mass.: University of Harvard Press.

Richter, Dieter. 1984. *Schlaraffenland: Geschichte Einer Populären Phantasie*. Cologne: Diederichs.

Rodari, Gianni. 1996. *The Grammar of Fantasy: An Introduction to the Art of Inventing Stories*. Translated by Jack Zipes. New York: Teachers and Writers Collaborative.

Rogers, Rex Stainton, and Wendy Stainton Rogers. 1992. *Stories of Childhood: Shifting Agendas of Child Concern*. London: Harvester Wheatsheaf.

Röhrich, Lutz. 1987. *Wage es, den Frosch zu küssen: Das Grimmsche Märchen Nummer Eins in seinen Wandlungen*. Cologne: Diederichs.

Rosen, Betty. 1988. *And None of It Was Nonsense: The Power of Storytelling in School*. London: Heinemann.

Rosen, Harold. 1985. *Stories and Meanings*. Sheffield: National Association for the Teaching of English.

Rosen, Harold. 1993. *Troublesome Boy*. London: English and Media Centre.

Rubright, Lynn. 1996. *Beyond the Beanstalk: Interdisciplinary Learning through Storytelling*. Portsmouth, N.H.: Heinemann.

Sapon-Shevin, Mara. 1999. *Because We Can Change the World: A Practical Guide to Building Cooperative, Inclusive Classroom Communities*. Boston: Allyn & Bacon.

Sax, Boria. 1990. *The Frog King: On Legends, Fables, Fairy Tales and Anecdotes of Animals*. New York: Pace University Press.

Schwartz, Marni, Ann Trousdale, and Sue Woestehoff, eds. 1994. *Give a Listen: Stories of Storytelling in School*. Urbana: National Council of Teachers of English.

Shenkman, Richard. 1988. *Legends, Lies, and Cherished Myths of American History*. New York: William Morrow.

Shumar, Wesley. 1997. *College for Sale: A Critique of the Commodification of Higher Education*. Washington, D.C.: Falmer.

Sierra, Judy, and Robert Kaminski. 1989. *Twice upon a Time: Stories to Tell, Retell, Act Out, and Write About*. New York: Wilson.

Sima, Judy, and Kevin Cordi. 2003. *Raising Voices: Creating Youth Storytelling Groups and Troupes*. Westport, Conn.: Libraries Unlimited.

Simons, Elizabeth Radio. 1990. *Student Worlds, Student Words: Teaching Writing through Folklore*. Portsmouth, N.H.: Heinemann.

Slaughter, Sheila, and Larry Leslie. 1997. *Academic Capitalism: Politics, Policies and the Entrepreneurial University*. Baltimore: Johns Hopkins University Press.

Sobol, Joseph Daniel. 1999. *The Storytellers' Journey: An American Revival*. Urbana: University of Illinois Press.

Spolin, Viola. 1963. *Improvisation for the Theater: A Handbook of Teaching and Directing Techniques*. Evanston, Ill.: Northwestern University Press.

Spolin, Viola. 1986. *Theatre Games for the Classroom: A Teacher's Handbook*. Evanston, Ill.: Northwestern University Press.

Stephens, John, and Robyn McCallum. 1998. *Retelling Stories, Framing Culture*. New York: Garland.

Stone, Kay F. 1998. *Burning Brightly: New Light on Old Tales Told Today*. Peterborough, ON: Broadview.

Stowell, Laurie. 2000. Building Alliances, Building Community, Building Bridges through Literacy. In *Promoting Literacy in Grades 4–9: A Handbook for Teachers and Administrators*, edited by Karen D. Wood and Thomas S. Dickinson. Boston: Allyn & Bacon.

Taggart, James M. 1990. *Enchanted Maidens: Gender Relations in Spanish Folktales of Courtship and Marriage*. Princeton, N.J.: Princeton University Press.

Tarlington, Carole, and Patrick Veriour. 1991. *Role Drama*. Portsmouth, N.H.: Heinemann.

Tatar, Maria. 1992. *Off with Their Heads! Fairy Tales and the Culture of Childhood*. Princeton, N.J.: Princeton University Press.

Taylor, Eric K. 2000. *Using Folktales*. Cambridge: Cambridge University Press.

Thompson, Stith. 1946. *The Folktale*. New York: Dryden.

Tucker, Nicolas. 1981. *The Child and the Book*. Cambridge: Cambridge University Press.

Turner, Patricia A. 1993. *I Heard It Through the Grapevine: Rumor in African American Culture*. Berkeley: University of California Press.

Vos, Gail de. 1996. *Tales, Rumors, and Gossip: Exploring Contemporary Folk Literature with Young Adults*. Westport, Conn.: Libraries Unlimited.

Vos, Gail de. 2003. *Storytelling for Young Adults: A Guide to Tales for Teens*. 2nd ed. Westport, Conn.: Libraries Unlimited.

Vos, Gail de, and Anna E. Altmann. 1999. *New Tales for Old: Folktales as Literary Fictions for Young Adults*. Westport, Conn.: Libraries Unlimited.

Vygotsky, L. S. 1978. *Mind in Society: The Development of Higher Psychological Processes*. Edited by Michael Cole, Vera John-Steiner, Sykvia Scribner, and Ellen Souberman. Cambridge, Mass.: Harvard University Press.

Weigle, Marta. 1982. *Spiders and Spinsters: Women and Mythology*. Albuquerque: University of New Mexico Press.

Wilde, Oscar. 1912. *The Soul of Man Under Socialism*. Edited by Robert Ross. London: Humphreys.

Wilson, Michael. 1997. *Performance and Practice: Oral Narrative Traditions among Teenagers in Britain and Ireland*. Aldershot, U.K.: Ashgate.

Wolf, Shelby Anne, and Shirley Brice Heath. 1992. *The Braid of Literature: Children's Worlds of Reading*. Cambridge, Mass.: Harvard University Press.

Wood, Karen D., and Thomas S. Dickinson, eds. 2000. *Promoting Literacy in Grades 4–9: A Handbook for Teachers and Administrators*. Boston: Allyn & Bacon.

Zipes, Jack. 1973. Building a children's theater, 2 documents: Asja Lacis/Walter Benjamin. *Performance* 1: 22–27.

Zipes, Jack, ed. 1976. *Political Plays for Children*. St. Louis: Telos, 1976.

Zipes, Jack. 1994. *Fairy Tale as Myth/Myth as Fairy Tale*. Lexington: University Press of Kentucky.

Zipes, Jack. 1995. *Creative Storytelling: Building Community, Changing Lives*. New York: Routledge.

Zipes, Jack. 1997. *Happily Ever After: Fairy Tales, Children, and the Culture Industry*. New York: Routledge.

Zipes, Jack. 2001. *Sticks and Stones: The Troublesome Success of Children's Literature from Slovenly Peter to Harry Potter*. New York: Routledge.

Zipes, Jack, ed. 2000. *The Oxford Companion to Fairy Tales: The Western Fairy Tale Tradition from Medieval to Modern*. Oxford: Oxford University Press.

Notes

Chapter 1

1. Richard Chase, ed., *The Jack Tales: Folk Tales from the Southern Appalachians* (New York: Houghton Mifflin, 1943), xi–xii.
2. Cf. Jack Zipes, ed. and trans., *Beautiful Angiola: The Great Treasury of Sicilian Folk and Fairy Tales Collected by Laura Gonzenbach* (New York: Routledge, 2003), 96–102.
3. Herman Pleij, *Dreaming of Cockaigne: Medieval Fantasies of the Perfect Life*, trans. Diane Webb (New York: Columbia University Press, 2001), 26.
4. Oscar Wilde, *The Soul of Man under Socialism*, ed. Robert Ross (London: Humphreys, 1912), 45.

Chapter 2

1. Mario Vargas Llosa, *The Storyteller*, trans. Helen Lane (New York: Farrar, Straus and Giroux, 1989), 244.
2. Barnaby J. Feder, "Biotech Industry Bets Its Future on Storytelling," *International Herald Tribune*, 25 June 1999, p. 13.
3. Roland Barthes, *Mythologies* (London: Granada, 1973), 142–43.
4. Karl Kroeber, *Retelling/Rereading: The Fate of Storytelling in Modern Times* (New Brunswick, N.J.: Rutgers University Press, 1990), 187.
5. "If we understand that storytelling did not simply disappear with the advent of the twentieth century, we open the way to different kinds of critical understanding that might enable us to break free from constrictive theoretical conceptions." Ibid., 188.
6. Hermann Hesse, *The Fairy Tales of Hermann Hesse*, trans. Jack Zipes (New York: Bantam, 1995), 190.
7. Kroeber, *Retelling/Rereading*, 4.
8. Ibid., 9.
9. This is fully documented in Richard Alvey's study, "The Historical Development of Organized Storytelling for Children in the United States" (Ph.D. diss., University of Pennsylvania, 1974).
10. Joseph Daniel Sobol, *The Storytellers' Journey: An American Revival* (Urbana: University of Illinois Press, 1999), 14.
11. Ibid., 15.

12. Kay Stone, *Burning Brightly: New Light on Old Tales Told Today* (Peterborough, ON: Broadview, 1998), 8–9.
13. Sobol, *The Storytellers' Journey*, 29.
14. Lynn Rubright, *Beyond the Beanstalk: Interdisciplinary Learning through Storytelling* (Portsmouth, N.H.: Heinemann, 1996).

Chapter 3

1. For Ewald's original version, see "A Fairy Tale about God and Kings," in *Fairy Tales and Fables from Weimar Days*, ed. and trans. Jack Zipes (Hanover: University Press of New England, 1989), 34–35.
2. Michael W. Apple, *Educating the "Right" Way: Markets, Standards, God, and Inequality* (New York: RoutledgeFalmer, 2001), 29.
3. Diane Ravitch, *The Language Police: How Pressure Groups Restrict What Students Learn* (New York: Knopf, 2003), 159–60.
4. Anthony W. Marx, "Review of Derek Bok's *Universities in the Marketplace*," *International Herald Tribune*, 22 May 2003, p. 18.
5. Jen Webb, Tony Schirato, and Geoff Danaher, *Understanding Bourdieu* (London: Sage, 2002), 36.
6. Ibid.
7. Nina Jaffe, "Bringing Storytelling and Folk Narrative into Classroom Life," in *Revisiting a Progressive Pedagogy: The Developmental-Interaction Approach*, ed. Nancy Nager and Edna K. Shapiro (Albany: State University Press of New York, 2000), 162.
8. See Mary Jane Smetanka, " 'U' Hails Success of Capital Campaign: 7-Year Effort Yields $1.656 Billion," *Star Tribune*, 11 September 2003, pp. B1, B7.
9. Zygmunt Bauman, *Community: Seeking Safety in an Insecure World* (London: Polity, 2001), 144.
10. Laurie Stowell, "Building Alliances, Building Community, Building Bridges through Literacy," in *Promoting Literacy in Grades 4–9: A Handbook for Teachers and Administrators* (Boston: Allyn & Bacon, 2000), 82.
11. Cf. Viola Spolin, *Improvisation for the Theater: A Handbook of Teaching and Directing Techniques* (Evanston, Ill.: Northwestern University Press, 1963).

Chapter 4

1. Jerome Bruner, *Making Stories: Law, Literature, Life* (New York: Farrar, Straus and Giroux, 2002), 64.
2. Ibid., 65.
3. Jerome Bruner, *The Culture of Education* (Cambridge, Mass.: Harvard University Press, 1996), 81–82.

Chapter 6

1. K. L. Nichols, "Native American Trickster Tales," http://www.pittstate.edu/engl/nichols/coyote.html, p. 1.

Chapter 7

1. Gianni Rodari, *The Grammar of Fantasy: An Introduction to the Art of Inventing Stories*, trans. Jack Zipes (New York: Teachers and Writers Collaborative, 1996).

Chapter 9

1. *Political Plays for Children: The Grips Theater of Berlin*, ed. and trans. Jack Zipes (St. Louis, Mo.: Telos, 1976), 2.
2. For information on Grips, see Jack Zipes, ed., *Political Plays for Children: The Grips Theater of Berlin*, a translation of three plays with an introduction about the history of the Grips Theater (St. Louis, Mo.: Telos, 1976). Gerhard Fischer has just published an excellent social history of Grips. See *Grips: Geschichte eines populären Theaters (1966–2000)* (Munich: Iudicium, 2002).
3. These essays, including "Programm eines proletarischen Kindertheaters," can be found in Walter Benjamin, *Über Kinder, Jugend und Erziehung* (Frankfurt am Main: Suhrkamp, 1970). All the page citations in the text are taken from this volume. For a translation of "Programm eines proletarischen Kindertheaters," see "Program for a Proletarian Children's Theater," trans. Susan Buck-Morss, *Performance* 1 (March/ April 1973): 28–32. I have not used Buck-Morss's translation because there are problems with it. To begin with, the title is wrong. Benjamin did not write a program for a proletarian theater, he wrote a program of or about it. A minor point, perhaps, but the fact is he was writing about the work that Lacis had already accomplished. It was a description of a potential theater that had already shown its potency. At any rate, I have consulted Buck-Morss's translation at times, but all the translated passages in this essay are mine.
4. For information about their relationship, see "Building a Children's Theater, 2 Documents: Asja Lacis/Walter Benjamin," *Performance* 1 (March/April 1973): 22–27.
5. Benjamin, *Über Kinder*, 81.
6. Ibid.
7. Ibid., 85.
8. For excellent critiques of consumerism, see Charles McGovern, Susan Strasser, and Mattias Judt, eds., *Getting and Spending: European and American Consumer Societies in the Twentieth Century* (Cambridge: Cambridge University Press, 1998); Charles McGovern, *Sold American: Inventing the Consumer, 1890–1945* (Chapel Hill: University of North Carolina Press, 2002); and Gary Cross, *An All-Consuming Century: Why Consumerism Won in Modern America* (New York: Columbia University Press, 2000).
9. Oskar Negt and Alexander Kluge, *Öffentlichkeit und Erfahrung* (Frankfurt am Main: Suhrkamp, 1974), 466–67.
10. Benjamin, *Über Kinder*, 73.
11. Guy Debord, *The Society of the Spectacle*, trans. Donald Nicholson-Smith (New York: Zone Books, 1995), 19; first published as *La Societé du spectacle* (Paris: Buchet-Chastel, 1967). Debord, who died in 1994, wrote a preface for the third French edition of 1992, included in the U.S. edition.
12. Ibid., 23.
13. Zygmunt Bauman, *Globalization: The Human Consequences* (New York: Columbia University, 1998), 18.

14. I have amply discussed homogenization tendencies in my book *Sticks and Stones: The Troublesome Success of Children's Literature from Slovenly Peter to Harry Potter* (New York: Routledge, 2001).
15. See Alex Molnar, *Giving Kids the Business: The Commercialization of America's Schools* (Boulder, Colo.: Westview, 1966).

Index